The Family Support Handbook

Ann Wheal
with Gerry Emson

Russell House Publishing

First published in 2002 by:
Russell House Publishing Ltd.
4 St. George's House
Uplyme Road
Lyme Regis
Dorset DT7 3LS
Tel: 01297-443948
Fax: 01297-442722
e-mail: help@russellhouse.co.uk
website: www.russellhouse.co.uk

© Ann Wheal and Gerry Emson and the various contributors of documents and examples.

The moral right of Ann Wheal, Gerry Emson and the various contributors to be identified as the authors of this work has been asserted by them in accordance with The Copyright Designs and Patents Act 1988.

All rights reserved. No part of this publication may be reproduced, stored in a retrieval system or transmitted in any form, or by any means, electronic, mechanical, photocopying, recording or otherwise, without the prior permission of the copyright holder and the publisher.

British Library Cataloguing-in-publication Data:
A catalogue record for this book is available from the British Library.

ISBN: 1-903855-08-X

Design and layout by Jeremy Spencer, London
Printed by Bell and Bain, Glasgow

Acknowledgements

The authors would like to thank all the people and organisations who have helped or contributed in many different ways in the compilation of this book particularly:
- The parents.
- The staff at the Willows Nursery School, (see Useful Groups and Organisations), and in particular Meriel Mann who was our critical reader.
- Sarah Bray, Hilary Day, Julie Leckey, Kate Roberts, Gloria Russell.
- Our husbands for their patience and tolerance, particularly towards the end of the project!

About Russell House Publishing

RHP is a group of social work, probation, education and youth and community work practitioners and academics working in collaboration with a professional publishing team. Our aim is to work closely with the field to produce innovative and valuable materials to help managers, trainers, practitioners and students. We are keen to receive feedback on publications and new ideas for future projects.

Contents

List of model forms and documents	vi
Children's rights	x
About this Handbook	**xi**
How to use this handbook	xi
What is in this handbook	xii
Supporting Families: A Guide for Those Helping Parents to Help Themselves	**xiv**
Preamble	xiv
Background	xiv
Section 1 – Issues	**1**
The child	1
Parents	4
Confidentiality	10
Child protection	11
Ensuring safety when working with families	14
Section 2 – Children and Families	**20**
Understanding children	20
Meaningful milestones for under fives	21
Understanding adolescents	21
Other family members including fathers and grandparents	23
Behavioural problems: the child's or the adult's?	24
Children who have been abused and how to help	25
Young people who have abused	27
Children with disabilities	29
Addictions	30
Loss and bereavement	34
Living with a new or different family	36
Victims of domestic violence	36
Section 3 – Parenting Skills and Methods of Family Support	**52**
Parenting skills and what influences them	52
Parenting programmes	54
Preventative work	55
Methods of family support	58
Who might facilitate family support?	58
Meeting parents	59
Practical suggestions for working with parents	59
Section 4 – Keeping the Family Together	**62**
Getting the family 'on board'	62
Supporting families in their own home	63

The family support handbook

Support care	65
Coping with crisis	66
Family group conferences	66
Family assessments	67
Living away: working with parents whose children are unable to live with them	67
Managing contact with parents and other family members	69

Section 5 – Organising and Planning Family Support — 75

Choosing a location	75
Setting the rules	76
Parents helping parents	77
Ground rules for groups	78
Planning for groups	79
Types of group	82
Managing groups	86
Helping families to help their children get the most out of school	86
Teenage parents groups	88
Providing support after visits cease	88

Section 6 – Personal Development: All the Family — 93

Self-esteem and self-image	94
Coping strategies	97
Learning to play: the family	98
Behaviour management	101
Cooking, menus and diets	106
Mentoring	109
Mediation	110
Brief therapy	110
Counselling and therapy	111
Anger management	115
Conflict resolution	116
Parents' factor 85	117
Language, words and praise	118

Section 7 – Cultural, Disability and Family Issues — 123

Respecting race, creed, culture and disability	123
Discrimination	124
Practical suggestions for working with disabled children or parents	126
Families and friends	128
Developing positive approaches	129

Section 8 – Inter-agency working — 131

Who's who in helping families	131
The key worker	131
Child Development Team	132
Connexions	132
The children's guardian	132
Social service workers	133

Education workers	134
Health workers	134
Other referrers	136

Section 9 – Management Issues — 138
Recruiting staff and volunteers	138
A person specification	139
The new worker or volunteer	140
Volunteers	140
Characteristics of a team	142
Training	142
Appraisals	143
Delegation	143
Goals	144
Using time effectively	144
Communication	145
Record keeping	151
Visitors – pain or pleasure?	152
Complaints	153
What happens if things go wrong?	155

Section 10 – Policies, Procedures, Evaluation and Monitoring — 161
Policies and procedures	161
Evaluation and monitoring	161

Section 11 – Conclusion — 190

Useful names and addresses — 191

The family support handbook

List of model forms and documents

Section 1   The Child
Family support checklist	Checklist	18
Developing effective partnerships with parents	Form	19

Section 2   Children and Families
Child Development: birth to 16 years old	Guidance	40
Meaningful milestones for under fives	Guidance	43
Practical suggestions for working with young people	Information	48
Welcome to Holland	Story	49
Audit of needs: working with a child with disability	Checklist	50

Section 3   Parenting Skills and Methods of Family Support
Parenting programmes review checklist	Checklist	61

Section 4   Keeping the Family Together
Model family group conference	Information	73
Tips for successful contact	Tips	74
Practical suggestions for a safe contact	Guidance	74

Section 5   Organising and Planning Family Support
Group planning example	Example	90

Section 6   Personal Development: All the Family
Behaviour plan	Example	120
Emergency coping strategies	Checklist	121

Section 9   Management Issues
Volunteer training plan	Example	157
Staff and volunteer training needs assessment checklist	Checklist	158
Staff and volunteer training priorities: checklist	Checklist	159
Keeping records of training	Example	160

Section 10   Policies, Procedures, Evaluation and Monitoring
Beacon Policy	Example	165
Policy for outreach work	Example	166
Home/outreach agreement	Example	167
Outreach monitoring	Example	168
Outreach monitoring – Record of Feedback	Example	169
Playscheme procedures	Example	170
Questionnaire for 'new' parents	Example	172
Questionnaire for parents	Example	173
Questionnaire for visiting professionals	Example	174
Questionnaire on our outreach service	Example	175
Questionnaire for parenting groups	Example	176
Students and professional visitors policy	Example	177

Complaints:

Stages for handling complaints	Example	178
How to listen to complaints	Example	179
Guidelines for parents	Example	180
Guidelines for staff	Example	181
Guidelines for governors	Example	182
Complaints procedure	Example	183
Record of complaint	Example	184
Summer school for teenagers: risk assessment	Example	186
Confidential staff questionnaire	Example	188
Example of presenting your findings	Example	189

Children and families are entitled to social provisions that help them live together peacefully and satisfactorily. If there are new programmes anywhere that better achieve this goal, families should have access to these programmes and improved services as soon as they are available.

Juergan Hermann, 2001, *Social Work in Europe*, Volume 8, Number 2, p18.

Children's rights

All children have the right to love and care.
All children are equal.
All children have the right to adequate and healthy food.
All children have the right to education.
All children have the right to health care.
All children have the right to play.
No child should be exploited at work.
No child should be maltreated.
No child should be the victim of war.
No child should be abused in any form, sexually, emotionally or physically.
Children have the right to express their own opinions.
Children have the right to practice their own religion.
Children have the right to associate with others.
Children have the right to information.
Children without families have the right to special protection.
Refugee children have the right to special assistance.
Disabled children have the right to special care.
Children in conflict with the law have the right to special assistance.

From postcard entitled 'The Rights of the child' produced by Defence for Children International (DCI), a worldwide movement for children's rights. It is based on the main articles of the United Nations Convention on the Rights of the Child.

The Family Support Handbook will help anyone working with families to ensure that children's rights are upheld.

> **We should never be complacent.**
>
> **We should always strive to improve both the quality, level and appropriateness of the service offered to children and families.**

About this Handbook

How to use this handbook

This handbook is for anyone:

- Working with parents and other family members, including grandparents.
- Training people in working with parents.
- Studying in the area of family support or working with parents.

The book is not a training manual, as such, so we have not gone into the theories of family support, or given detailed guidance on what you should or should not do. The book is based upon our views, ideas and experience as well as extensive reading. However, we are sure other people will have equally valid and useful opinions.

This handbook is a series of:

- checklists
- guidance sheets
- notes
- charts
- diagrams
- further reading suggestions
- examples

These can be 'dipped' into at any time, used in any order and developed for use to help staff who have differing levels of ability, knowledge or experience. Some of these documents may also be given to parents as a reminder of issues discussed or work done.

The aim is for the book to act as an 'aide mémoire' for individuals. It will also help those involved in employing staff or utilising volunteers and managing a team to make judgements about their team and to help to develop them as people working with, and supporting, families.

Much of the material has been produced so that it may be copied or used as OHP foils. It may also be adapted to meet specific needs or given as handouts to staff, volunteers, visitors or parents.

At the end of each section is a bibliography or suggested further reading.

This book seeks to discourage unfair discrimination on the grounds of age, gender, disability, including the use of sign language, race, ethnic origin, nationality, sexual orientation, social class, religion or language.

The family support handbook

What is in this handbook

Supporting families is a very sensitive area of work: it should not be undertaken lightly. It needs care, planning and thought, so that parents may be helped in turn to help the child. It is also important to be wary of imposing one's own values, beliefs and attitudes rather than enabling the parents to develop their own personality and identity. Finally, and most importantly, we should not lose sight of:

- What does the child want?
- What is in the child's best interests?
- What will enable the child to thrive, develop and grow so that they are able to fulfil their potential and take their rightful place in society?

Section 1 – Issues

This section looks at the many issues relating to working with parents:

- The child
- Objectives of family support
- Parents:
    - Developing effective partnership with parents including checklist
    - Barriers to working well with parents
    - How do you see parents?
    - What do parents want?
    - What do parents need?
    - Different types of parents and different types of families
- Confidentiality
- Child protection
- Ensuring safety when working with families
- Family support checklist

Section 2 – Children and families

This section discusses child development and understanding children before moving on to look at the many different types of needs of both parents and children. When most people think of parenting or parenting groups it is the mother that first comes to mind so this section also examines the roles of other family members including fathers and grandparents.

Section 3 – Parenting skills and methods of family support

This section discusses the whole question of parenting skills including what we mean, how judgements are made, who is right and whether there may be other, equally important and successful ways of parenting, including joint working with parents. The importance of preventative work is also discussed.

Many parents today do not have appropriate role models of 'good enough' parenting; they may lack self-esteem or confidence or other basic parenting skills. This section looks at ways of personal development for parents as well as providing coping strategies and simple techniques for managing situations and difficult behaviour.

Section 4 – Keeping the family together

No matter what hard times or difficulties children and young people have experienced, for most of them the place they wish to be is with their family (NFCA, 1999). We therefore look at ways of keeping the family together.

Section 5 – Organising and planning family support

This section looks at who might facilitate family support, setting the rules as well as some of the barriers preventing success. A large part of this section discusses working with groups before moving to supporting families to organise and run their own groups. Teenage parent groups are also discussed.

Section 6 – Personal development: all the family

Here there is a broad section which covers areas such as building confidence and self-esteem, learning to play, coping strategies, anger management and conflict resolution. This section also looks at what outside help may be available to parents and how it might be utilised.

Section 7 – Cultural, disability and family issues

Important issues around respecting race, creed, culture and disability are considered and ways noted of avoiding discrimination. The importance of understanding other people's family values and developing positive approaches to these issues is discussed.

Section 8 – Inter-agency working

The role of the wide and disparate groups who may be involved with parents is examined and brief descriptions of their roles included. In this section there is also a discussion around contact and referral and ways of ensuring appropriate co-ordination of services are examined.

Section 9 – Management issues

This section looks at basic management issues around setting the rules, recruitment and retention of staff, record keeping and team building, as well as the practical implications of setting up and running groups and what happens if things go wrong. The efficient and sensitive use of volunteers in working with parents is also examined including the importance of their training and appraisal.

Section 10 – Policies, procedures, evaluation and monitoring

Without evaluation and monitoring it is not possible to know how you are doing, what you could do to improve and whether the service is meeting the needs of the children and their families. This section provides examples of evaluation and monitoring tools and looks at the importance of giving feedback and using the information obtained to improve the work. Sample forms are included.

Section 11 – Conclusion

At the end of this book there is a list of useful groups and organisations from whom more detailed information on a particular topic may be obtained.

If we are to have a fairer society where families can live happily together then we have to find ways of supporting those who may need help either in the short-term or on an ongoing basis. Hopefully this book will make a small contribution to helping to achieve these goals.

The family support handbook

Supporting Families: A Guide for Those Helping Parents to Help Themselves

Preamble

In order to feel able to write this book the authors, experienced practitioners, have read a vast amount of literature and talked to many people working in the field and in academia. They have also visited many different locations both in the voluntary and public sector.

The places, groups and people visited that stand out are those that have the indefinable quality of 'atmosphere', 'feeling of warmth', being 'snug', 'caring' or 'comfortable'. It is not possible to describe this feeling or how to create it but if some of the suggestions in this book are followed with commitment and enthusiasm then the rest should follow.

Background

> *...Parenting is not about patting yourself on the back for being understanding and liberal, it's about Guidance, Education and Training to help the child you love become a man or woman you can respect.*
> (Grandparent Times, May 2000)

The vast majority of parents are very capable people. We should be empowering them to take control of their lives. This may be in helping them develop skills by:
- Actively involving them in decisions that affect their children's lives.
- Providing opportunities to share responsibilities for the welfare of their child if this will help to maintain family life.
- Providing opportunities for them to help others by using their own skills to care for other people's children.
- Teaching them how to cope in times of illness, bereavement or at other times of stress in their life.
- Letting them know that support is there if needed, and how to access that support.
- and most importantly, ensuring that parents are not disempowered by the system, but are confident in their own child rearing skills and knowledge.

John Hudson says in his paper *Working with Parents* 1997:
> *There are very few inherently bad parents. Most parents who find themselves unable to carry out their responsibilities are being affected by circumstances...such as lack of knowledge, experience of satisfactory role models; resources; stigma or social isolation or long-term stress through unemployment, poor conditions or chronic illness.*

Family support helps to promote the welfare of children and their families. It:
- Enables families to take control of their lives.
- Helps families help their children develop and grow.
- Gives both the family and the child the opportunity to take their rightful place as active citizens in society.

The potential impact of family support was summarised very clearly by one parent who said, when she realised that her special needs child was going to a play-day for a whole day: *'have I died and gone to heaven?'*

The book is suitable for training people and working with people who are employed in a variety of circumstances. It can be used by:
- Family centre staff.
- Family groups.
- Parenting groups.
- Those working with families whose children have special needs.
- Home visiting groups.
- Portage workers.
- Health visitors.
- People delivering outreach work in different locations.
- Family support workers working in the child/parent's home or elsewhere.
- Foster carers working with parents.
- Social workers and others working with the parents of:
  - children who might otherwise be taken into the care system, or
  - children who may be preparing to return to the family home.
- Anyone studying, or working towards a qualification in, working with parents.

As long ago as 1989, S17 (1) of the Children Act stated that:
It shall be the general duty of every local authority...to safeguard and promote the welfare of children within their area who are in need; and so far as is consistent with that duty to promote the upbringing by their families, by providing a range and level of services appropriate to those children's needs.

Yet today courts still recommend in many cases that children should be 'taken into care' based on the advice of professionals. Often by the time a case comes to court, carrying out any preventative work is no longer a possibility. As Maria Ruegger notes in her research:

...I come across great numbers of records of investigations dealt with on a duty basis and then closed. Usually little, if any consistent help or support is offered to these families as a result of the investigations...when eventually the growing number of incidents of concern leads the local authority to institute legal proceedings parents feel betrayed and let down...Sadly it is often the case that specialist help is only available late in the day to families when proceedings are underway...If such help could be offered at an early stage then it is reasonable to assume that at least some families would never need to experience legal proceedings.

(Working with Parents, 2000)

If we really do wish to meet the needs of children then one of the first things we should do is to consider the views, feelings and situation of the parents as well as the children. We should provide all necessary help to assist and support parents to enable them to care for their children.

Further reading

Alexander, T. (1997) *Empowering Parents: Families as the Foundation of a Learning Society.*
A report for policy makers, parents and practitioners, which presents a summary of the views and recommendations from over 1,000 parents and people who work with families in fifteen parts of Britain. It contains ideas about how to support parents and children and sets out the priorities for action as seen by parents and workers on the ground.

Association of Metropolitan Authorities, and Children's Rights Office (1995) *Checklist for Children: Local Authorities and the UN Convention on the Rights of the Child*. Luton, Local Government Management Board.

Childline (1998) *Unhappy Families: Unhappy Children*. London, Childline.
Written for adults, this is a child's eye view of troubles and unhappiness within families. It addresses a number of questions, including: what do children identify as problems in family life, where and whom do they turn to for help, what are their expectations of family life?

Penn, H., and Moss, P. (1996) Playing to Win. *Community Care*. 1131, 24-5.
This article argues that it is imperative that we work towards an integrated children's day care service if we are to meet the educational, physical and emotional needs of all children.

Useful resources and bibliography

Hermann, J. (2001) Families First: Comparing Child Care Developments in the Netherlands and Germany. *Social Work in Europe*. 8: 2, 18.

Hetherington, R., Cooper, A., Smith, P. and Wilford, G. (1997) *Protecting Children, Messages from Europe*. Lyme Regis, Russell House Publishing.

Home Office (1998) *Supporting Families*. London, HMSO.

HMSO (1989) *The Children Act*. HMSO.

HMSO (1995), *The Children Act (Scotland)*. HMSO.

Kitz, H., Old, D.L., Henderson, C.R. et al. (1997) *Effects of Prenatal and Infancy Home Visitation by Nurses on Pregnancy Outcomes, Childhood Injuries and Repeated Childbearing. A Randomised Controlled Trial*. JAMA.

Millham, S., Bullock, R. and Little, M. (1993) *Going Home*. Dartmouth, Devon.

National Foster Care Association (1999) *National Standards in Foster Care: Report on Findings Of Children and Young People's Questionnaires*. London, NFCA.

Trevelyan, J. (1996) Father's Day. *Health Visitor*. 69: Jun. 213.

Wheal, A. (2000) *Working with Parents*. Lyme Regis, Russell House Publishing.

Section 1
Issues

The child

Both children and adults have needs, though they may be very different ones. Children, which in this book, means anyone between birth and the age of 16, have physical, emotional, social, environmental and developmental needs.

Physical needs include:

- Food and drink.
- Warmth and shelter.
- Protection from harm.
- Clothing.

Emotional needs:

- To feel approval.
- To have the opportunity for self-expression.
- The ability to love.
- To feel loved.

Social needs:

- To communicate, through language and gestures.
- To benefit from caring adults.
- To learn boundaries and rules.
- To play, with and without direction.

Environmental needs:

- To have a safe, clean, space to live and play in.
- To be stimulated, both mentally and physically.

Developmental needs:

- To be able to play.
- To have learning opportunities, to solve problems.
- To be able to socialise, make friends.
- To have quality, safe, play equipment appropriate to the age of the child.

A child needs ... Time:

to be	to use	to laugh
to do	to look	to enjoy
to ask	to listen	to work
to feel	to touch	to play
to learn	to taste	to make mistakes
to say	to smell	

A child needs ... Love:

You can help:

- Be there for the child.
- Say yes, as often as possible.
- Realise how important it is to be a child.
- Invent pleasures together.
- Giggle a lot.
- Surprise them.
- Say 'no' when necessary.
- Teach about feelings.
- Learn about parenting.
- Make loving safe.
- Teach them to play.
- Reveal your own dreams.
- Search out the positive.
- Keep the gleam in your eye.
- Encourage being silly.
- Open up to the child.
- Stop yelling.
- Express your love – a lot.
- Speak kindly.
- Handle them with care.

There are many more…

Figure 1: Children's needs

Different parents have different wants, which may include:

- Choices
- Confidential advice
- Confirmation
- Counselling
- Help in solving problems
- Help with discipline
- Knowledge
- Peer support
- Peer or family approval
- Support
- Someone to talk to
- Self awareness
- To be in charge
- To have an enjoyable family life
- To acquire new skills
- To develop nurturing skills
- To communicate better
- To learn by example
- To manage behaviour
- To feel less isolated
- To be assertive
- To manage anger
- To be confident
- To grow

Figure 2: Developing parenting programmes

Objectives of family support

To:

- change attitudes
- improve parenting skills
- improve coping skills
- increase knowledge and understanding
- improve parent's confidence and self esteem
- build family relationships
- recognise parents' own needs
- empower parents
- share views, ideas and information with others
- raise child's self esteem
- improve quality of life for parents and child
- improve two-way communication
- develop child's abilities
- promote positive parenting
- improve nurturing
- advise about family relationships
- make choices

may also help to:

- change parents' behaviour
- change child's behaviour
- understand and respect child's needs
- be more child centred
- manage difficult behaviour
- change parenting style
- encourage parents to value and praise children
- improve home-school links
- prevent abuse
- allow parents to recognise their own skills
- provide support in a crisis
- allow parents to look at their life/child/family in 'another way'
- provide practical support eg when a new baby arrives
- handle stress
- develop problem solving skills
- provide appropriate information eg child with special needs
- understand teenage years
- understand grandparents and their roles

At the beginning of the 21st century there has been a shift away from Child Protection issues immediately a family is a 'cause for concern' to a proactive family support system of operating. What this means in practice is that professionals have realised that some families may need a little or a lot of outside help at some time in the lives of their children. This support, whether one-to-one or in groups will, in most cases, prevent a child being taken away from the family and placed into the care system.

The aims and objectives of family support should be SMARTER:
- **S**tated
- **M**easurable
- **A**chievable
- **R**ealistic
- **T**imed
- **E**valuated
- **R**eviewed

Family support must be in the child's best interest.

We should remember that parents are a child's first educator. Any help we give parents should therefore benefit the child. We may be helping parents to improve their parenting skills **but** they must want help, it should not be imposed.

Some parents will attend a group or meeting of their own accord. Others will have been referred by any of a variety of individuals (see Section 8). However, if a child or family is referred to your group or organisation, then you should know the reasons for the referral.

If you do not receive this information, then the checklist at the end of this section should enable you to identify the areas where a family might need help. The parents could complete the form on their own or they might wish to complete it with you – either because they have reading difficulties or purely because they wish to talk things over with you.

They could put ticks in more than one box if they wish or they could number the items in order of the highest priority to them. Sometimes health visitors, for example, will complete a similar form on behalf of the parents. It may be interesting to compare the parent's perceptions of need with that of the professionals.

Parents

Developing effective partnership with parents

Most parents who need family support may be unable to carry out their responsibilities as they are being affected by circumstances. These may include:
- Lack of knowledge, experience or satisfactory role models.
- Lack of resources to feed, clothe, house, teach or support their family.
- Lack of opportunity through, for example, stigma or social isolation, to provide the wide range of experiences a child or young person needs.
- Long-term stress through unemployment, poor working conditions or chronic illness.
- Short-term stress through redundancy, bereavement or other crisis.
- Relationship difficulties whether at home or in wider society.

- The consequences of such relationship difficulties including separation, divorce, remarriage and step-parenting.
- The indirect consequences of stress or relationship difficulties, such as alcoholism, self-abuse and mental illness.

Parents may need:
- practical support
- reassurance
- to learn skills
- to develop new ways of dealing with situations
- to acknowledge differences without feeling a failure
- to realise that acknowledging this as 'normal' can go a long way to solving, or at least reducing, the differences to manageable proportions

In the UK the average life of a marriage is now under ten years which means that an increasing number of young people will not be living or cannot remember living, with their family of origin. The trauma for families of broken relationships and the development of new ones must be addressed by both children, young people and the families.

Before working with parents it must be decided:
- Why this is necessary.
- Should the child or young person be there or do the parents wish to be alone – discuss with all concerned.
- What it is hoped the partnership will achieve.

When working with parents it is important to look at:
- What the child or adolescent wants.
- What the parents want.
- What it is possible to achieve and then make a plan.

You may think either party needs to change their way of behaving but everyone's feelings must be considered.

If you go to the parent's home, it will give you an opportunity to learn about the family at home which may show the children, young people and parent(s) you know, in a very different light.

When you meet parents, in whatever location, treat them as equals. It should be a two-way process. Assume they have a long-term positive interest in their child's future – whatever the short-term evidence to the contrary might be. This may have arisen from the stress of their present situation.

You may also need to encourage them to remain as involved with their child as they feel able and as the child will permit. They need to be involved in decision-making and kept in touch with progress even where they have no or minimal involvement with them for example.

Sometimes other family members or family friends can be used as 'go-betweens' to help the situation. They might also act as a mediator where communication has broken down within the family. Family group conferencing may also help.

Sometimes you may decide to offer counselling to parents. Explain what this means and what the implications might be. Whatever happens, you cannot force the pace. You have to allow time for parents to come to you.

Where you meet parents will have an affect on the likelihood of a successful outcome. Many parents will have adverse memories of school for example, so meetings in schools may cause fear or be unsettling. A student once said that the one thing her mother was looking forward to when she left school was not having to come to parents' evenings.

If you are invited to the parents' home then it is important to remember that you are the guest in their home and should behave accordingly. You should also respect their way of life.

When – many parents work and day time groups and meetings may mean a loss of pay or the goodwill of an employer. It may also mean that the father may not be able to attend. Meetings should be called that are convenient to all parties and if they must be during normal working hours should either be at the beginning or the end of a working day. Meetings that involve young people should be held after school.

Child care provision and interpreters should also be offered if this is appropriate for any meetings.

Why – it may be to help, assist, ameliorate, guide, arbitrate or just support the family. *'I just thought I'd come to see how things are going'* may be all that is needed or may be the trigger to the family telling you about other concerns where they think you may be able to help.

Building up trust – the police, for example, know the value of building up trust with families. Often they will call round to visit a family who are likely to be called to give evidence. This moral support, which families find very beneficial, usually means that the police have a better chance of obtaining a conviction.

What you wear – is it important? Some would say no. However, if you wish to create the right atmosphere in order to achieve success then you need to think about the family and respect what you judge to be appropriate dress – very casual may be right for one family and equally inappropriate for another. Cultural dress codes should be honoured, which may mean women covering arms and legs in order not to give offence.

How you behave – always treat the family with respect. Meet them on time if you have made an appointment, say how long the meeting will be, listen to what is said even if you don't agree. You don't have to accept the offer of a cup of tea if you think the standard of cleanliness leaves something to be desired! On the other hand it may be culturally offensive to refuse. Do your homework before you meet the family.

Tell parents that anything they tell you will always be confidential. If you feel you have no alternative but to pass on any information, always tell them what you are going to do. Also let them see what you have written down and give them a copy.

Any suggestions you make must suit the family's way of life. Some parents may shout. You must keep calm and try to work out alternative strategies with which they are happy.

Alone or accompanied – sometimes visiting a family alone is the best strategy. At other times for your own safety it may be better to be accompanied. If someone else is with you, one of you can talk and work with the parents and the other with the child or young person.

Strategy – have a plan before the meeting and try not to allow circumstances to make you digress. Have a safety strategy too!

Concluding – at the end of the meeting or visit state what has been agreed, what has to be done and when contact will be made again.

Partnerships with parents will only develop successfully if the parents respect, trust and believe in you. By following the above guidelines you will have a better chance of success.

Barriers to working well with parents

This list is not factual. Sometimes, however, it may be the parents' or other people's perception of why things are not going well:
- Lack of experience of working with different groups of adults.
- No experience of parenthood.
- Experience of parenthood different to that of some parents.
- Limited experience of working with those who have failed academically.
- Life experience may be quite different from that of the parents.
- Stereotypical idea of parents.
- Discriminatory views of certain groups.
- Culture – some professionals jealously guard their professional autonomy and do not understand the need, or wish, to work in partnership with parents.
- Poor interpersonal skills.
- Lack of empathy.
- Poor listening skills.
- Prescriptive or judgemental approach.
- Poor preparation.
- Having a different agenda to that of the parents.

How do you see parents?

How do you see parents? Do you see them as a single group or as individuals who may be:
- Confined to a wheelchair?
- Muslim?
- In receipt of welfare benefits?
- Afro-Caribbean?
- Carers not parents?
- Partially sighted?
- Mothers?
- Step-parents?
- Unable to read?
- Asylum seekers?
- Fathers separated from their children?
- Academic failures?
- Unemployed?
- And so on, you get the idea.

or

Do you see them as people, equal partners, who want the best possible life chances for their children?

The family support handbook

Different parents have different wants but they may include:

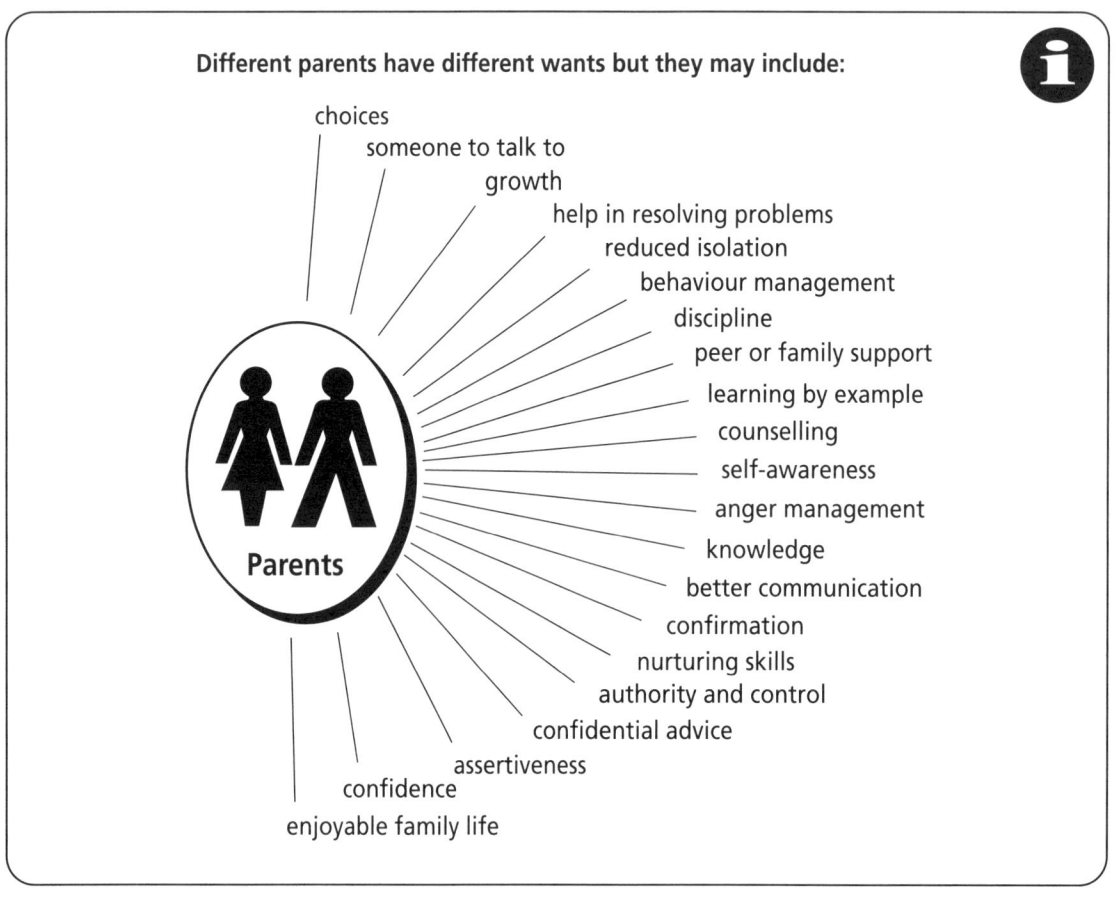

- choices
- someone to talk to
- growth
- help in resolving problems
- reduced isolation
- behaviour management
- discipline
- peer or family support
- learning by example
- counselling
- self-awareness
- anger management
- knowledge
- better communication
- confirmation
- nurturing skills
- authority and control
- confidential advice
- assertiveness
- confidence
- enjoyable family life

Figure 3: What do parents want?

Eg, parents need:

1. To know themselves, and to understand:
   - their own values and beliefs
   - what these mean in practice
   - how committed to them they are
   - how they might change themselves, and their practice

2. Understand the influences:
   - background, environment
   - expectations
   - their friends
   - the media
   - how they have become e.g. authoritative, over-protective, permissive

3. Practical information:
   - health (their own and their children's)
   - child development
   - where to go for help
   - rights
   - ailments
   - accidents
   - education

4. Skills:
   - bonding and attachment
   - empathy
   - self-awareness
   - touching
   - discipline
   - unconditional love, honesty and respect
   - developmental knowledge

Figure 4: What do parents need?

Parents need information, knowledge and learning about how to:
- Win and keep love and affection.
- Develop sensitivity and confidence in a child's worth and abilities.
- Have appropriate expectations of their child.
- Enjoy sharing meals, games, and outings together.
- Be consistent, reliable and dependable, set clear rules and stick to them.
- Supervise and encourage children to set their own boundaries.
- Communicate openly and honestly.
- Listen and reflect.
- Make decisions and accept responsibility for them.
- Cope with stress and deal with conflict.
- See things from a child's perspective.
- Avoid harsh punishment and reinforce good behaviour.

Children need help with and to receive:
- basic physical care
- affection
- security
- stimulation
- independence, responsibility
- consistency, fairness
- guidance and control
- boundaries and routines

Different types of parents and different types of families

Reproductive technology such as IVF and social change have generated new ideas of parenting. Whilst two parent families where both parents have produced their child and are living together are still the norm, many children are now brought up by a single parent, usually the mother.

We also have:
- Children conceived from anonymous donors.
- Surrogate motherhood.
- Gay couples who have become parents.
- Many young girls who are still technically children, becoming mothers.
- Families that have been reconstituted more than once often being the norm.
- Children adopted via the internet without stringent checks being made.
- Children cared for by other family members such as grandparents.
- Shared care and support care for parents who cannot bring up their child unaided.
- Foster carers and residential carers looking after children where the courts have decided the local authority rather than the parent should have parental authority.
- Private fostering where the parents pass the responsibility for looking after their children to another individual whilst they continue their study or return to their country of origin, for example.

All or any of these groups may need individual or group help, therapy or counselling, to learn new skills, to understand themselves or their situation better or just plainly someone to talk to in our modern often very lonely society.

Religious, moral, ethical beliefs may also affect parenting styles and practice. Some examples are:
- **Sikhism** – mothers are required to rest for 40 days after childbirth and are given rich food. They are forbidden to prepare food during this time.
- **Judaism** – childbirth is always considered a life-threatening situation. After the baby's head has been delivered the child is considered to be a separate human being whose life may not be sacrificed even to save the mother's life.
- **Jehovahs Witnesses** – do not believe in anyone receiving a blood transfusion in any circumstances. This may affect the lives and wellbeing of the parents and or the child.
- **Roman Catholics** – do not believe in abortion or in using birth control. Some sectors of the Catholic church also actively encourage families to have several children.

It is important therefore to be tolerant and understanding of all families and to find out as much as possible about their beliefs.

Confidentiality

Everyone is covered by the same confidentiality rules as everyone else.
- leaders
- workers
- helpers
- volunteers
- visitors
- caretakers and cleaners
- tea makers
- children and young people
- AND other parents

Constant reminders may be necessary of what is unacceptable:
- Gossiping.
- Repeating what has been said in apparent confidence.
- Leaving written documents lying around for others to see.
- Not closing the door securely if a private telephone call is being made or private meeting is being held.
- Repeating secrets.

You may learn something that concerns you
{
- In general conversation
- During group discussions
- As a disclosure
- Someone deliberately telling you something
- Someone accidentally telling you something
- Overheard – accidentally or whilst eavesdropping
- Whilst observing a situation
- In written documentation

Figure 5: Confidentiality

Many people are very secretive, keeping their worries and concerns to themselves.

Other people love chatting and like nothing better than to tell others their most intimate secrets.

Some people hate the idea that they are being discussed by others, whilst it would not concern others in the slightest.

> **Relevant information should only be passed on to others on a 'need to know' basis.**

However, some secrets cannot be kept. If you are worried that a child or a young person has suffered or is likely to suffer significant harm, you may have to take the matter further, but you should tell the person concerned what you intend doing and why, and that they will be kept informed.

Child protection

Child abuse

The main forms of abuse are:
- **Physical abuse:** where children are physically hurt, injured, given poisonous substances or drugs.
  90% of children who are physically abused have visible injuries, for example, different ages of marks, marks from beating, black eyes, burns or scalds, unexplained fractures and head injuries.
  Physical abuse should be suspected where the explanation of the injury does not fit the facts, or if the child is reluctant to say how the injury happened. However, it is important to remember that children do hurt themselves accidentally sometimes. It is when the same event seems to occur more than once that you should be wary.
- **Neglect:** where a child's basic needs are not met such as food, warmth, medical care, shelter.
- **Emotional abuse:** where a child suffers as a result of a constant lack of affection, verbal attacks, bullying, racial and other harassment, which undermine a child's confidence and self-esteem.
- **Sexual abuse:** where children are exploited by others to meet their own sexual needs. This may be sexual intercourse, fondling, masturbation, oral sex, anal intercourse and exposure to pornographic material including videos.

Child Protection Conference (CPC)

This is a meeting called by social services if they, or the police, a teacher or someone from the health service such as a doctor thinks a child may be suffering, or might be at serious risk of suffering significant harm because of abuse and that they may need protection.

The first child protection conference is called to exchange information and to decide whether the child should be placed on the **Child Protection Register**. If so, then a keyworker will be appointed to:
- Co-ordinate a plan.
- Help the child and parents to take part in the plan.
- Keep the child informed of what is going on.

The plan is made to ensure the child is kept safe and well and that they get any help needed. The plan will also show any other action that may be necessary. Whatever is agreed at the meeting should be carefully explained to the child.

CPC meetings must be held at least every six months and more often if necessary.

The Child Protection Register
- Is a list of children and young people who are considered to be at risk or who may be at risk of abuse.
- Is a central point of reference for professionals who are worried about a child and want to know quickly whether a child protection plan exists.
- Is a source of information for all the professionals concerned.

A child or young person's name comes off the list if:
- It is considered the child or young person is no longer at risk.
- The reasons which originally led to the registration no longer apply.
- The child has moved to another area and that area has accepted responsibility for the case.
- The young person is 18 years-old.
- The young person has married.

Information for parents
(Staff and volunteers should know this too!)

What are the early signs of abuse? Children who suffer abuse of any kind **may**:
- Show aggressive behaviour, have severe tantrums.
- Give an air of 'detachment' or don't care attitude.
- Exhibit overly compliant behaviour or have a 'watchful' attitude.
- Not join in school social activities, and have few friends.
- Not trust adults, particularly those who are close.
- Have 'tummy pains' or other symptoms with no medical reason.
- Have eating problems including over-eating, loss of appetite.
- Suffer from disturbed sleep, nightmares, bedwetting.
- Run away from home, attempt suicide or inflict self-harm.
- Revert to younger behaviour, become depressed or withdrawn.
- Have relationships between adults and children that are secretive and exclude others.

Children who have been sexually abused **may**:
- Show sexually explicit behaviour (e.g. playing games and showing awareness which is inappropriate for the child's age).
- Continually masturbate openly or be aggressive.
- Take part in inappropriate sex play.
- Have soreness in their vagina or genital area – often spotted during nappy changing.

However, many of these signs may have a simple explanation not related to abuse. Conversely there are other signs that may indicate abuse. What is important is to be vigilant.

What are the consequences of abuse?
Some of the above signs may persist into adulthood. Adults may also experience personal problems such as difficulties in personal relationships with both men and women; difficulties in sexual relationships; conflicts with parents and difficulties in responding to their own children.

A parent may ask 'Can I touch my child'?
Yes, of course. Children depend on their parents for warmth, security and love. It is natural for parents to cuddle, hug, kiss and stroke their children when showing love and affection.

What is wrong is for adults to subject their children to sexual activities for their own gratification. If a parent becomes worried about sexual feelings towards their child then they need to get help.

How can I help my child?

> **Experience shows that children very rarely lie about abuse.**

Listen very carefully to what your children tell you, they may be telling you that they are worried. If your child tells you that they have been abused:
- Believe them.
- Tell them that they are not to blame for what has happened.
- Tell them that they are not alone and you are there to protect them.
- Tell them that you will make sure that the abuse does not happen again.
- Reassure them that you believe them, you are their friend and can be trusted.
- Seek advice and help and act to protect your children.

Who should I tell?
If you suspect your child is being abused contact:
- social workers
- health visitors
- family doctors
- police

or you may want to discuss it first with someone you can trust.

Will my child be taken away?
Only a minority of circumstances require the child to be removed from their family for immediate protection. Full and thorough investigations take place and then if there is sufficient evidence the case will be taken to court for the judge to decide what is best for the child.

Do social workers have a right of entry to my home?
No. But, if you don't give permission without a very good reason it may give the impression you have something to hide, in which case, a warrant will be produced by the police.

Can my child be medically examined without my consent?
If the social worker or the police have grounds to suspect that some form of abuse has occurred they may apply to court for a medical examination to take place if the parents refuse to give their permission.

How can I help my child avoid being abused?
- Let them know you will believe them – they shouldn't be worried about telling you anything.
- If they don't need to be accompanied by an adult, children should wherever possible go around in pairs or in groups.
- They should always take the same route home.
- A young child should not be allowed to go to public places such as lavatories on their own.
- Baby-sitters and child minders should be checked to ensure they are reliable and can be trusted.
- Tell them they can do anything they like if they think they are in danger or someone is hurting or threatening them:
  - run away
  - scream
  - shout
  - kick
  - punch
  - or lie.

- Their safety is all that matters.
- Children should know they can choose for themselves who they want to kiss, cuddle and hug them. They shouldn't be made to do these things against their will, particularly if they feel it is wrong.
- Parents should always know the three Ws:
  - **W**ho their children are going out with.
  - **W**here they are going.
  - **W**hen they are going to be home.

> **Don't keep it to yourself – if you know, or suspect, that a child is being mistreated or neglected you must tell someone even if the perpetrator is someone you know or even love.**

Child protection

- 60% of women aged 16-21 years had previously received unwanted sexual attention:
  - 4% had been forced into physically invasive sexual acts
  - only 2% had been to any official support agency.
- 90% of children had been hit by parents by the time they were eleven:
  - 75% of children aged one had been hit
  - 15% of all physical punishments could be categorised as severe.
- Referrals:
  - 23% from education including school nurses
  - 17% from health
  - 17% from general public and family members
  - 13% from social services
  - 12% from the police and probation
  - 6% were anonymous
  - 12% unknown.
- Six out of seven children who were the subject of child protection referrals did not get placed on the child protection register:
  - 44% of those investigated led to no further action.
- Combinations of more than one type of abuse, or persistent abuse, led to more negative outcomes for children.
- Parents' attitudes to social work systems were soured if they found out that an investigation had taken placed behind their backs.
- There is a strong link between child abuse and mental illness; substance misuse and domestic violence.

(Steve Hayes, Portsmouth City Council)

Ensuring safety when working with families

Whilst offering family support to parents or carers part of the role will include working with children and young people. It is of paramount importance that issues of safety are always considered. There may be slightly different issues from those when working with adults.

The following parameters should be followed at all times to ensure the safety and protection of everyone.

General

- Read over carefully any notes received on the children and young people for whom you are responsible.
- Familiarise yourself with the programme.
- Identify any child or young person who has a medical condition or special needs.
- Ensure you are aware of the information on all the emergency procedures to be undertaken.
- Establish who is to administer any medication to the child or young person.
- Ensure a police check is made on everyone working with children and young people before they begin.
- For your own protection and that of the child you should never be alone with the young person except in public rooms unless agreed staff and helpers procedures have been set up and followed.

Tips

- Never leave keys in the door – you may get locked into the room.
- When visiting a new place, quickly look around and make a safety plan for exit if you think this might be necessary.
- Take someone with you if you have a doubt about safety.
- Make a professional decision about whether to enter someone's home or not.
- Find out if anyone else is in the house if you visit alone.
- Use all safety locks provided on any premises – to prevent unwanted visitors entering as well as ensuring the safety of everyone and stopping children 'escaping'.
- Read all safety procedures for the building you are using. If there aren't any, then devise some and get them approved.

Working 'off-site', going on a visit or working within a group

- Keep a list of those for whom you are responsible and check this regularly.
- If dealing with a distressed child or young person, always stay within sight of your group.
- Always make sure you are aware of where the children or young people are going and offer a time limit for their return – if not tell them you will contact a group leader and report them missing.
- If you feel a child or young person would benefit from time out of the group, ask for assistance.
- Decide what is an acceptable number to allow out of your sight to use the toilet at any one time and stick to it.

Disclosure

Some people (child, young person, parent) may tell you or one of the other helpers something difficult that is happening or has happened to them. It could be they are unhappy where they are staying; it could be they have suffered abuse in the past or are suffering abuse at present or they think or know their children are suffering abuse.

These are very serious things for anyone to be saying and it is important to respond appropriately. It is not appropriate for you or any of the staff to ask questions about the abuse – that is a task for social workers and the police. What is needed is to support the person making the disclosure if they are distressed and to let the nominated person in your organisation know as soon as possible so that they can take the appropriate action.

The following are some important points to remember in your contact with a child, young person or parent telling you about possible abuse:

- Listen carefully to what you are being told.
- Explain to them that you cannot keep secret what they tell you because you must try to get them or their children the protection they need.
- Some children, young people or a parent may decide that they are not going to tell you something because you cannot guarantee them confidentiality. This is always hard but it is not appropriate for you to carry the burden of keeping confidential something that may mean the child or young person continues to be hurt.
- If it is possible and the child, young person or parent wants to talk to you about a difficult topic try to find a quiet space. It may well be that you don't feel confident to open the topic further – that is fine and you should contact a group leader as discreetly as possible and ask them to come to help you.
- If the child, young person or parent does tell you something it is important to reassure them that they are right to tell you about something that is worrying them.
- Find out if they have spoken or feel able to speak to anyone else.
- So you can pass on information, you may ask a very few open questions – questions which ask where? who? when? what? These questions do not put words into anyone's mouth but help them to recall what has happened. It is a good idea to jot down anything the child, young person or parent tells you for referring on if this is decided as necessary.
- Let them know why and what you are doing and will do.
- It is important to try and stay calm, as the child, young person or parent may be upset.

Remember you are not responsible for investigating any abuse that may be disclosed. You are responsible for making sure that the correct people are told so that they can put in process any child protection procedures.

There may be children, young people or parents who have had very difficult times and who are angry and resentful about what has happened to them. They may try to take it out on others so be alert to the possibility that they may be a risk to others.

If you see anything that makes you think a child or young person is acting inappropriately, e.g. bullying, hitting or sexually assaulting another child you must act immediately to prevent this situation continuing. You may also see parents behaving in a similarly inappropriate way. In these situations the leader should be asked to take the child, young person or parent away from the group until there has been time to discuss the next move.

Sometimes telling whoever is trying to bully or hurt others that this is unacceptable and you will be closely watching what is happening may be enough to stop the problem. Sometimes extra help may be needed and you should find out the procedure for offering this service.

Talk to a leader about handling the different needs of all those involved.

Always record in writing any concerns that you may have as this information may be useful in the future.

Further reading

Armstrong, H. (1997) *Refocusing Children's Services Conference*. Department of Health/Association of Directors of Social Services. 43pp. London, Department of Health.
Proceedings of a conference held to discuss how to achieve the refocusing of child protection practice envisaged in *Child Protection: Messages from Research*, so that the emphasis is on preventative and family support work.

Association of Directors of Social Services, and NCH Action for Children (1996) *Children Still in Need: Refocusing Child Protection in the Context of Children in Need*. 40pp. London, NCH Action for Children.
Examines how, in the light of recent research findings, the child protection process and support services to families and children in need can be improved and integrated in order to achieve better outcomes for children and families.

Batty, D. and Cullen, D. (Eds.) (1996) *Child Protection: The Therapeutic Option*. 126pp. London: British Agencies for Adoption and Fostering.
All too often children who have been abused are subject to repeated interviews and examinations prior to court hearings, their parents are disempowered and antagonised, their home lives are disrupted and there are longer and longer delays before the provision of any support that can be described as therapeutic.

Useful resources and bibliography

Wheal, A. (1997) *Adolescence, Positive Approaches to Working with Young People*. Lyme Regis, Russell House Publishing.

Wheal, A. (Ed.) (2000) *Working with Parents, Learning from Other People's Experiences*. Lyme Regis, Russell House Publishing.

Wheal, A. (2000) *The Foster Carer's Handbook*. Lyme Regis, Russell House Publishing.

Model forms and documents

Family support checklist

Please put a tick at the side of one or more of the descriptions which you think fits your needs best:

You need help with:

- Your child(ren)'s health and wellbeing. ❏
- Your child(ren)'s stability. ❏
- Managing your child(ren)'s behaviour. ❏
- Being involved in your child(ren)'s development. ❏
- Your emotional health and wellbeing. ❏
- Your self-esteem. ❏
- Your own health and wellbeing. ❏
- Stress caused by conflict in the family. ❏
- The day-to-day running of the house. ❏
- Managing the household budget. ❏

You feel isolated. ❏

You are already using other services ❏

You are coping with extra work caused by having:

- Children under five ❏
- A multiple birth ❏
- A child with special needs ❏

If there are other reasons why you might need family support, please tell us about them:

Developing effective partnerships with parents

Action	Whose responsibility?	Date completed/ To be completed	Date of next review
Establish a policy that sets out the values underpinning the relationship and acknowledges the differentiated nature of the parents			
Identify a named person responsible for developing effective relationships with parents			
Establish transparent procedure and practice for working with parents: – meetings – telephoning/e-mail – use of language (inc. foreign language) – style of dialogue – provision of information – managing situations – complaints			
Establish a focus group to meet regularly			
Develop systems for parents to contribute to all aspects of improvement of the organisation/ group			
Produce written material that: – is written in a style providing access for all parents – contains contribution from parents			
Establish procedures for meetings that offer: – minimal formality – opportunities to take advantage of existing parent activities/skills			
Develop systems that: – directly involve parents – ensures reflection on the progress/ development of the child and involves all concerned			
Develop parent consultation procedures that offer parents clear opportunities to have pre-determined input e.g. behaviour management, conflict resolution			
Analyse the child's performance to identify social patterns of achievement that may affect the way the child interacts with the parent			

Section 2
Children and Families

Understanding children

A child enters the world with a combination of genes inherited from both parents, which will influence development of skills and preferences. This is just part of the story for, from the moment of birth, pressures outside the child begin to affect the way they react to surroundings. These pressures include:

- the physical environment
- the level of care and stimulation received
- health
- material circumstances
- cultural differences
- religious preferences

A child born prematurely or ill may not catch up with peers for several years. A child who lacks attention and stimulation will also be disadvantaged. In the western world, parents are persuaded to part with their hard-earned money to buy toys regarded as educational, in the hope that development will be accelerated. We all know that sometimes the child in question rejects the toy but has hours of fun with the box. In other parts of our globe, where survival is precarious, higher value may be placed on skills which might appear less necessary to us.

There are certain basic needs common to all children, however, without which progress can be patchy or arrested. These might be listed as:

- Knowing and feeling that their parents or carers love and want them.
- Being given time and attention when they need it.
- Living in a calm and happy environment.
- Having clear and consistent care and reasonable expectations of progress.
- Being set a good example by adults.

Perfection is something for which we strive but rarely achieve, therefore peaks and troughs are likely to occur in the best-run households. It is the overall pattern of care which is the single greatest influence parents or carers have on a child's development.

When the two major factors, heredity and environment, combine, they do so in an infinite variety of patterns. Every child has a different range of experiences and skills, resulting in a marvellous tapestry of progress which can be classified as 'within normal development'. Therefore, beware. Developmental checklists (page 40) give a flavour of what is appropriate at each age. A single step outside the range does not always need to be dealt with, for every child is different. It should not be ignored, but a little time often sorts out the problem. When there are a variety of concerns, a plan of action will be needed, which includes support from professionals.

Meaningful milestones for under fives

Many parents want to know how their child should be developing. At the end of this section is a Guidance Sheet, *Meaningful milestones for under 5's*, which is a guide to the general pattern of development of a child at different ages. It may also be useful for those working with families, either as a guide for themselves or as a way to help parents with child development.

Some children will achieve some milestones earlier than predicted for their age but may be behind in others. If one or two of these milestones are not reached by the time of their next birthday, it is certainly nothing for the parent to worry about. However, if a child is behind with quite a few of these milestones then a parent should discuss their concerns with a health visitor or GP, for example.

Understanding adolescents

When Andy was 16 and kicking over the traces, I thought that provided I gave him food, clothing and shelter, he would be happy, and anyway I was busy getting on with my own life. Eventually he left and went to live with his father…I thought he would soon come back, but he did not. Now 24, he has told me that what he hated most when he was 16 was that I wasn't there. (Parent)

I hate it when my parents go on holiday. There's no-one there to talk over what you've done in a day. (Young person)

There is no such thing as a 'normal' adolescent but some of the following characteristics may be displayed at different times during adolescence:
- Increased aggressiveness.
- More direct expression of their own opinions about clothes, entertainment, politics, activities etc.
- Forgetting to do chores or not taking their responsibilities seriously.
- Complaining about chores and other activities.
- Messing about or being silly, especially in front of friends.
- Making decisions which they know will cause disagreement.
- Keeping secrets.
- Stubbornness.
- Periods of a critical or condemning attitude towards anyone in authority.

Many young people may also exhibit any or all of the following:
- Chronic irritability and negativism.
- Rebellion or defiance.
- 'Don't care' attitude.
- An inability to work co-operatively, even with their peers.
- Frequent depression or outbursts of rage.
- Prolonged anger.

Young people need you to:
- Establish clear expectations and limits.
- Discipline fairly.
- Deal with negative behaviour in a positive way.
- Reward good behaviour.
- Promote and encourage a relationship with birth family if appropriate.
- Encourage their cultural and religious heritage and behave in a way which does not discriminate.
- Ensure that their educational needs are met.
- Promote their self-esteem and positive self-image.
- Respect them and their birth family.
- Work with all concerned, including themselves, to help them achieve their potential.
- Help them to learn to live independently.
- Help them to speak up, to be heard and to be listened to.
- Listen, understand and relate to them.
- Be available when needed.
- Encourage independent thinking.
- Be knowledgeable about sexuality.
- Beware of over or under stimulation.
- Allow them their own space and privacy.
- Learn to handle hypersensitivity.
- Provide stability and structure.
- Share your own adolescent experiences.
- Know their friends.
- Set realistic limits.
- Encourage responsible choices.
- Be sensitive to sensitive areas.
- Encourage and support them.

The **emotional growth** of adolescents is the process of becoming aware that they are an individual. This may manifest itself as argumentativeness, silence or questioning as they discover who they are. As they become less dependent on others and learn to think for themselves, they still develop their own uniqueness and individual character; choosing their own clothes, friends, music, hobbies and food and ways of saying 'This is who I am'. All the physical, intellectual, emotional, social and spiritual growth teenagers have experienced throughout their lives will pull together into a relatively stable and enduring personality, enabling them to take their place in the community as responsible adults. For teenagers whose lives have been disordered in some way, this is probably the hardest stage to achieve and where the most help will be needed.

Adolescents need to:
- Develop their own distinct identity and sense of uniqueness and individuality.
- Progressively separate themselves from their childhood dependency on others.
- Develop meaningful relationships with peers and others.
- Crystalise their sexual identity and develop their capacity to relate well to others.
- Gain confidence and skills to prepare for a career, economic independence and adult responsibilities.
- Fashion their values, beliefs and attitudes toward life.

But they often want the privileges of adulthood without the responsibilities!

Teenagers also need to:
- Become comfortable with their feelings, both positive and negative.
- Become less troubled by strong feelings of love and happiness as well as intense feelings of fear, discouragement and anger.
- Learn that strong and even conflicting emotions can exist together without causing damage.
- Find out they can love someone and still be angry with them.

Early adolescents, for example, may angrily announce 'I hate him. I never want to see him again'. Older adolescents may be more able to admit 'I love her and hate her. She makes me so mad' or 'I wish I didn't like him'.

> **There is no such thing as a 'normal' adolescent.**

> **Safety tips**
>
> For your own safety, remember the following four points:
> 1. You may be vulnerable; know your organisation's policy on punishment and restraint.
> 2. Beware of corners of rooms or standing between large pieces of furniture as you may get trapped by a young person or a group.
> 3. Don't flirt or allow yourself to be taken in by young people flirting with you.
> 4. Some young people may appear to be articulate, confident and well behaved so may not get the attention they deserve.

> **If you want young people to respect you then you have to respect them.**

For practical suggestions for working with young people, see page 48.

Other family members including fathers and grandparents

When I went along to the playscheme I was just ignored by everyone including the helpers. I presume it was because I was a man. (Father)

My wife and I are caring for our grandchild. We didn't know anyone else who had young children so I took...along to the local playgroup. No-one spoke to me and several people eyed me suspiciously ...'why has an old man like that got such a young son?' I felt they were saying. (Grandfather cover)

When we think of working with parents, many people think of working with women, as the Department of Health report 1995 noted:

Although researchers were sensitive to this issue it was frequently easier to interview mothers in the studies than fathers, other relatives or resident partners and this should be borne in mind when interpreting results. (Department of Health, 1995, p17)

Trevelyan, interviewing representatives from the Institute of Public Policy Research (1996) cites their comments:

> The attitude of professionals is crucial. In practice, it appears that they almost invariably target services at mothers, many are ambivalent about engaging with fathers and evidence suggests that many actively avoid them. Fathers then sense how they are 'defined out' of the childcare equation.

However, it is not just the attitude of professionals, it is also the attitude of fathers. Staff at the Lawrence Weston Family Centre, where 70 per cent of the children are on the Child Protection Register, became aware of the importance of involving fathers in work with children. The found that fathers' and children's groups were the most successful way of engaging fathers because fathers felt excluded from mother-focused groups. They have engaged fathers by encouraging agencies to identify the needs of the fathers, as well as mothers, at the referral stage, ensuring fathers are involved at all introductory visits and contact meetings. They also offer fathers a range of services at the initial stage.

Recent research by the Family Rights Group and others has also highlighted the need to include grandparents and other family members within family support schemes. This should not just be within the decision making process such as family group conferences as many grandparents are now caring for their grandchildren, often full-time, and will want, and need, guidance and help.

Some fathers and some grandparents may be happy to participate in services that have primarily been designed for mothers. However, for some this may be extremely difficult so it is important to be alert to individual needs and to develop services that may be adapted for differing circumstances and differing groups.

Behavioural problems: the child's or the adult's?

Much of the behaviour of a child or a teenager that is classed as a 'problem' may actually be the result of the behaviour of the parents or other adults:

Carer-related
- a lack of discipline
- too much shouting
- too little listening
- too busy
- treating different children in a family, a school or a club better than others
- ignoring the physical, emotional and social needs of the child or adolescent
- lack of supervision of the content of tv, videos or computer games
- arguments and disputes
- lack of coping skills

Child-related
- few opportunities for play
- worries
- non-stimulating environment
- poor nutrition
- inappropriate tasks
- lack of exercise
- too much time spent watching TV or computer games or on the internet
- lack of praise
- lack of confidence or self-esteem
- jealousy of others
- instability in the home environment (house moves, changing families)
- lack of good role model

Other causes may be:
- peer pressure
- media pressure
- illness
- **a physical condition that prevents communication and causes frustration**

Whatever the cause, those working with these children need to first of all find out and understand what is causing the child's or young person's behaviour. They then need to work with all concerned, including parents and the child to find ways of improving or changing the situation.

Children who have been abused and how to help

> **Most abused children or young people are abused by those they know and even like.**

Children and young people who have been abused may behave in such a way that it is often not possible to know that they have problems. This may be because of the coping strategies they learnt during the time that they were being abused. Others may exhibit violent, sexual or emotional behaviours which may be difficult to cope with. Whatever behaviour they exhibit they may need additional help to cope with their past.

Parents who discover that their partner or someone close to them has been abusing their child, or just the fact that their child has been abused, may also need professional help to enable them to cope with the situation and to help their child.

Child Protection in Section 1 highlights some of the behaviour patterns of an abused child and also gives some pointers to watch out for. As explained in that section there are four types of abuse:

Physical   **Neglect**
Emotional   **Sexual**

Children and young people are entitled to be protected from all forms of abuse:
- Let them know they are not alone and that you are there to protect them.
- Many children and young people will find it hard to talk about being abused.
- They need to know that you can be trusted.
- They need to know that you will believe them.
- They need to know they are not to blame.
- But most importantly they need to know that some 'secrets' cannot be kept.

The signs of abuse are repeated here in another form from that in the Child Protection Section. However, any of the following may be purely symptoms of distress:
- Poor or deteriorating school work.
- A reluctance to go to school or frequent early morning minor illnesses.
- Problems with sleeping, nightmares.
- Complaints of hunger, lack of energy, apathy.
- Possessions are often 'lost', dirtied or destroyed.
- A desire to either stay around or avoid adults.
- Reluctance to attend health assessments.
- Appearing unhappy, withdrawn or isolated.
- A new tendency to stammer.
- Lack of appetite, or 'comfort eating'.
- Aggression.
- Constant attention seeking, over-pleasing or compliant behaviour.
- Indications of substance misuse.
- Attempted suicide.
- Running away from home.
- Low self-esteem.

Unlikely excuses to explain any of the above, or refusing to give any reasons for the above should ring 'alarm bells'.

Common signs of sexual abuse

These are:
- Injuries or soreness in sexual areas or mouth.
- A wide range of emotional problems.
- Inappropriate sexual behaviour; overly sexual or extreme fear of intimate contact.
- Knowledge and understanding of sexual matters beyond their age.

When it is suspected a child or young person has been a victim of sexual abuse, they may be interviewed at a safe place by trained staff, one of whom may be from the police. A video or tape recording may be made of this interview, so the child doesn't have to keep repeating their experiences.

If you suspect abuse?
- Record your concern.
- Share the concern with a senior member of staff, a social worker or the police.
- Consult the child/young person protection manual if you have one.
- In some cases you may have to speak to someone outside your own organisation if you suspect abuse is occurring within your organisation.

Breaking confidentiality is a big problem. Some children or young persons will tell you their problem, begging you not to tell anyone else. If you have evidence that the child is being abused, then you **must** pass this on. You will have to explain this to them. They'll hate you at first but will be relieved when they know that something is being done. Keep them informed.

You can help a child or young person who may have been abused by:
- Listening to what they say.
- Avoiding asking too many questions or asking for unnecessary detail.
- Being alert and observant.
- Making notes ASAP during or after your talk.
- Trying to find out what they are afraid of.
- Following the procedures for protecting them when they are in danger of serious harm.
- Telling them what you are going to do and what will happen next.
- Never telling lies.
- At the end note the time of starting and finishing the conversation and the circumstances described, using the child's language wherever possible. Sign and date it. Keep your original notes whether typed or hand written.
- Referring to social services.

Follow up in writing using social services proforma which covers:
- The child's developmental needs.
- Parenting capacity.
- Family and environmental factors.

Who are the abusers?

Most abused children or young people are abused by those they know and even like, such as older friends, parents, relatives, carers or neighbours. This is particularly difficult for the child to cope with as they do not want to cause a problem to those close to them. Nevertheless, action must be taken as the abuser may go on to abuse others. You will have to help them to understand this, and that what abusers do is wrong. It should be made quite clear that they are in no way to blame.

The effects of abuse are:
- Physical scars heal, but the emotional trauma takes many children and young people longer to recover from and they usually need professional help.
- Children and young people who have been sexually abused over a long period of time may have little understanding of what is appropriate sexual behaviour. This will have to be learnt. Be aware of this and ensure that you do not place yourself in situations which could be misinterpreted.
- Victims of sexual abuse may act out their abuse on younger child. Be alert.

Young people who have abused

This section has been written from the perspective of a parent. In this way it is hoped that anyone working with parents in this situation will have a better understanding of some of the difficulties faced by the parents concerned and may feel better able to help them.

To know someone who abuses children is a dreadful experience for most people. To know someone who you love who abuses is even worse. To know that that person is your own child is often the worst experience a parent has ever had, or is ever likely, to have.

Background to the abuse

The vast majority of young abusers are boys. However, occasionally the abuser is a girl. In the early teens, boys, just like girls, go through changes in their life known as 'puberty'. These changes are both physical and emotional. It is a natural part of maturing into adulthood. Boys enjoy playing with their penis and will often have an erection and both boys or girls may masturbate. They may become overtly interested in all things sexual, including pornographic magazines, TV and internet channels and in discussion with their friends. They may also become uncouth and vulgar about such matters.

All the above are a normal part of a child's development. However, a young abuser's fantasies are around young boys or girls. Keep a watchful eye. Young abusers may be any, or all, of the following :
- Immature for their age.
- Short in stature.
- Thin or fat.
- Shy.
- Have low self-esteem.
- Quiet.
- Secretive.
- Have been subject to ridicule at school because of their appearance, their ability or their lack of confidence.
- Not very popular or successful with members of the opposite sex.
- Have been abused themselves.

Of course, many children may exhibit some of these characteristics but are certainly not abusers.

What can parents do to help prevent their child being an abuser?

- Tell them in an open way what is, and is likely, to happen to their body during puberty. This is most important as what they hear from others may not be correct.
- Create an environment where teenagers can talk freely to you about sexual and other matters.
- Have time to listen, to share their worries and concerns.
- Be interested and concerned.
- Be available. Parents often think that once a child becomes a teenager they are no longer needed. This is not true. They are needed in a different way.
- Find ways to give them confidence.
- Help them to succeed.
- Have some control over the TV and internet channels they watch.
- Know what they are reading, where they are going, who they will be with and when they will be back.
- Help them take part in a wide variety of activities and hobbies.

If your child is an abuser

- You will feel anger, shame, remorse, blame yourself, blame others and hate.
- You will ask 'why?'
- Your relationship with your partner may suffer, either temporarily or sometimes permanently as you each try to come to terms with what has happened.
- You will worry about the safety of the other children in the house.
- You will feel angst and pain for the victim and their family.
- Neighbours and so-called friends will reject you.
- You may be subject to verbal abuse as others blame you.
- People will talk about you.
- You will be visited by the police, social workers and other professionals.
- You may have to attend court.

In addition to coping with the above you will also have to come to terms with your feelings for your own child:

- Will you ever be able to trust them again?
- Do you love them?
- Do you despise them?
- Can they be 'cured'?
- What will happen to them?
- 'Where did I go wrong, what could I have done differently?'
- How do they feel now?
- Will I ever feel the same about them again?

This will be an extremely difficult time for all the family. You, and other family members, may need professional counselling. Your son or daughter will almost certainly be required to attend regular counselling sessions to help them think about:
- The problem.
- How things have worked out for themselves and for the victims.
- What a mess they have got themselves into.
- What the future holds.

What is certain is that your life will never be the same again. You will have to make plans, develop coping strategies and hope that you and your child will be able to work something out together to enable your lives to continue in a way that is acceptable to both of you.

Children with disabilities

I'll never walk her down the aisle. (Parent just told of his child's severe brain damage.)

Disabilities come in many forms and combinations. A child may have a single difficulty or a combination of several. Syndromes may cause a variety of physical and learning problems. There are five main points to remember and be mindful of:

1. **The child is a child first**. The disability will be secondary to the child's natural disposition. You may still have expectations of behaviour and performance from the child. All too often, misguided parents try to make up for the disability by not imposing rules and indulging the child. This in itself leads to an unhappy child who is unsure what boundaries exist, or whether they have to follow them as other children do.

2. Eighty per cent of what you would do for a non-disabled child is OK for a disabled child. For the other twenty per cent, you will need to seek the advice of all those experts out there who are only too willing to let you know what to do in direct response to the nature of the disability.
   The Code of Practice for Special Educational Needs 2002 gives four categories:
   - Communication and interaction: children with speech and language delays and disorders would come within this category, as would some aspects of autistic spectrum disorders.
   - Cognition and learning: all learning disabilities, whether moderate or severe.
   - Behaviour, emotional and social: as well as those who find it difficult to respond to boundaries, this would also include traumatised children and some aspects of autistic spectrum disorders.
   - Sensory and physical needs: these are the children whose disabilities are often more obvious, e.g. the wheelchair bound, combined with those whose sensory deprivation is not quite so apparent, e.g. the partially sighted and those with hearing loss.

3. You cannot always see disabilities. A child may be seen to behave differently, with the result that the parents are blamed for poor child-rearing skills. The truth of the matter may be that the child has an unseen disability. Imagine how you would feel if your child had a problem, then try to be more understanding next time you see that child yelling in the supermarket.

4. Consider the parents who:
   - Will have been through a period of mourning for the perfect baby they expected.
   - May feel guilty for causing the disability by passing on genes or suspecting what was eaten or done during pregnancy.
   - May feel that they have failed in the most basic human drive for reproduction by producing a less than perfect child.
   - May have had a very black picture painted, or have been informed insensitively of the disability.
   - May have very real worries about the future of their child and both the child's and their own ability to cope.
   - May show increased anxiety about their child's care away from them.
   - May have to cope with a stringent daily medical routine.
   - May have to cope with a child who is in constant pain or who has a terminal condition, or who wrecks the house.
   - Will have had far more outside interference in their lives than they might normally expect.
   - May experience relationship problems. The arrival of a child with special needs often causes anguish and marital difficulties. One parent may find it far easier to accept a disabled child than another. One parent may be unable to express their feelings, to the distress of the other.
   - Will continue to feel distress at each new stage of development. All around, other children will reach life stages and develop skills which their child may be unable to gain until much later, if at all. Remember how parents compare their children constantly and what it might feel like to be the parent of the child who is being compared unfavourably.

   When I was first learning about disabilities, a wise person used an onion to explain what parents might feel. Think how, as an onion grows, it has to produce another and another layer to enclose its core. When you have a child with a disability, as each little stage is reached and your child does not follow the usual pattern, you have to grow another layer on your onion.

   On the positive side, read *Welcome to Holland* at the end of this section.

5. Children have rights in law according to the SEN and Disability Act 2001. One of the basic rights is to be included with non-disabled children in education. Access has to be managed so that children with disabilities are made to feel valued and respected members of their communities, no matter what their combination of difficulties. This will mean attendance at a mainstream school for most children if their parents so wish.

Addictions

We all have addictions at some time in our life. It may be:
- eating chocolate
- drinking tea
- dieting
- watching TV
- surfing the internet
- smoking tobacco
- drinking alcohol
- taking prescribed medicines
- sniffing substances
- smoking pot
- taking illegal drugs

In most cases, people generally realise what they are doing and find a way of stopping, sometimes by themselves. Sadly, some people cannot stop their addiction. Some people seek help, others will seek help that will not be successful, others do not seek help and the damage to their body and mind is irretrievable.

Parents and carers

In the past it was government policy to take children away from serious substance misusers or send the adult to a re-habilitation clinic in order to wean them off the drugs. It is now realised that some drug addicts can still parent their children adequately so a new emphasis has evolved. Professionals gather information about the children and family and then make judgements as to whether or not the cumulative picture of concern in relation to the child warrants intervention under the child protection framework or family support framework.

Substance misuse is defined as:
> ...use that is harmful, dependent use or use of substances as part of a wider spectrum of problematic or harmful behaviour   (H.A.S. 1996)

Substance misuse by parents or carers does not on its own automatically indicate that children are at risk of abuse or neglect, although it is essential that workers recognise that this is a high risk group. Adults who misuse substances may also be faced with multiple problems including:
- homelessness
- accommodation or financial problems
- difficult or destructive relationships
- lack of effective social and support systems
- issues relating to criminal activities
- poor health

Assessment of the impact of these stresses on the child is as important as the substance misuse itself. It is important to know whether the childcare has changed for the better or worse from when the parent or carer was a non-user. Detoxification or ceasing of substance misuse does not in itself necessarily lead to better childcare, family life or functioning. In households where there are two adult carers, drug or alcohol use may be organised to enable one carer to assume responsibility for childcare when the other is intoxicated, with little intervention being necessary.

Withdrawal from drugs for some people can significantly impair their capacity to tolerate stress and anxiety. Detoxing can be difficult and a drug or alcohol using parent may require additional childcare support during this process. The child should receive support in their own right to help them deal with their feelings as well as their physical wellbeing.

The parent or carer's perception of the situation is extremely important. If they are aware of the effects their substance misuse may be having on their children they are more likely to try to lessen the impact by stabilising or changing their use. The importance of stability should be stressed rather than insisting parents or carers detox. It must not be assumed that when a parent or carer becomes drug or alcohol free they will be a better parent or carer.

A parent seeking treatment is frequently seen as the solution to preventing continuing risk. However, entering treatment for a variety of complex reasons can actually increase substance misuse temporarily or increase the risk to the child. For similar reasons, leaving treatment even when abstinent and fully motivated is not necessarily a positive factor when the care of the child is considered.

The child or young person

Children as young as eight may start to 'glue sniff' or smoke and some children as young as 11 will have been totally under the influence of alcohol. With easy access to all these substances children and teenagers are becoming addicted at much earlier ages. Also in some households where drinking is the norm, children are actively encouraged to drink alcohol, often quite heavily, by the adults.

A recent government initiative, offering nicotine patches to 12 year-olds to help them give up smoking highlights the size of the problem. General observation also shows that some 14 year-olds regularly get drunk at weekends. There is obviously a good deal of work to be done around re-education and use of leisure time if young people are going to be able to take their place in society as active citizens.

The following may be helpful for parents and for others working with children and young people.

Drug and substance mis-use

Many young people will have experimented with drugs in some form before they leave school.

Why do they use solvents or take drugs?
- It's an alternative to alcohol.
- They like the excitement, the element of danger.
- If adults are shocked, that can be an attraction.
- They like experimenting with new sensations which can be seen as interesting and exciting.
- Hallucinations can also be dangerous, unpleasant and frightening, but even this can be enjoyable (think of horror films).
- Drugs allow young people to escape – if only temporarily and only in their imagination.
- They may be lonely, feel inadequate, lack self-esteem or confidence and think drug taking will help.
- They think it will help them blot out problems.
- They are encouraged by their friends or made to look small if they refuse.

Solvent abuse
After smoking and alcohol, 'glue sniffing' as it is commonly called, is the most common form of teenage experimentation. Children often start as young as eight or nine years but the peak age is thirteen or fourteen years. Most children only do it a few times and then stop. Sadly some do not.

What to look for
There are no clear-cut signs and many of the effects are hard to distinguish from normal growing up. Moodiness may be a result of sniffing but many children are moody without having tried solvents. Look out for:
- Finding quantities of empty butane, aerosol or glue cans, or plastic bags in a place where you know children have been.
- Chemical smell on clothes or breath.
- 'Drunken' behaviour.
- Sudden change in behaviour or lifestyle, for example, going around with a new set of friends.
- Wide swings in mood or behaviour.
- Spots around nose and mouth (glue sniffers rash only occurs with some glues and may not be as common as acne!).
- Loss of appetite.
- Asking for money from their friends or carers without explaining what it is for or with feeble explanations.
- Secretiveness about leisure-time activities.
- Frequent and persistent headaches, sore throat or runny nose; a quick visit to the doctor would be useful.

Don't jump to conclusions but be alert to the signs

Drugs

The drugs have 'street' names which may change with fashion. Your local drugs advisory service will give you a leaflet showing the latest names.

Injecting drugs can be most dangerous because of the risks of:
- Infection where injecting equipment is unsterile and shared. The most serious infections are HIV (which can develop into AIDS) and hepatitis. If a young person is injecting drugs they may get hepatitis B or C. Make sure children know the dangers.
- Abscesses, thrombosis and other conditions from injecting drugs that were never intended for injection.
- Gangrene from hitting an artery instead of a vein.
- Blood poisoning caused by a wound becoming infected.
- Overdose when a drug of unknown strength is delivered directly into the bloodstream.

What to do if someone is 'high' on drugs
- Keep calm and patient – you have got to try to bring them down.
- Talk to them about how they feel at the moment.
- Ask them questions about where they are or what they can see – pink elephants?
- Gradually, slowly, quietly explain where they are, who you are.
- Keep talking, don't threaten, be pleasant – the time, if appropriate, for punishments and explanations may be later.
- Sometimes the best solution is just leaving them to themselves but you will need to stay alert.

What to do in an emergency
- Make sure they've got fresh air.
- Turn them on their side so they won't choke on their vomit.
- Don't leave them alone.
- Get someone to dial 999 and ask for an ambulance.
- Collect any powders, tablets or anything else that may have been used and give it all to the ambulance driver.

Tips to help prevent drug, solvent and alcohol abuse

- Talk to the children and young people about their views on drugs, drink, smoking and sniffing.
- Help them have new, interesting and challenging experiences.
- Get them to think about how they might refuse these drugs (they are all drugs) without losing their friends.
- Teach them to care for and value their health.
- Help them build up their self-esteem and respect for themselves.
- Treat them with respect.
- Take an interest in their opinions and worries.
- Check out any problems they may have.
- Arrange other activities and help them take part.
- Seek support from your local advisory centres.

Be a good listener.

Eating disorders

Some very young children have a physical condition around eating which they may have had since birth. Other children and young people may develop an emotional eating disorder. Many people who have an eating disorder will have begun this at around the age of 13 years, though sadly some will begin even earlier.

My brother tries to be perfect in every way. He worries all the time about what other people think of him. (Young person)

My friend sometimes starts eating and just can't stop. (Young person)

My sister has become very distant from us. She seems to keep herself away from us.
(Young person)

Some of the above signs might mean that someone has an emotional eating disorder. People with an eating problem may eat too much, or refuse to eat, or make themselves sick after food because they are unhappy. This can lead to emotional and physical problems. People often think that eating disorders are just about food and weight – but they are not. They are about feelings too. People often don't think they could have this illness.

Eating disorders are a way of coping with feelings that are causing unhappiness or depression. It may be difficult to face up to, and talk about, feelings like anger, sadness, guilt, loss or fear. The eating disorder is an unconscious attempt to avoid these feelings, or keep them under control. It is a sign that the child or young person needs help in coping with life and shows how they see themselves as a person.

There are many reasons why people develop eating disorders. Often there is no one cause, but a series of events that makes them unable to cope. Examples are:
- changes in the family
- the death of someone special
- problems at school, e.g. exams or being bullied
- lack of confidence, e.g. adolescence
- emotional or sexual abuse

If you know someone who has, or who you think might have, a particular problem with eating they should seek advice. It may be there is quite a simple reason that can easily be put right or they may need specialist help.

Loss and bereavement

At any age losing someone or something you love even for a short time may be a very painful experience. Talking and listening is the best tool for helping someone at this time but there are some practical things that can be done too.

Bereavement

For children, it is sensible to develop the idea of death from quite an early age:
- a dead bird
- a dying cat
- what does it mean?
- what causes it?
- what happens afterwards?

You could talk about the ageing changes that occur throughout life; how illnesses cause different changes; and why people die. They may not remember but if the time came when someone died, the words would at least be familiar.

If you know someone close to the child is likely to die then the child should be prepared. What the following words, for example, mean to someone may be a useful topic for discussion:
- death
- bereavement
- burial
- cremation
- funeral
- mourn
- cancer
- AIDS

It may also be possible to talk about the feelings and emotions of the different people involved; how different people will react in different ways. When a death occurs it may also be necessary to remind a child what the words mean and also explain, probably more than once, what is happening.

Rituals around death vary depending on the culture or religion. It is important to have information so the child, young person or parent can be helped and supported. The better prepared people are the more control they will have. On hearing the news of the loss of someone they know and love there may be feelings of shock and disbelief – a numbness. This may be followed by:
- misery
- anger
- questioning
- sadness
- self-blame
- blaming others

If people, child and adult alike, know in advance that the loss is to occur they will have time to prepare themselves mentally. The immediate impact of the loss is much greater if the loss is sudden.

When the time is right, talk to them or let them talk to you as talking helps to dispel wrong ideas and make good sense of the loss. Talk naturally or ask a question but don't put pressure on anyone to talk. If they don't answer, accept this. Remember, even if they don't talk they are likely to be thinking about the dead person or may even be silently speaking to the dead person.

Don't try to make people get over it too quickly. There is no set time that bereavement lasts. The bereaved feel desolation and despair. They will feel there is no sweetness, no purpose, no point in their lives:

Who am I?
What does it mean for me?
may be said many times.

The pain will recur again and again – at birthdays, anniversaries, at Christmas, at holiday times and at other times that were special for the particular family.

Some children or young people may want to go to the funeral service, others may not. Some may want to visit the cemetery or crematorium, others may not. Whatever their wishes, these should be respected and if at all possible acted on. It may be necessary to check that the child understands the occasion if they wish to attend the funeral.

Different religions or cultures practise and use different rituals in relation to death and you may find *Caring for Dying People of Different Faiths* by Julia Neuberger to be useful. Help children and adolescents find practical things they can do, such as collecting mementoes or photographs or writing down how they feel. They may want to keep a particular item that belonged to the person who has died, such as a sweater or a pair of slippers. Let them choose.

Remembering the person is important, so too is feeling proud of that person.

Losing a pet they have loved can be just as traumatic for a child as losing a loved one. Just buying a replacement probably won't solve the problem.

Children and adolescents who enter the care or criminal justice system may experience similar feelings of loss and so too will their parents.

Divorce

Divorce or separation is very much like death to children and young people in many ways. They may be losing someone they love. They often blame themselves. They will need to be prepared and know what is going on and be allowed to be involved in discussions if they are old enough to understand.

A form of grieving may also take place. Be a good listener. Talk to them. Be prepared.

Living with a new or different family

Most children will live with a family of some kind.

Living with a family will have different meanings to different people. It may mean:
- A couple living alone.
- A couple and child.
- An extended family such as grandparents or uncles and aunts.
- A single parent, possibly with visiting partner.
- One parent and a step parent plus parents' child.
- One parent and a step parent plus both parents' children.
- Two parents' children plus foster children.
- A household with pets.
- No pets when the child is used to pets.

No two families are the same. There may be different:
- customs and traditions
- atmospheres – formal or informal
- attitudes to noise, shouting and play
- acceptances
- values
- expectations
- religions or no religion

Victims of domestic violence

Almost a million incidents of domestic violence in England and Wales were uncovered by the British Crime Survey (1996). 680,000 involved men's violence towards women. Domestic violence is a form of abuse inflicted on a person by someone they know. This might be a:
- current or ex-spouse
- partner
- relative
- child towards parent or relative

Domestic violence is not class, gender, age, race or sexual orientation biased.

Domestic violence can be in the form of physical, emotional or sexual abuse, vary in severity and frequency and can be punished by law. Victims may suffer injury which may need hospital treatment (including death), unconsciousness, sleep problems, anxiety, depression, loss of confidence and low self esteem

Children may, as a result of being exposed to domestic violence:
- Suffer disability from violence during pregnancy.
- Be at risk of physical harm or death.
- Be at risk of other forms of abuse which may accompany violence, e.g. sexual abuse, emotional abuse.
- Suffer short or long-term distress.
- Become depressed.
- Become confused in their loyalties and relationships.
- Have their education and home lives disrupted.

What can we do to help?
- Ask if you suspect someone is experiencing domestic violence.
- Give priority to ensuring the safety of those involved.
- Give positive response and support.
- Discuss their fears in a sensitive way.
- Believe them.
- Reassure them that they are not to blame.
- Emphasise how strong they are to have coped with the abuse.
- Tell them they are not alone.
- Be aware of problems due to racial, language and cultural barriers.
- Contact specialist agencies.
- Discuss with them whether they can be sent mail at home.
- Respect their wishes if they do not want you to make contact with them.
- Help them to decide what they want and what steps might achieve it.
- Let them know they can talk to people at a refuge without having to leave their home.
- Provide a listening ear when it is asked for.
- Talk about the best ways to maintain their safety.
- Inform them of the help they might expect from other agencies.
- Be personally responsible when you refer them elsewhere and follow through.
- Try to maintain some contact.
- Offer help no matter how you are asked; it may be a throwaway remark or an angry outburst.

What are the barriers?
- Fobbing people off when they ask for help.
- A flippant, cynical or sceptical response to what they tell you.
- Asking what they did to provoke the violence.
- Thinking only of what they can do on their own in the situation.
- Making choices for them.
- Ignoring your intuition if you suspect someone is a victim.
- Giving up on them when things are taking longer than you had hoped.
- Insisting on them having joint meetings with the abuser.
- Letting the abuser have their address or telephone number.
- Promising to pass on a letter to them from the abuser or arranging contact between them.

Further reading

Adams, P. (1999) Towards a Family Support Approach With Drug-using Parents: The Importance of Social Worker Attitudes And Knowledge. *Child Abuse Review*. 8:1 Jan. 15-28.
Considers social worker attitudes to drug using parents in the context of developing a family support approach. A minority of social workers seem to hold attitudes that appear to be inconsistent with family support for drug using parents and are likely to discriminate against them. The need for staff training is clearly indicated.

Bartlett, D. (1999) The Future for Fathers? *Outlook*. 4: 14-5.
At a time of great interest in the role and status of fathers, the NEWPIN Fathers Programme Manager asks: Are fathers part of the problem or of the solution? Looks at government policies and initiatives concerning fathers and the role of fatherhood.

Bastiani, J. (1998) *Family Upheaval and Change: Schools Pack*. London, National Stepfamily Association.
A pack of leaflets designed to support schools in the way they respond to issues of family change. Included are guidelines to review and develop good practice; questions to review practice; facts and figures on family life; an information sheet on stepfamilies; a list of resources for children and families; a publications catalogue and a book list for children.

Berry, M. (1996) Services to Prevent Child Placing-out for Cocaine-affected and Non-affected Families. *Child & Family Social Work*. 1:4 Nov. 219-31.
Reports on an evaluation of the effectiveness of the 'In-Home Family Care' programme of Children's Home Society of California in Alameda County, particularly regarding the emphasis and impact of services for cocaine-affected families. Berry discusses the implications for risk assessment and placement decisions. She concludes that issues of poverty and parenting skills are more direct correlates of family stress and family breakdown than is the incidence of drug use by a parent.

Carten, A. (1996) Mothers in Recovery: Rebuilding Families in the Aftermath of Addiction. Social Work (US). 41:2 Mar. 214-23. New York City has implemented the Family Rehabilitation Program as an alternative to placement. Carten reports on the outcomes for some of the women who successfully completed the programme and discusses implications for policy in this area.

Dunne, M., and Ellery, M. (1997) Drink Problems. *Community Care*. 1181 Jul. 29.
Describes the NSPCC's Kilburn Family Support Project, which focuses on prevention when working with families where a parent is misusing alcohol.

Ghate, D., Shaw, C., and Hazel, N. (2000) *Fathers and Family Centres: Engaging Fathers in Preventive Services*. York, Joseph Rowntree Foundation.
Study examining what helps or hinders fathers' involvement with family centres. Fathers who chose not to be involved in centres were questioned, as well as those who were actively involved. Many centres often cater well for fathers in particular situations, such as being lone parents, but the authors suggest that a greater clarity is needed about who family centres are really intended for.

Ivory, M. (1995) Fathering Perceptions. *Community Care*. 1085 Sep. 27.
Workshops to help black fathers cope in what are sometimes hostile surroundings are to be launched by Exploring Parenthood.

Johnson, K. et al. (1998) Preventing and Reducing Alcohol and Other Drug Use Among High-risk Youth by Increasing Family Resilience. *Social Work*. 43:4 Jul. 297-308.

Mulroy, E.A. (1997) Building a Neighborhood Network: Interorganizational Collaboration to Prevent Child Abuse and Neglect. *Social Work* (US). 42:3 May. 255-64.
Mulroy describes and analyses how cooperation was used as a method to build a new service network, the characteristics of the network, and factors that facilitated the collaborative process.

Renshaw, J. and Perfect, M. (1996) Out of Order. *Community Care*. 1151 Dec. 20-1.
Youth justice services can play a crucial role in reducing crime. Renshaw and Perfect discuss the findings of their Audit Commission report – Misspent youth: young people and crime on the worrying level of offending by young people.

Ryan, M. (2000) *Working with Fathers*. Department of Health. Abingdon: Radcliffe Medical Press.
Describes the impact of fathers on children's development and explores aspects of the father's role as parent.

Shepherd, J.P., and Farrington, D.P. (1995) Preventing Crime and Violence. *British Medical Journal*. 310:6975 Feb. 271-2.
The best ways to prevent crime and violence seem to be by family support, training of parents, preschool education and modifying opportunities for crime. Interventions that have been shown by randomised

experiments to produce long term benefits have targeted single parent, low income, and poorly educated households with preschool children.

Thompson, A. (2000) The Trouble with Teenagers. *Community Care*. 1318 Apr. 26-7.
Reports on what is being done by social services to help parents who are finding it difficult to cope with their adolescent children.

Useful resources and bibliography

Bowlby, J. (1971) (1975) (1981) *Attachment and Loss*, Vols 1-3.

Calder, M. with Peake, A. and Rose, K. (2001) *Mothers of Sexually Abused Children, A Framework for Assessment, Understanding and Support*. Lyme Regis, Russell House Publishing.

Calder, M. C. (Ed.) (1999) *Working with Young People Who Sexually Abuse, New Pieces of the Jigsaw Puzzle*. Lyme Regis, Russell House Publishing.

Cleaver, H. and Freeman, P. (1995) *Parental Perspectives in Cases of Child Abuse*. HMSO.

Delaney, R. J. (1991) *Fostering Changes, Treating Attachment Disordered Foster Children*.

Fahlberg, V. (1994) *A Child's Journey Through Placement*.

Goulding, S., Hanks, H., Regan, L., Rose, K., Skinner, J. and Wynne, J. (2000) *The Complete Guide to Sexual Abuse Assessments*. Lyme Regis, Russell House Publishing.

Green, C. (1992) *Toddler Taming*. Vermilion.

Hacket, S. (2001) *Facing the Future, A Guide for Parents of Young People Who Have Sexually Abused*. Lyme Regis, Russell House Publishing.

Harbin, F. and Murphy, M. (2000) *Substance Misuse and Child Care, How to Understand, Assist and Intervene When Drugs Affect Parenting*. Lyme Regis, Russell House Publishing.

Hooper, C. (1992) *Mothers Surviving Child Sexual Abuse*. London, Routledge.

Howe, D. et al. (1999) *Attachment Theory, Child Maltreatment and Support*.

Howe, D. (1995) *Attachment Theory for Social Work Practice*.

Jewett, C. (1995) *Helping Children Cope with Separation and Loss*.

Parkes et al. (1991) *Attachment Across the Life Cycle*.

Peake, A. and Fletcher, M. (1997) *Strong Mothers, A Resource for Mothers and Carers of Children Who Have Been Sexually Assaulted*. Lyme Regis, Russell House Publishing.

Sgroi, S. (1989) *Handbook and Clinical Intervention in Child Sexual Abuse*. USA, Lexington Books.

Sheridan, M. *Children's Developmental Progress*. NFER.

Stern, D. (1985) *The Interpersonal World of the Infant*.

Verny, T. (1981) *The Secret Life of the Unborn Child*.

Verrier, N. (1993) *The Primal Wound*.

Wheal, A. (1997) *Adolescence, Positive Approaches to Working with Young People*. Lyme Regis, Russell House Publishing

Wheal, A. (Ed.) (2000) *Working with Parents, Learning from Other People's Experiences*. Lyme Regis, Russell House Publishing.

Wheal, A. (2000) *The Foster Carer's Handbook*. Lyme Regis, Russell House Publishing.

Winchester and Eastleigh Healthcare NHS Trust, *Personal Child Health Record*. Winchester and Eastleigh Healthcare NHS Trust.

The family support handbook

Model forms and documents

Child development: birth to 16 Years

The next part of this section *Meaningful milestones for under fives* gives more information for this age group.

Birth to one year old
In the first year of life, children begin to develop a sense of security and trust.

Expected development:
- rapid physical growth
- the beginnings of language development
- gaining muscular control
- trust begins to develop, basic needs are met (food, warmth, affection)
- a strong attachment to key people begins, and wariness of strangers

Interrupted development could mean:
- a failure to thrive, both physically and emotionally
- poor language development
- insecurity
- mistrust

Resulting behaviour may include:
- being passive
- a lack of response
- poor muscle control
- little movement or speech
- constant crying

One to three years old
These are years when children develop self-confidence and a sense of being a separate human being.

Expected development:
- standing, walking, picking up small objects, being 'into everything'
- the need to use primary carers as a base from which to explore the world
- trying to gain some control over the world

Interrupted development could mean:
- poor physical development and co-ordination
- a lack of trust in the carer may result in the child becoming very fearful of exploring
- too independent of adults and a danger to themselves
- an inability to control anger and frustration

Resulting behaviour may include:
- a return to baby development (regression), including sucking and use of baby language
- being very clingy and dependent, wanting to be close to adults all the time
- being stubborn, very resistant to control and temper tantrums

Four to six years old

These are years when children are finding out about themselves and the world around them.

Expected development:
- rapid language development
- curiosity and eagerness for information – lots of questions
- enjoyment of physical activity
- play, using imagination as a way of finding out about the world
- sharing and co-operating with others
- enjoyment of the company of other children and adults
- increasing self-reliance, for example, the ability to dress themselves and use the toilet

Interrupted development can mean:
- delayed language development
- a lack of curiosity
- social isolation
- poor physical co-ordination – fear of physical activity
- feelings of being 'bad' and to blame for what has happened
- feelings of being out of control
- a lack of control over bodily functions

Resulting behaviour may include:
- a lack of interest – acting as though 'frozen'
- nightmare terrors
- extreme clinginess
- restless energy – hurtling around the room
- aggression towards self, other children and objects

Seven to ten years old

These are years when children are trying to gain greater understanding and control of life outside the family.

Expected development:
- growing reasoning skills
- new physical skills – working hard and playing hard
- beginning to see a sense of order in the world
- developing a clear sense of right and wrong

Interrupted development could mean:
- being overwhelmed by a sense of loss and grief
- poor concentration at school, as grieving takes energy and leaves little time to develop new skills
- finding it hard to make friends

Resulting behaviour may include:
- feelings of sadness, anger, guilt and depression; 'Why has this happened to me? It's not fair'
- being very withdrawn or bossy with other children
- difficulties in developing greater reasoning skills
- telling lies to cover up lack of skills
- trying hard to 'get in' with older peers, acting streetwise

Eleven to sixteen years old
These are years when young people are making sense of who they are and finding out more about their place in the world.

Expected development:
- the onset of puberty
- a need to make important relationships outside the immediate family
- trying to make sense of strong emotional feelings, including sexuality
- the questioning of adult values
- changing views of the world
- changing views about themselves
- establishing a clearer sense of identity
- exploring from a secure base

Interrupted development could mean:
- feelings of insecurity
- having a low opinion of themselves
- greater intensity of emotions
- an inability to make lasting friendships or to develop peer group bonding
- identity confusion

Resulting behaviour may include:
- being uncommunicative
- rudeness
- unsuitable friends
- drinking alcohol
- smoking
- experimenting with drugs
- secrecy
- spending a good deal of time in own room
- not participating in usual family occasions
- exploring sexually and sexual experimentation

Children and families

Meaningful milestones for under fives

Between 0 – 3 months
- first smile
- follows with eyes
- cooing
- holding toys
- looking at hands
- chewing hands

Points to watch out for:
- not paying attention to what is going on around them
- no reaction to sudden noises
- lack of bonding
- poor head control
- not smiling responsively

Between 3 – 6 months
- good head control
- rolling over
- reaching for toys
- smiling
- observing the world
- kicking and rolling
- holding toys for longer
- enjoys bouncing – either by adults or in a baby bouncer
- starting to sit up unaided for short time – surrounded by cushions
- plays with rattles
- follows moving object with eyes
- starting to eat solid food

Points to watch out for:
- Poor head control.
- Not able to bear any weight on legs.
- Not rolling over or reaching.
- Not turning to voice.
- Not reaching for toys out of range or looking at small items.

Between 6 – 12 months
- sitting unsupported
- pulling to stand
- crawling
- walking around furniture – or holding someone's hand as they try to walk
- recognising people
- using a cup
- eating finger foods
- clapping
- waving
- babbling
- naming words – mummy, daddy
- throwing things down or dropping them
- waving 'bye bye' and enjoying 'peek a boo' games
- picking up small objects such as raisins

Points to watch out for:
If any milestones have not been reached this should be discussed with parents and with their permission the health visitor

Between 1 and 1½ years
- walks reliably without any support
- squats down to pick up a toy
- pushes wheeled toys around the floor
- loves to put objects in and out of containers
- able to pick up crumbs and other small objects
- holds a pencil like a dagger and scribbles without purpose
- talks tunefully to self in own language
- uses between 3 and 20 appropriate words. (Note: appropriate does not include repeats of what someone has just said)
- most start to show preference for one hand – right or left
- points to shoes, hair, nose, feet on request
- responds to a simple one-part verbal command
- points to objects in a picture book, e.g. dog
- holds a spoon securely and is reasonably reliable in feeding
- manages a feeding cup unaided
- piles 3 blocks on top of each other
- starts to show discomfort when wet or dirty
- starts to go upstairs holding on tightly
- fluctuates between being very clingy and resisting attention
- not in the age of reason. Does not know what he wants but knows he wants it immediately
- starts to imitate significant others e.g. helping in the house
- starting to play e.g. passing a ball

Points to watch out for:
- no tuneful babble
- hearing seems to be a problem, doesn't turn head to noise, i.e. music or voices
- no interest in the environment or people
- not yet standing upright beside furniture
- not using the finger/thumb grip
- does not 'feel right' in any way, or is significantly different to a brother, sister or friend at that age

Between 1 and 2 years
- walks reliably holding furniture
- some may be walking alone (average age 13 months – range of normal between 9 and 18 months)
- walks backwards
- picks up small objects
- understands the word 'No!'
- knows name and will usually turn when it is used
- babbles in a tuneful, foreign-sounding way
- understands 'Give it to Mummy', but only if accompanied by gesture
- uses up to 50 words
- uses a drinking cup confidently
- can hold a spoon but may be unable to load it at the plate and navigate without spillage to the mouth
- if a toy is hidden as he watches, he immediately knows where it is

Points to watch out for:
- not able to take sock or shoe off
- poor co-ordination, e.g. should be able to kick a ball, and starting to run
- not able to combine words by the age of two – 'all gone'
- not sure about and not able to relate to body parts – hair, head, mouth, hands
- generally should be coming more sociable beings – so be concerned if not

Between 2 and 3 years
- uses 200 or more words
- uses pronouns, 'I', 'Me', 'You'
- holds pen with a reasonable adult-type grip and imitates a circle and horizontal line
- builds a tower of 7 blocks
- pulls pants down for toileting but usually unable to get them back up
- knows full name
- may stutter in eagerness to get information out
- plays alongside in parallel to other children
- little idea of sharing playthings or adults' attention
- won't wait, expects everything immediately
- walks well. Runs reliably
- walks upstairs holding to a rail. Almost able to come down again in walking position
- enjoys rides on toys
- pushes toys along
- walks backwards
- drags a wheeled toy on the end of a string
- attempts to kick a ball
- removes a wrapper from a biscuit or sweet
- holds a pencil almost correctly
- scribbles in a circular manner
- can imitate a vertical line
- enjoys looking at picture books
- turns one page at a time
- can usually point out 'Which girl is happy?'
- hand preference is mostly established
- puts 2 and occasionally 3 words together
- refers to self by name
- joins in nursery rhymes and songs
- delivers simple messages, 'Daddy, come'
- chews food well
- spoon feeding a success
- usually dry by day
- usually tells when wants to go to the toilet
- imitates mother doing household duties
- will help tidy away toys
- real help with dressing
- demands parent's attention constantly
- plays beside, but not directly with, other children
- clingy – plays in another room, but checks every couple of minutes to ensure parent is still there
- rebellious when does not get own way
- possessive of toys and attention
- not a time for sharing and seeing another's point of view

Points to watch out for:
- there is minimal or no speech
- toys are still being mouthed
- toys are being thrown in an unthinking way
- play is always repetitive – e.g. spinning wheels and banging blocks
- interest in environment is not being shown
- there is a lack of 'body language'
- there is unusual irritability
- knowledge of body parts is lacking
- speech is not understandable by people outside the family
- poor co-ordination of movement

Between 3 and 4 years
- walks upstairs using alternate feet on each step and comes down using 2 feet per step
- jumps off bottom step with 2 feet together
- runs around obstacles with speed and accuracy
- pedals tricycle
- can walk on tiptoe
- can catch a ball with arms outstretched
- copies a circle and imitates a cross
- matches 3 primary colours, but still confuses blue and green
- cuts with scissors
- speech intelligible even to a stranger
- uses most plurals correctly
- will volunteer full name and sex
- still talks to self at length at play
- able to say who their own friends are
- able to describe an event that has happened, simply but reliably
- questions start – 'Why?' 'Why?' 'Why?'
- listens eagerly to stories and likes a favourite one repeated, and then repeated once more
- recites several nursery rhymes
- counts to 10, but only understands counting of 2 or 3 objects
- washes hands but needs supervision to dry
- can dress self except for buttons, tight tops and shoes
- likes to help adult with home activities
- behaviour is less impatient and self centred
- able to wait for a short time before getting what wants
- understands sharing toys, sweets and attention
- plays directly with other children
- vivid imagination, loves pretend play
- separates reasonably well from mother, but this varies greatly

Points to watch out for:
- there is an inability to communicate through appropriate speech
- body language is poor
- repetitive play shows little imagination, or richness
- behaviour is still like an 18-month-old
- movement is difficult or clumsy

Between 4 and 5 years
- walks and probably runs up and down stairs without holding on
- throws and catches well; starts to bounce a ball
- piles blocks, 2 to the side and 1 on top, to copy a bridge
- holds a pen like an adult
- draws a man with trunk, head, legs and usually arms and fingers
- draws a reasonable likeness of a house
- names 4 colours
- grammar and speech construction is usually correct
- a few sounds still mispronounced and immature
- can describe an occurrence in an accurate and logical way
- can state address and age
- questioning is at its height. Constantly asks 'Why? When? How?'
- listens intently to stories
- tells stories, often confusing fact with fiction
- may have imaginary friends
- understands yesterday, today, tomorrow, i.e. past and future
- rote counts to 20 and understands meaningful counting of up to 5 objects
- enjoys jokes and plays on words
- eats with skill and cuts with a knife – children rarely use a knife and fork before age 4+
- washes and dries own hands
- brushes teeth with supervision
- blows nose reliably
- wipes bottom after toileting
- can fully dress and undress except for inaccessible buttons, bows and shoelaces – shoelaces are rarely tied before the age of 5 and with the advent of Velcro for many children it is much later
- plays well with other children
- now argues with words rather than blows
- verbal impertinence and bickering are developing fast
- understands taking turns, sharing and simple rules
- starts to believe in justice and everyone keeping to the rules
- many become 'bossy boots'
- shows concern for younger siblings, playmates in distress
- usually separates well from parent

Points to watch out for:
- not speaking in sentences
- difficulty with concentration, e.g. for 4 – 5 minutes on one activity
- not able to use climbing equipment effectively
- eating problems around a varied diet or trying new foods
- barring accidents, toilet trained both night and day
- not willing to experiment with pencil skills and not interested in puzzles
- not able to put small pegs into a peg board
- ignores other children

Practical suggestions for working with young people

Young people
- be proud
- only accept the best
- be on the side of the young person
- advocate
- explain what is going on
- consult
- discuss
- don't punish everyone unless you are absolutely sure everyone is to blame, not just because you can't find the culprit
- compliment the young people, say how nice they look when they smile
- thank them when they are helpful
- make them feel wanted
- help them to have a positive attitude
- many young people you work with may be the product of poor parenting; don't punish the young people because of this

Adults and the young people
- set clear boundaries
- make the young people feel good about themselves
- explain to the young people what you are doing, what you expect and what you would like
- let young people know you will stick your neck out for them, that you will not let them down. Help them to understand that in return they shouldn't let you down.
- say 'thank you'
- acknowledge achievements, no matter how small
- don't talk **at**, talk **to** young people

Adults and themselves
- be punctual
- avoid irritating habits
- don't gossip
- you may have to occasionally 'bend' the rules
- always have something else ready that you can use if what you planned doesn't work out
- be prepared
- say it and mean it
- make sure any materials you use are fresh and up-to-date, not from last year or dogeared
- set standards; don't say 'that'll do', either it is up to standard or not
- make the place look good
- adults don't always know best
- sometimes young people may come to apologise, give them a chance to speak
- don't leave keys in the doors of rooms or walk-in cupboards as you may get locked in!
- don't put temptation in a teenager's way by leaving valuables lying around

Welcome to Holland

By Emily Pearl

I am often asked to describe the experience of raising a child with a disability – to try to help people who have not shared that unique experience to understand it, to imagine how it would feel.

It's like this…

When you're going to have a baby it's like planning a fabulous vacation trip – to Italy. You buy a bunch of guide books and make your wonderful plans. The Coliseum, Michaelangelo's David, the gondolas in Venice. You may learn some handy phrases in Italian. It's all very exciting.

After months of eager anticipation the day finally arrives. You pack your bags and off you go. Several hours later the plane lands. The stewardess comes in and says, 'Welcome to Holland'.

'Holland?' you say. 'What do you mean Holland? I signed up for Italy! I'm supposed to be in Italy! All my life I've dreamed of going to Italy.'

But there's been a change of flight plan. You've landed in Holland, there you must stay.

The important thing is that they haven't taken you to a horrible, disgusting place full of pestilence, famine and disease. It's just a different place.

So you must go out and buy new guide books. And you will learn a whole new language. And you will meet a whole new group of people you never would have met.

It's just a different place. It's slower paced than Italy. But after you have been there a while and you catch your breath you look around and you begin to notice that Holland has tulips. Holland even has Rembrandts.

But everyone you know is busy coming and going from Italy and they're all bragging about what a wonderful time they had there. And for the rest of your life you will say, 'Yes, that's where I was supposed to go. That's what I had planned'.

And the pain will never go away, because the loss of that dream is a significant loss.

But if you spend your whole life mourning the fact that you didn't get to Italy, you may never be free to enjoy the very special, very lovely things about Holland.

The family support handbook

Audit of needs: working with a child with a disability

General
- Have you sufficient information and advice from where the child was previously?
- Do you have a comprehensive list of involved professionals?
    - educational psychologist
    - speech and language therapist
    - physiotherapist
    - occupational therapist
    - dietician
    - medical
    - social worker
    - school
- Have you met the child?
- Have the previous carers sent on programmes used by the child?
- Have the previous carers sent on equipment on loan from physiotherapy?
- Have you contacted the respective specialist, teacher adviser?
    - visual impairment
    - hearing impairment
    - physical difficulties
    - speech and language difficulties
    - behaviour support
- Do you need training?
- Do you need advice from therapists?
- Do you have programmes from therapists?
- Do you need more or different specialist equipment?
- Does your building need to be modified?
    - ramps
    - access, e.g. gates and doorways
    - bathroom or toilet
- Do you need to adjust any rules (e.g. for peanut allergy)?

The child is not toilet trained
You may need:
- disposable gloves
- bags and method of disposal
- nappies, wipes or special pants
- potty or specialist toilet seat
- spare clothing which is practical for the disability

The child has a physical disability
You may need:
- a risk assessment for manual handling
- space to store bulky equipment when not in use
- hoist and sling
- specialist seating
- standing frame or other specialist equipment
- wheelchair access throughout the (parts of) building used by the child, including wide doorways, slopes and lowered thresholds.
- training in the use of equipment and manual handling
- training to remove or replace splints and specialist footwear

- specialist utensils for eating, etc.
- advice of physiotherapist or occupational therapist
- programmes for the child, plus training and equipment needed to use them effectively
- protocols for undressing and dressing children with stiff or floppy limbs

The child has an autistic spectrum disorder
You may need:
- advice on regime from previous carers
- behaviour management programmes in operation
- child's method of communication and training to use it, e.g. Makaton, Picture Exchange Communication System (PECS)
- advice on unusual behaviours and likes or dislikes, e.g. spinning, textures
- advice on sound sensitivities and potential distress triggers
- advice on proximity of other children, e.g. the child may need to play alone, or may not cope with other children
- advice about ability to cope outside the home
- advice on eating
- advice on structures and routines to assist the child

The child has communication or speech and language difficulties
You may need:
- advice from the speech and language therapist
- programme to work on, equipment to carry it out, training
- awareness of level of understanding
- alternative communication methods training e.g. Makaton signing, Symbols, PECS or Time lines

The child has a hearing impairment
You will need:
- the advice of the specialist teacher adviser
- the chosen route of the child's family, e.g. signing or non-signing
- advice on acoustics
- advice on care and fitting of hearing aids

The child has a visual impairment
You will need:
- the advice of the specialist teacher adviser
- awareness of the need to wear and care for glasses
- advice on wearing of caps, etc. to reduce glare
- blinds if the child is light sensitive
- advice on adaptations to home environment, e.g. sharp corners
- training in specialist skills which may include braille, touch-typing, mobility, tactile awareness

The child has a medical need, e.g. epilepsy, allergy, eczema
You may need:
- full medical details
- written protocol which states what to look for and what to do including dosages etc. for life threatening conditions, e.g. use of Epipen for allergy or rectal medication for epilepsy
- written instructions for prescription drugs, inhalers, etc. which are taken regularly or for short periods
- agreed location for prescribed drugs, etc.
- list of allergies

Section 3
Parenting Skills and Methods of Family Support

Parenting skills and what influences them

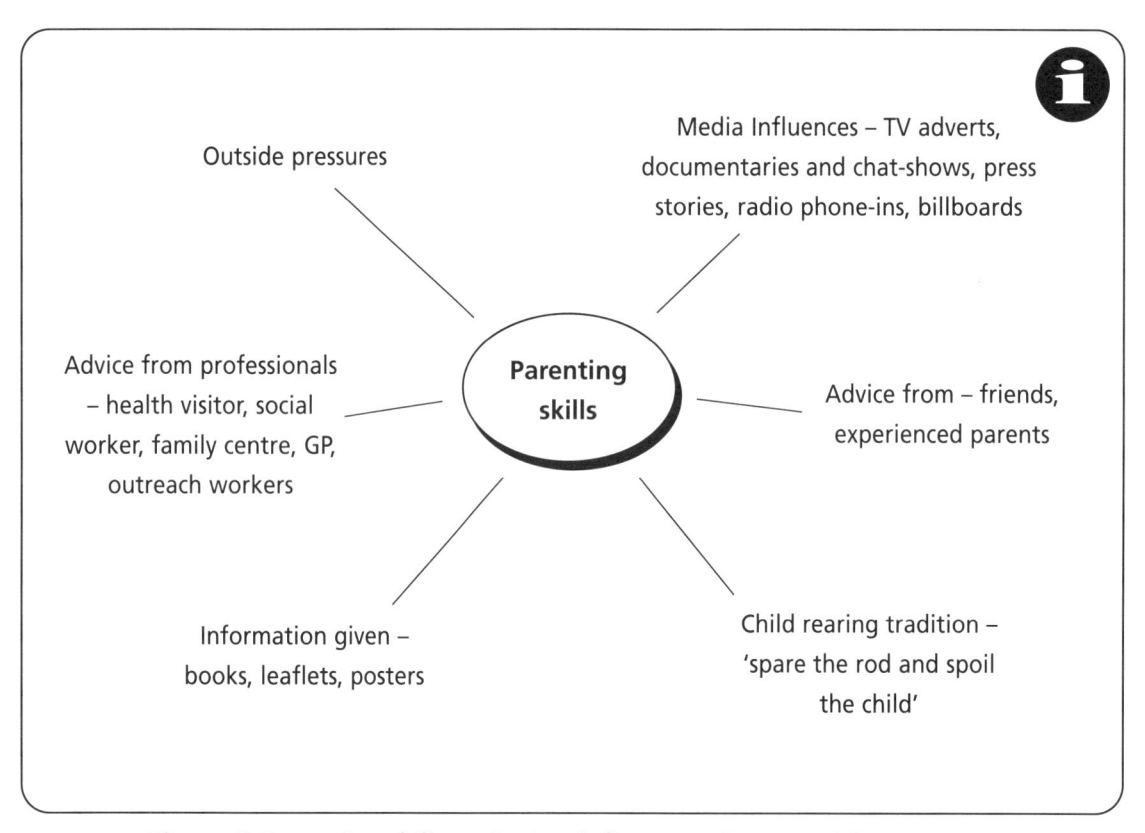

Parenting skills influences:
- Outside pressures
- Media Influences – TV adverts, documentaries and chat-shows, press stories, radio phone-ins, billboards
- Advice from professionals – health visitor, social worker, family centre, GP, outreach workers
- Advice from – friends, experienced parents
- Information given – books, leaflets, posters
- Child rearing tradition – 'spare the rod and spoil the child'

Figure 6: Parenting skills and what influences them: ouside pressures

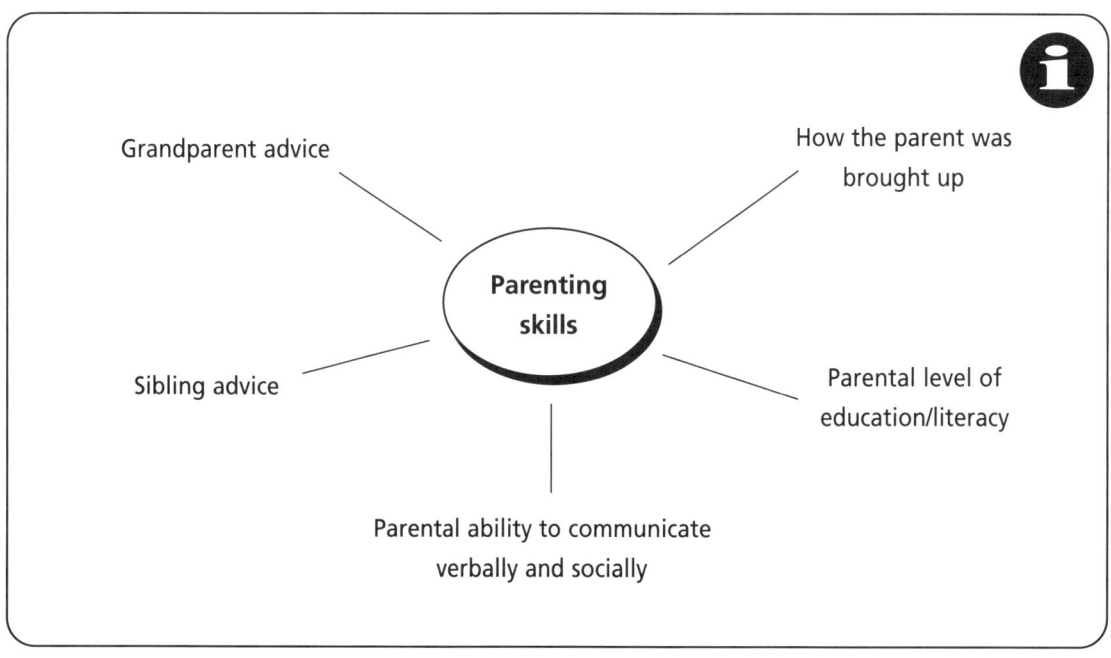

Parenting skills influences:
- Grandparent advice
- How the parent was brought up
- Sibling advice
- Parental level of education/literacy
- Parental ability to communicate verbally and socially

Figure 7: Parenting skills and what influences them: family pressures

Parenting skills diagram

Central concept: **Parenting skills**

Surrounding skills and influences:

- Managing finances
- Bedtime and sleep patterns – routines, sufficient sleep, place to sleep, wakefulness
- Managing behaviour – in the home, outside, rules, boundaries
- Attitude to physical skills and play – encourage, discourage
- Health – immunisation, managing ill health, awareness of signs of illness
- Promoting food and eating – purchase, preparation, suitable provision/catering
- Play skills – joining in at child's level, stimulation, relaxation, fun
- Promoting good nutrition and eating habits, behavioural use of food
- Managing leisure – TV, Computers, outside lessons e.g. music or drama, social groups e.g. cubs, youth clubs etc., sports, outdoor safety
- Attitude to education and schools – skills, teachers, the law, civic duties and responsibilities
- Responsiveness to – injury, questions, bullying, peer problems, anxiety, affection
- Fostering self-esteem – praise not put downs
- Organisation – time for children, clothes, household
- Expectations – parents of children, children of parents
- Hygiene – clothes, house, personal
- Ability to recognise and nurture talents and aptitudes

Figure 8: Parenting skills and what influences them: skills, attitudes. and preferences

Who provides parenting programmes?

- Local education authorities.
- Educational psychologist.
- Parent partnerships.
- Sure Start.
- Portage.
- Health authorities.
- Community councils.
- Child guidance.
- Social services – nurseries, family centres.
- Voluntary organisations such as NCH Action for Children, Barnardos.
- Religious groups.
- Home Office – young offenders, prison.
- Academic institutions.
- Private business.

Sometimes the service is free to the parents, sometimes they are required to pay a small sum towards the costs, and at others, fund raising events are the norm to ensure the group survives.

The family support handbook

Parenting programmes

There are many different types of parenting programmes in existence in the UK today, some doing invaluable work and others where the quality leaves a good deal to be desired even though the people concerned are doing the best possible job as far as they are aware.

Some groups are firmly entrenched in evaluating their work and looking to improve its quality, whereas other groups continue unchecked. Some of the groups:
- Are voluntarily run.
- Require the parents to pay a contribution for attending.
- Are supported by both local and national government.

As Celia Smith says:
> *The groundswell of interest in parenting programmes shows no sign of abating…In several areas this important topic has been built into Children's Services Plans. Parenting is no longer being treated only as a personal and private issue, but also as a political one.*
> (Developing Parenting Programmes, 1997)

Some parenting groups have become well known both nationally and internationally. In fact Home-Start has been a victim of its own success as in many areas there is a waiting list for support for parents.

Home-Start is a voluntary organisation committed to promoting the welfare of families with at least one child under five years of age. Volunteers offer regular support, friendship and practical help to families under stress in their own homes, helping to prevent family crisis and breakdown.

Newpin, another voluntary organisation, runs groups for parents, providing crèche facilities for the children. It aims to empower mothers to take control of their lives and helps them to run the groups themselves.

However, because the mothers are trained by the mothers themselves there is sometimes a danger of a lack of new ideas evolving, and myths around situations may be perpetuated. Also new mothers often find it hard to walk into a new place with new people:
> *I walked round and round and then went home. I eventually plucked up courage to go in the following week.* (Mother)

The Department for Education and Skills has funded **Early Excellence Centres** throughout the country. These may offer:
- Pre-school training for early years providers.
- Drop-in groups for parents with special needs children.
- Groups to help parents whose children are late talkers.
- Individual support to families concerned about the development of their child.
- Summer play schemes.
- Saturday play schemes, especially at difficult times such as Christmas.

Sure-Start is another government initiative. This is a needs-led scheme offering support for families in different locations. The aim is that in the future all families with children under five will have an opportunity to participate in the scheme and receive appropriate support.

Safe Caring is a joint social services and voluntary sector initiative. The aim is to identify needs and develop services for young people and their families where sexual abuse is an issue.

They seek to provide a framework for adults to ensure safe caring for children:
- The adults develop an understanding of the inherent vulnerabilities of the children they look after.
- The adults consider their thoughts, feelings and actions and how these impact on children.
- The adults are able to make decisions about parenting that are based on these understandings.
- Most importantly, the process that the adults use to explain their decisions to the children they are responsible for, is monitored and reviewed as to the appropriateness of those decisions.

Living with Risk seeks to offer a framework for understanding the conflicts and dilemmas faced by all mothers and carers who wish to maintain contact with perpetrators of abuse.

Family Centres are run by social services. They provide a variety of support to families in need, including managing contact with children where a court order is involved, developing parenting skills, carrying out assessments or just a place for families to meet.

The Penn Crescent Family Centre in Horsham runs a scheme known as 'Feeding to Thrive'. This is where families meet at lunch time and sit down with their children and other families and are all provided with a two or three course meal. Staff or visitors sometimes join them or offer help and advice. At other times there are only families. The children learn to eat regularly and well, the parents see what other children do and are also able to help their children who sit with them, the families converse and a pleasant social and learning occasion occurs.

Parenting programmes and groups may come in any shape, size or form; be formally run or just provide a drop-in centre. What is important is that they are regularly evaluated and monitored and improvements and changes made in the light of the information obtained. Causes for concern should always be recorded and appropriate action taken.

Parenting programmes review checklist

Section 10 deals with Evaluation and Monitoring and contains sample forms and questionnaires.

At the end of *this* section is a Parenting programmes review checklist. The aim of this document is to help staff adapt the service to ensure it is appropriate for each individual. It is intended to be used verbally as a way of getting the parent to join in a conversation. It can also be used in sections or in any order. As it is an informal document, records may be kept or not as appropriate.

Preventative work

When J was a toddler, we didn't know what we was supposed to do. Now we have K we are trying all the things you showed us with him, and she is doing really well.
(Parent of child with special needs)

Why do preventative work?

The old saying goes 'prevention is always better than a cure', which is why we immunise our children against diseases. The same is true of supporting families. The work done to make life better for families at one stage will have long lasting effects, not only on this generation, but also on those to come. Research in America on early start programmes, such as HighScope and

Portage, suggests that working with families at the pre-school stage can often bring about changes in life expectations and eventual achievements. A note of caution, however. The way in which this work is carried out will either motivate parents, carers and children to make the most of what they have learned, or alienate them if carried out insensitively. All families have the right to lead their lives in the way that they wish, provided that no abuse to themselves or others is involved, and the law of the land prevails.

We must guard against:
- Providing social solutions to problems which do not fit the family circumstances:
    Miss T was always showing us how to use a hankie. She did it at least once a week. But we didn't have hankies in our house, so I just carried on using the end of my shirt.
- Seeing problems where the family is comfortable with the status quo, because in our own homes we do things differently:
    Mr G says we must eat at the table, with a tablecloth and a proper knife and fork, but we always have our dinner on our laps because we all watch 'Neighbours' together.
- Believing that there is nothing we can do:
    We don't get very good results, but what can you expect with the type of families we deal with.

Living is a continuous learning process, which stops only when we die. We all have the potential and the capacity to respond to new ideas. For some people the resultant changes may be small and hard won, but they will no less have an impact.

Preventative work may be about:
- Increasing adult skills and self-esteem.
- Improving parenting skills, including behaviour management.
- Increasing home management skills, e.g. budgets and catering.
- Enhancing child skills for those who have delays, have suffered trauma, etc.

Who does preventative work?

Personnel from health, social services, education and voluntary services all engage in forms of preventative work:

- health visitors
- community mental health team
- therapists
- teachers
- school outreach teams
- education welfare service
- social workers
- social work assistants
- family centre staff
- personnel from organisations such as SCOPE, MENCAP, etc.

The type of service offered will differ in terms of:
- Length of intervention – it may be a single visit, or a series, or be ongoing.
- Place of intervention – it may take place at home, in a meeting place or at school.
- Type of intervention – it may be group, individual, drop-in or statutory.
- Cost of intervention – it may be free, low cost or subsidised by funding.
- Access to intervention – it may be open or via referral systems.

How is it accessed?

In some schemes, there needs to be a connection between the person and the intervention offered, e.g. you may need to be a parent of a child in the school to access some school-based interventions. In other schemes, there may be referral processes or limited access due to numbers allowed. This may be particularly true of some school-based groups. Where the system involves home visiting, there may be limits on the availability of staff who run it, due to low funding, or a lack of trained volunteers. Some services, which do not involve visits to continuously staffed sites such as schools and offices, are generically termed 'outreach'. They are generally open to those in the surrounding neighbourhood, cheap or free, and may be advertised by:

- Posters in surgeries, health centres, schools, family centres, etc.
- Adverts in free newspapers.
- Flyers distributed locally.
- Leaflets given to other professionals or families for distribution.
- Telephone calls to prospective attendees.
- Word of mouth via satisfied customers.

When should it take place?

- When there are younger children involved groups, visits, etc. are best organised within school hours, so that there are no childcare expenses or difficulties with older children at school.
- Events in the afternoons should be arranged so that there is adequate time for the adult to collect children from school punctually. It is extremely upsetting for a child to be the last one left at school or group, anxiously wondering whether they will ever see mum or carer again. A small child lives in the 'here and now' and five minutes may seem an eternity. Older children may be afraid to be alone and waiting, particularly if it is dark. Young people left to wait will feel let down and devalued.
- Where the meeting is for adults only, there should be provision for preschool children such as a crèche or an equipped room with trained staff, not just the office person who has other duties to perform. Older children need more to occupy them than last year's dog-eared comics, or toddler toys.
- Evening meetings are possible if a crèche or group for older children is provided. It is not enough to give them the run of the outside area whilst the meeting or group takes place. The children should have sufficient toys or equipment to make the event pleasant for them, or they may well prevent your adults from returning for further sessions.
- Meetings which straddle meal times give rise to catering needs and expenses.
- Home visits should always be prearranged at a mutually convenient time.

What is provided?

- Regular or drop-in groups for families, parents, young persons and children to meet, learn and socialise.
- Individual visits to help with family concerns.
- Services for families which include a disabled member.
- Advice on family matters and issues.
- Links to other professionals, families and services.

Remember...
Whatever the service offered, people will not access it if it does not meet their personal or social needs. It is important to know what your families want, rather than deciding this for them. So, ask them first!

The family support handbook

Methods of family support

Group discussion	Reading
Information giving	Sharing views, ideas, information
Audio tapes	Parents and children working together
Video tapes	Modelling behaviour
Role play or drama	Mediated learning
Self-analysis	Prayer
Self-reflection	Psychotherapy
One-to-one discussion – either in own home or elsewhere	Counselling
	Therapy
Exercises	Mentoring
Activities	Behaviour management
Improving own skills, e.g. numeracy, literacy, cooking, menu planning	Anger management
	Building self-esteem
Improving own knowledge, e.g. hygiene, nutrition, family planning	Learning to cope with crisis
	Learning coping strategies
Role play	Family group conferences

Figure 9: Methods of family support

Who might facilitate family support?

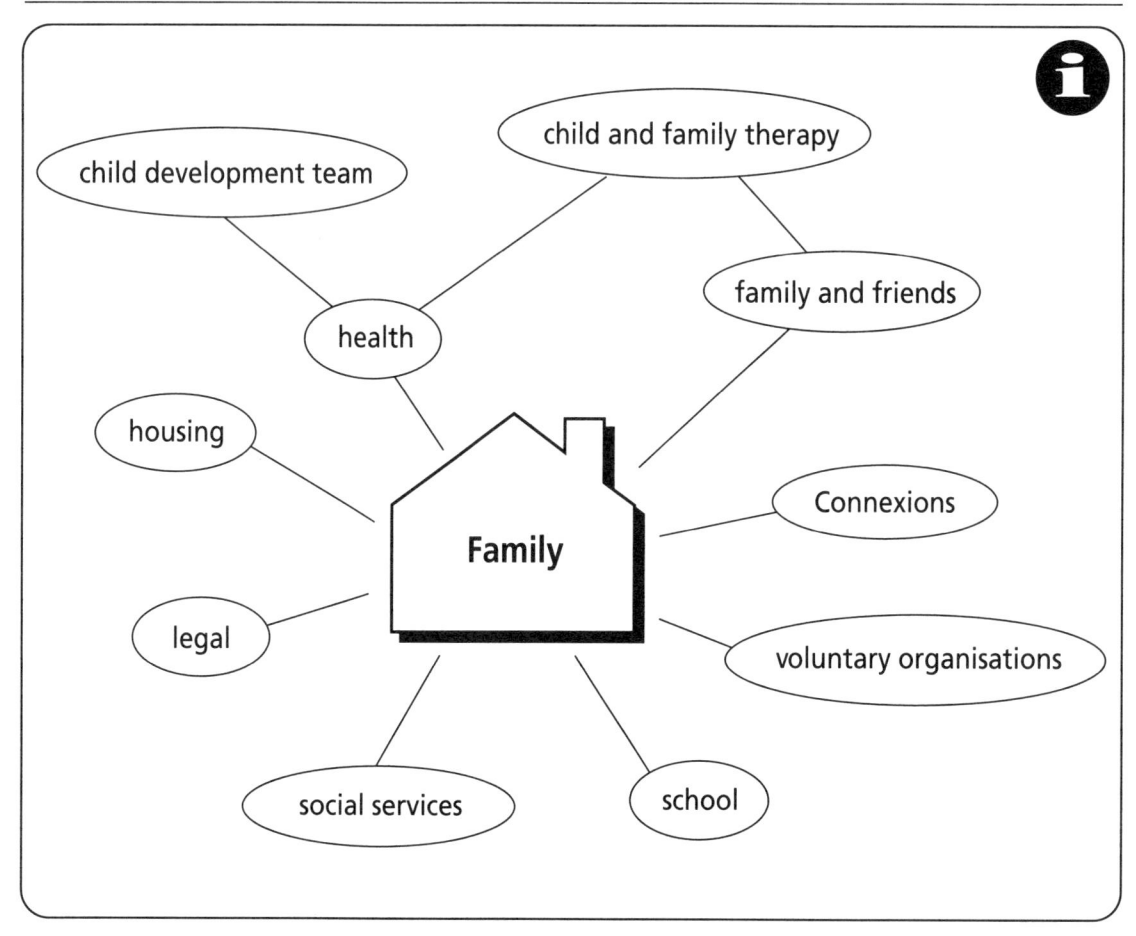

- child development team
- child and family therapy
- health
- family and friends
- housing
- Connexions
- legal
- voluntary organisations
- social services
- school
- Family

Figure 10: Who might facilitate family support?

The number and type of professionals involved will vary from family to family, as will the influence each has on family dynamics. In many cases, the pressure of numbers has an adverse effect. A key worker would:

- Regulate the flow of visitors.
- Reduce pressure on family time and emotion by arranging joint visits.
- Avoid repetition of assessments and history taking.
- Give the family a 'one stop' contact point.
- Provide a spokesperson to indicate the family's preferences.
- Allow more efficient sharing of information on a 'need to know' basis.

Meeting parents

One of the first things that will be needed when working with parents is to find out:

- What is the parenting ethos?
- What are their expectations?
- What do they see as being their responsibility?

Before meeting parents it must be decided:

- Why a meeting is necessary?
- Should the child or young person be there?
- Will crèche or childcare facilities be provided?
- What it is hoped the meeting will achieve?

When meeting parents it is important to look at:

- what the young person wants
- what the parents want
- what it is possible to achieve

…and then make a plan.

When you meet parents you must meet as equals. It should be a two-way process. You must assume they have a long term positive interest in their child's future, whatever the short term evidence to the contrary might be.

Practical suggestions for working with parents

- Thank the parents for their contribution, no matter how small.
- Don't get involved or sidetracked by other events.
- Although you have a plan you may have to 'play it by ear'.
- Sometimes what you see and hear will be emotionally disturbing and take its toll on you – be prepared.
- Be focused – what you hear may be interesting but not relevant to the task you wish to successfully achieve.
- Don't be shocked by the home environment.
- The young person may not want you to meet the parents or may not want to maintain contact. Respect their wishes. Try again at a later date.
- Other members of the extended family may be the starting point.
- Be sensitive – parents may not accept, know or care whether there is anything wrong.
- Always maintain confidentiality unless you are concerned about child protection issues.

Further reading

Edwards, J. (1995) Parenting Skills: Views of Community Health and Social Service Providers About the Needs of their 'Clients'. *Journal of Social Policy*. 24:2 Apr. 237-59.
The wider social factors which may influence the conduct and practice of parents in relation to their children are screened out of discussion in the rhetoric of 'educating parents'; instead, difficulties are located in the individual's own abilities and capabilities.

Evans, G. and Grant, L. (1995) *Moyenda Project Report 1991-94*. London, Exploring Parenthood.
Describes the development and progress of a project set up to consider the specific needs of Black parents for information and support. Planning and working participatively with Black parents and community groups in London, the project made links to set up group-work parent support. Understanding was gained about how race, ethnicity and culture affect parenting and parent support.

Hall, L. (1995) Positive Parent Power. *Community Care*. 23 Nov. 21.
Community-based care for parents and children together, with the emphasis on prevention, has proved a great success in Wiltshire.

Hurd, T., Lerner, R. and Barton, C. (1999) Integrated Services: Expanding Partnerships to Meet the Needs of Today's Children and Families. *Young Children*. 54:2. 74-80.
In the USA the concept that teaching, nurturing and caring for young children is a community process is becoming widely accepted, and new kinds of partnerships between the various constituents concerned with supporting children are being attempted. Approaches traverse school and community boundaries, and include university collaborations with early education settings. Features of effective integrated programmes are set out, and implications for practice and training discussed.

Inglis, S. (1995) *Take Ten Families: Parents' Experience of Problems and Sources of Help in Scotland*. 43. Edinburgh, Children in Scotland.
A study which contributes to the development of family support by examining the problems experienced by ten Scottish parents and their experience of the help available to them. Not designed to be a definitive or comprehensive study, it points to some key issues and considers their implications for further research designed to inform both policy and practice development.

Iwaniec, D. (1997) Meeting Children's Needs: Adequate and Inadequate Parenting Style. *Child Care in Practice*. 3:3 Mar. 49-57.
Discusses the needs of children, the needs of parents and parental responsibilities, assessing parenting, helping neglectful parents and helping children.

Joseph Rowntree Foundation (1995) *Family and Parenthood: Supporting Families, Preventing Breakdown*. Social Policy Summary. York, Joseph Rowntree Foundation.
Summarises the main findings of David Utting's report on changing family patterns.

Langley, J. (1998) Successful Parenting: How To Live With Children. *Community Practitioner*. 71:9 Sep. 289-91.
Describes an evaluation of the Living with Children project which offers support and training for parents experiencing problems bringing up their children.

Linehan, T. (1996) The Family Way. *Community Care*. 22 Feb. 10.
Discusses the work of Kensington and Chelsea's Family Partnership Scheme. The multidisciplinary team works in partnership with families which are experiencing difficulties with their children's emotional, behavioural or physical development.

Link, R.J. (1995) Parent Participation in British Family Centres. *Community Alternatives*. 7:1 (Spring) 81-105.
Explores social work practice in family centres which are developing strategies to promote parent participation and empowerment.

Statham, J. (1996) Don't Count Your Chickens: Rural Poverty and Family Support. *Family Support Network Newsletter*. 7 (Autumn) 16-7.
Family support services are just as important for rural families as those in urban areas, especially given the widespread but often hidden nature of rural poverty. Flexible ways need to be found to make such support available to families who are geographically or socially isolated, building on the strengths of their local communities.

Useful resources and bibliography

Home-Start (2000) *Home-Start Ethos and Approach*. London, Home-Start.

Smith, C. (1997) *Developing Parenting Programmes*. London, National Children's Bureau/Joseph Rowntree.

Wheal, A. (Ed.) (2000) *Working with Parents, Learning from Other People's Experience*. Lyme Regis, Russell House Publishing.

Model forms and documents

Parenting programmes review checklist

The Group

Were you given enough information about the service?

Was it helpful?

What were your hopes and expectations at the start?

When you met the staff, did their approach fit in with your hopes/expectations?

If you were referred by someone else, was the time between referral and the visit acceptable?

What were your fears, anxieties or worries whilst waiting?

How do you feel now?

Do you think that the staff understood your problems?

Do you think the staff understood what your feelings were?

Home visits

Do you feel the frequency of visits was OK?

Were you able to make contact with someone between visits if necessary?

Did you feel comfortable with the time and length of the home visits?

Do you have any other comments to make about the home visits?

General

Have you ever been unhappy about any part of our work? Please tell us about it.

Did you tell the staff at the time?

Do you know what happened?

If you didn't tell the staff at the time what would have made it possible for you to tell us?

What is helpful about our work?

What would make it more comfortable for you?

Please tell us about the benefits you have gained from working with us?

Please tell us about the benefits your child has gained from the work?

What is the most difficult part of working with us?

What is the best part of working with us?

Please tell us of any other comments you would like to make.

Section 4
Keeping the Family Together

Getting the family 'on board'

I went along but nobody talked to me so I didn't bother to go back. (Parent)

How the worker goes about getting the family on board may vary a little depending on whether the family is joining an established group, becoming a founder member of a new venture or coming to a meeting about their family concerns. When they are attending a meeting, it is easier to check for their arrival and put them at their ease. When they are coming to a group for the first time, leaders need to maintain awareness of who is arriving and be ready to greet them.

The following ground rules will help to ensure a well run and successful group meeting:
- Provide something parents might want via subject matter, activity, social aspects or meet them at home.
- Send out flyers to raise awareness of group events.
- Issue a personal invitation in writing followed by a 'phone call to confirm.
- Check that they know the time of the event.
- Welcome them on arrival and clarify forms of address.
- Show them to the correct venue for the group or meeting.
- Let them know where the loos and drinks are.
- Introduce them to other group members gently – no pressure tactics.
- Value group members equally.
- Provide adult size and comfortable seating if possible.
- Listen to concerns and be interested in what is said.
- Check that you have understood concerns correctly.
- Explain how the group works.
- State any rules, e.g. no smoking.
- Have sufficient materials and toys to complete activities.
- Involve them in planning future meetings.
- Say goodbye properly and thank them for their input.

Once contact is established nurture it by sharing and exchanging information.

Remember:
- How you felt when you last entered a strange room full of people you recognised only slightly or those you did not know at all.
- Some people take time to warm up – don't harangue them into joining in.
- Not everyone likes to use first names immediately.
- A carrot works better than a stick, so research what the group might be interested in.
- To take photos (with permission) to be viewed at the next session.
- To provide an interpreter if you know a member has difficulty understanding English.
- To ensure activities are culturally appropriate for all the group.

Beware of:
- Giving attention to some family members and ignoring others.
- Bending rules without asking all the participants.
- Failing to produce planned activities.
- Providing topics and activities which you think are best, without consultation.

Supporting familes in their own home

When...X came to visit me at home it was just wonderful. I shall never forget the help she gave me – and ...is 15 now and he was only three then. (Mother)

Early intervention

Early intervention is designed to create a climate in which parents and young people are able to seek advice and support before a particular need or problem requires drastic remedies. It should also occur in circumstances where no-one feels stigmatised by their use of a particular service.

The Doorstep Theory

A parent who finds it difficult to communicate opinions or feelings may resort to the 'doorstep' method. You may think that you have given every opportunity for this parent to:
- Share their thoughts and feelings.
- Ask for or share information.
- Make action plans with you concerning problems they may have.

It might seem to have been a very successful visit, as you rise to take your leave. Once at the doorstep, however, almost as a throwaway, the parent may divulge a very real concern of which you had no knowledge. There is little that you can do except stay and listen, for the concern is too vital to the family's wellbeing to ignore.

In order to respond fully to such situations, you need to:
- Acknowledge the immediate concern and listen to what is said.
- Make a further appointment if necessary.
- Beware of neighbours who may be eavesdropping.
- Allow time for such eventualities – don't make your schedule so tight that you have to use the 'can't stop now' response as this may ruin the trust between you.
- Be aware that you need to build your relationship with the parent so that any future concerns are shared within the general time frame of the visit.

Listening and talking to children and young people

Thank you for listening (Young offender when talking to a researcher)

When I realised that when she said 'that's rubbish' what she really meant was 'I don't understand', I was able to help her. (Newly qualified teacher)

On page 145 there is a section on general listening and communicating skills that are imperative to use for all people at all times if you wish to achieve success. Here we provide a few tips specifically for working with children and young people.

You cannot listen to children or young people all the time but you can often spot those who have something important to say by a change of behaviour or mood. If they say 'Someone I know...' that someone is usually them but by hiding behind 'someone' they hope you won't find out or they can sort the difficulty out without anyone knowing.

The family support handbook

Tips for listening

- Never be too busy to listen. Children and young people often have important things to say at the most inconvenient time of day.
- Listen to what is being said. Give them your entire attention.
- Don't anticipate what will be said next. Wait and listen. That way you'll be sure.
- Keep your thoughts to yourself as to what is being said. Don't let your mind jump away from the topic.
- Pay attention both to what is being said and how it is being said.
- If you have a question, make a note of it unless it disturbs the child or young person. Ask the question at the proper time. Don't interrupt or write while they are actually talking. Asking questions can certainly help but they require careful handling and good timing.
- If you disagree, don't get angry. Wait until they have finished as they may say something that makes your anger unnecessary or even embarrassing.
- If the child or young person is continuing for a long time, jot down a few notes when there is a pause or when they have finished speaking. This will help later on in remembering what was said.

Listening is as much an art as speaking. Both require practice: Both require attention.

A good listener will usually be listened to because they will have taken care to listen and will have thought about what they want to say.

If you want to talk to a child or young person:
- Plan the time and place to suit you both and if possible, tell them in advance. Don't choose a time when a favourite tv programme is on!
- Plan what you want to say.
- Jot down the main points.
- Have a pen and paper ready to make notes.
- Tell them at the start what you want to discuss.
- End by saying what is agreed and what action is to be taken.
- Don't gossip or pass on what you have heard to others.
- Show you are listening by eye contact, nodding or use of body language.

Respect confidentiality and privacy unless you feel they are at risk of significant harm.

If you feel you must pass on something you have been told:
- Tell them, explaining the reasons why, what you will do and how you will do it.
- Tell them why you are taking that particular course of action.
- Tell them when you will be doing so.
- At all times help keep them informed of what is happening.
- Be honest.
- Never make promises you can't keep.

Support care

Support Care may be known as **Shared Care**, **Respite Care** or **Short-term Programmed Care**.

Families who have children with special needs may be offered a period of respite away from their children. This may be to enable them to:
- Just have a break.
- Spend time with their other children.
- Spend time with each other.
- Cope in time of family crisis.
- Go on a stress-free holiday if that is what is needed to enable the parents to continue coping with the child or young person at home.

Support Care is a development of Respite Care and usually takes place in the home of the carer. However, visits may be organised and sometimes the carer will visit the home of the child or young person for whom they are responsible if this is appropriate.

The aim of support care is to respond flexibly to the needs of families and young people by offering negotiated part-time placements **before** *rather than after a situation has broken down.*

Support Care acknowledges that most families experience periods of difficulty at times. Many parents use an informal network of friends, family and childcare professionals at this time. Support care may be used for any of the above or it may be used:
- As a way of calming family disputes.
- To help social workers to work with both children and parents separately.
- As a period of respite whilst the opinions of other people, including family members and professionals, are considered and a plan drawn up as a way forward for the future for the family.
- Whilst a young person is excluded from school and would in normal circumstances be at home alone all day and possibly get into trouble with the law.
- When a child has a terminal illness and doesn't normally get out of the house. In this way the carer has a child, say overnight, and the child is happy to be with other people in different surroundings.
- To give black, Asian or dual heritage children a chance to familiarise themselves or maintain contact with a community that reflects their own racial or cultural identity. In this case, black and Asian carers act as befrienders.

Support Care may be offered for example:
- overnight once a week
- for a fixed period full-time
- during the day only, Monday to Friday
- at weekends
- during the evening

Almost any combination may be negotiated, whatever is most helpful to the situation and the family in need of support. Support carers may be male or female, live alone or in a family. The most appropriate option for the child or young person will be chosen.

Different local authorities use different people as support carers. Some use carers who are also foster carers, others use retired foster carers, some use child minders and others recruit people without previous experience of this type of work. However, they must all be suitably trained, checked, supervised and supported.

The family support handbook

Coping with crisis

Every so often, the best laid plans go wrong. This may be due to:
- accidents
- natural disaster or weather effects
- emotional crises
- illness
- stress
- unexpected or unwelcome visitors, e.g. banned persons trying to gain access

No matter what crisis occurs, you have to respond to it in some way. In order to help you there may be:
- rules laid down for such an occurrence
- anger management strategies to use
- people around who can assist
- people who are first aid trained if the crisis is medical

Whether the above are in place or not, what practical things can we do to avoid escalation and lessen the trauma?
- Don't panic. Review the situation quickly and calmly.
- Summon help if necessary, by phone or by calling out (but don't let panic seep into your voice).
- Give clear directions to emergency services if they have been called.
- Remove people from danger or harm.
- Use anger management strategies if appropriate.
- Reassure the persons in difficulty and anyone in sight of the crisis.
- Respond to needs, e.g. to talk, to explain, to show.
- Use your training and experience to decide on a course of action.
- Stay at the scene until help arrives.

When a family reaches crisis point:
- Acknowledge their difficulties and check that you understand them exactly.
- Listen to their concerns immediately – don't fob them off.
- Provide practical help -who might help and what they might do.
- Plan a way through with them, involving them completely in any decisions.
- Record decisions, sign and date them.
- Pass on information to relevant others, with the family's permission (unless it is a child protection issue, when you have a statutory duty to do so).

Family group conferences

Family group conferences are meetings set up to assist a family in drawing up a plan for the care of children. A typical model is set out at the end of this section.

Family assessments

When we work with children and meet the parents, we may be assessing them sub-consciously. Alternatively we may be assessing them informally and, for example, looking for signs that may give us a clue as to why a child or young person behaves in a certain way.

However, formal **Family Assessments** take place if:
- Abuse is suspected or has been proved.
- It is believed the family are, or will be, unable to cope with their responsibilities.
- A child has a particular need that will make it difficult for the child to live at home without the parent receiving additional support.

In fact any reason that may lead to the child being at risk should necessitate a family assessment taking place. These assessments may cover any or all of the following depending upon circumstances:
- pregnancy and preparation for birth
- emotional, physical or psychological development and relationships
- basic physical care
- significant past and present experiences
- family dynamics
- other agency involvement with the family
- the child or young person and their needs
- home management and life skills

Assessments may take the form of observations, note taking, video recording, questioning by staff and professionals as well as self-completion questionnaires and talking. The assessor should draw up a plan of how, when and where the work will take place and the agreed finishing time. This should form part of the formal agreement with the family.

Family assessments are frequently used alongside psychological assessments or assessments of specific risk such as abuse.

Assessment work is not value free. Workers should realise that they will bring their own racial, cultural, gender, class and religious values to an assessment. They should also be aware of different cultural variations in child-rearing patterns to ensure a balanced assessment. If it is not possible for someone from a similar background to carry out the assessment then cultural issues should be discussed to ensure understanding and acceptance of different childcare norms.

Different family members may be assessed if this will help to develop a plan of support, care and advice that is in the child's best interests.

When the assessment has been completed the outcomes should be discussed with the family and a way forward planned which will, hopefully, enable the family to stay together and develop skills and coping strategies and to receive any necessary outside support. The plan should be periodically re-assessed.

Living away: working with parents whose children are unable to live with them

The aim of this part of the Handbook is to help parents whose children are not living at home. It should also help social workers, staff in children's residential homes, foster carers, other carers and local councillors in their roles as 'corporate parents'.

Parents whose children are not able to live with them may feel:
- upset
- angry
- isolated
- confused
- overwhelmed

Their children too may feel bewildered, confused and frightened especially when they first move away from the family home.

A child may be living:
- with grandparents or a close friend
- with a foster carer
- in a residential home
- in a boarding school
- in an establishment for children who have special needs

Encourage parents to:
- Keep in regular contact with their child.
- Ask questions of anyone involved with their child's care.
- Ask about decisions that should involve parents.
- Let the child take their own belongings with them.
- Work with those caring for the child to ensure they settle and are able to achieve their full potential.
- Keep taking an interest in their child's schooling and other activities and attend such events as parents evenings if at all possible.
- Ensure their child's cultural and religious needs are being met.
- Ask about plans for their child and what part they can play in these plans.
- Attend meetings about their child; they can take someone along for support or to give their views if they wish.
- Visit their child regularly and often.
- Not make promises they can't keep.
- Remember their visits will need to suit the child's life and the person looking after them, as well as their own needs.
- Let relatives know when they can visit.
- Make sure their child has access to a telephone, for making and receiving calls.
- Let everyone know about special family occasions such as birthday parties which they would like their child to attend.

Give the carers as much information as possible about the child:
- their likes and dislikes
- pet names for things
- who is important to them
- their hobbies
- favourite TV programmes, food and lessons

Carers

Carers know it is **crucial** for them to make good links with a child's family within the first days and weeks of the arrangement. This can determine how often a child will meet up with the family in the future and the likelihood of the child returning home.

Carers can help by:
- Listening to what both sides have to say.
- Talking to the child regularly, about all sorts of things. A child will probably come round to talking about their family at some point.

- Listening if a child is talking to their teddy or their pet; they may be acting out a reality but don't jump to conclusions.
- Finding out all the facts.
- Taking things slowly, one step at a time. Don't rush.
- Talking to other people who may know the child so they can learn as much as possible about the child, such as their culture or religion.

Sometimes a brother, sister, grandparent, relative or friend can help too.

If a first meeting is arranged, carers should talk over with the parent where it should be. If either the child or the parent refuses to make contact at first, the carers should not give up, but be sensitive to the difficulties.

There may be feelings of hate and hurt. There may also be feelings of guilt – children often mistakenly think 'it's my fault'.

There are practical things that could be done to encourage making and maintaining contact with families:
- Don't rush the child into making contact too soon; the child may not be ready. Children may appear upset but may really want to see their parents.
- Letters and telephone calls are useful ways of passing on the news.
- Talk to the parents about the child; tell them the good things.
- Be honest; talk plainly; use suitable language.
- Don't make judgements.

Sometimes carers are the 'piggy in the middle' with the child playing the parent off against the carer and vice versa. Areas of conflict might be:

- clothes
- hairstyles
- speech
- manners
- money
- food
- sweets
- diet
- TV
- video games
- bedtimes

Carers must respect the child's family as in most cases the child will eventually return to live with their parents.

Managing contact with parents and other family members

I insisted that I see my real family. I wanted to cling on to my background. If I hadn't been able to see them I would have suffered strong emotional damage. (Parent)

I knew that things weren't good with my real family but bad as they were, I didn't want to let them go. It's best to know and see for yourself what's what – hard as it is. Otherwise your imagination can run riot. (Adoptee)

It was only when I saw my mum and auntie that I saw people who looked like me. (Adoptee from birth)

I really did not want this woman in my house. But then I saw that she loved her son. He is back home now and I feel really proud that I played my part. (Foster carer)

Retaining contact with family members after there has been a disruption within the family is one of the most contentious issues in childcare law today. Most people would agree that, where a child is likely to return home to the birth family there should be plenty of quality contact, both directly and indirectly with their family. There is much less agreement as to the kind of contact arrangements that should be in place with respect to the child who is unlikely to return home.

Children for whom contact is being made available may have been:
- neglected
- abused in a variety of forms
- rejected by their parents

Research also shows that many of the parents themselves will have had similar experiences in childhood to that experienced by their own children. See Catherine Macaskill in *Safe Contact*.

Other children may have been involved in:
- Family friction caused by the non-custodial parent after divorce or separation.
- Step-siblings wanting to see each other again.
- Wishing to meet the absent parent, usually the father.
- Wanting to know more about their family if they were adopted at birth.

Whatever the cause, it is vitally important that the whole question of contact is planned and managed with utmost care. The National Association of Child Contact Centres has produced the following code of practice:
- Contact must be child-centred. Work with parents should be aimed at making contact less stressful for the child.
- Impartiality is fundamental to the process.
- The contact process requires explicit confidentiality.
- Training must be provided for all staff and volunteers.
- Each member of the family is treated as an individual.
- Multi-cultural and multi-faith issues must be addressed and work with families should proactively reflect this philosophy.
- Health and safety guidelines must be followed.
- Practical considerations should be given to the provision of facilities for people with disabilities.
- A complaints procedure should be in operation.

A group of foster carers has produced their *Tips for successful contact* that could be used in a variety of situations: see the checklist at the end of this section.

**Important:
when dealing with contact, any child protection issues
or procedures must be followed implicitly.**

Further reading

ATD Fourth World (1996) *Talk With Us, Not At Us: How to Develop Partnerships Between Families in Poverty and Professionals*. London: ATD Fourth World (48 Addington Square, London SE5 7LB).
Describes the results of a three year project run by ATD Fourth World with support from the City Parochial Foundation. It explores the concept of partnership between disadvantaged families and those from the legal, health, social and community work professions who seek to help them.

Biehal, N., Clayden, J. and Byford, S. (2000) *Home or Away? Supporting Young People and Families*. London, National Children's Bureau.
Explores new developments in preventive services for teenagers and their families. This study evaluates the work of an adolescent support team covering their preventive work and their work with homeless 16 and 17 year-olds. It examines the characteristics and problems of the young people and families using the team and assesses the outcomes achieved and the costs of services provided.

Department of Health (2000) *Framework for the Assessment of Children in Need and their Families*. London, The Stationery Office.
One pack. Contains copies of: 'Framework for the Asessment of Children in Need and their Families'; 'Assessing Children in Need and their Families: Practice Guidance'; 'The Family Pack of Questionnaires and Scales'; sample assessment recording forms including referral and initial information record, initial assessment record, core assessment records, assessment recording forms and guidance notes and glossary.

Hamill, H. (1996) *Family Group Conferences in Child Care Practice*. Norwich, University of East Anglia. Social Work Monographs No.151.
Family Group Conferences are a model of partnership, decision making and family involvement in caring for children and young people in need of care and protection.

Higgins, K., Pinkerton, J. and Switzer, V. (1997) *Family Support in Northern Ireland: Starting Points: Report on Part One of the Northern Ireland Family Support Research Project*. Belfast, Queens University of Belfast.
Gives an overview of existing family support services in Northern Ireland prior to the commencement of the Children Order. Describes the Northern Ireland context and outlines the support needs of children and families there.

Hoyal, J. (1996) Making Sense of s.17. *Childright*. 128: Jul. 20.
Discusses Aldgate and Tunstill's study 'Making sense of Section 17' which provides a national overview of implementation of services for children in need.

Kelly, B. (1995) Children, Families and Nursery Provision. *Early Child Development and Care*. 108: 115-36.
Examines the relationship between families and nursery provision. Describes the features of families using the nurseries and illustrates how integrated nursery provision was supporting vulnerable families to cope better with their children.

Lupton, C., Barnard, S. and Swall-Yarrington, M. (1995) *Family Planning?: An Evaluation of the Family Group Conference Model*. Report no. 31. Portsmouth, The University, Social Services Research and Information Unit.

McCartt Hess, P., McGowan, B.G. and Botsko, M. (2000) A Preventive Services Program Model for Preserving and Supporting Families Over Time. *Child Welfare*. 79:3 May. 227-65.
Describes a programme to prevent the unnecessary placement of children in out-of-home care. The programme combines elements of both family preservation and family support services into a comprehensive yet individualised response to families in need.

Morris, K. (1995) *Family Group Conferences: An Introductory Pack*. London, Family Rights Group (replacement copy Sep 97).
Aimed at child care professionals, it provides details about the basic model of FRGs, references to relevant research, basic training suggestions, examples of the local use of FRGs, information for families, and where to go for further help.

National Youth Agency (2000) *Young people and the family. Research, Policy and Practice Forum on Young People*. Leicester, Youth Work Press.
This paper reports on the Forum programme which explored young people and the family, with contributions and research from the Cabinet Office Social Exclusion Unit, Young Minds, BMRB Qualitative and the Trust for the Study of Adolescence.

Statham, J. (1996) Don't Count Your Chickens: Rural Poverty and Family Support. *Family Support Network Newsletter*. 7 Autumn 16-7.
Family support services are just as important for rural families as those in urban areas, especially given the widespread but often hidden nature of rural poverty. Flexible ways need to be found to make such support available to families.

Useful resources and bibliography

Department of Health (2000) *You Can Help: Helping Your Child in Care*. Department of Health.

Howard, J. (2001) *Support Care, Context and Development. in University of Bradford/Bradford Social Services Conference Report*. Bradford Social Services/NFCA.

Macaskill, C. (2002) *Safe Contact*. Lyme Regis, Russell House Publishing.

Salford Community and Social Services (2001) *Conducting Family Assessments, A Practice Guide*. Lyme Regis, Russell House Publishing.

Wheal, A. (1997) *Adolescence, Positive Approaches to Working with Young People*. Lyme Regis, Russell House Publishing.

Model forms and documents

Model family group conference

Referral
Agree the need for a plan and appoint a co-ordinator, – matched with the family's race, culture, language and religion.

Stage one
The co-ordinator, in consultation with the child and immediate carers, identifies the 'family' and issues invitations, agrees venues, date, timing and prepares participants.

Stage two
At the start of the meeting the co-ordinator chairs the information-sharing. Professionals explain their roles, responsibilities and concerns and local resources. Family can seek clarification.

Stage three
This is private planning time for the family. Professionals and co-ordinator withdraw as the family needs to agree a plan, and agree contingency plans and review arrangements.

Stage four
The co-ordinator and professionals rejoin the family and hear the plan. Resources are negotiated and the plan agreed unless the plan places the child at risk of significant harm.

Note:
Family group conferences are only successful if the family 'owns' the solution. However, for this to happen, care has to be taken when planning and organising the meeting.

Staff running these groups should also be appropriately trained. It is a skilled task, not to be undertaken lightly.

The family support handbook

Tips for successful contact

1. Prepare yourself **and** the child for the visit.

2. Learn to be flexible.

3. Welcome the parent – into your home or other suitable venue. Where appropriate give the parent and child non-restrictive access where they can speak to each other.

4. If you go to the parent's house, take time to have a cup of tea or coffee if asked.

5. Ensure that you know what your role is and what is expected of you.

6. Be honest and open about your feelings and don't keep problems to yourself.

7. Back-up procedures should be in place if the situation becomes too stressful for either party.

8. Be clear about what is acceptable and what is not.

9. Be non-judgemental – a child will be scrutinising how you handle particular situations with their family.

10. Find some time for yourself afterwards to think about how the contact went. Ask the parents and the child separately how they felt the contact went. Make an agreed plan for future contact.

Practical suggestions for a safe contact

- Don't rush into getting the child or young person to make face-to-face contact too soon. A telephone call may help to 'break the ice'.
- Talk to the parents about the child or young person, tell them the good things.
- Be honest.
- Talk plainly.
- Use suitable language.
- Don't make judgements; find out the facts.
- Try to get communication going, at first by you leading the talking.
- Have some ideas for things the family and the child or young person can do together such as drawing, painting or playing with toys; beware of parents who want to show the child how to do it or to improve the child's picture. For a young person it might be discussions around favourite food, music, hobbies or clothes; for both groups just sitting watching the television may be enough on the first contact or going for a walk in the local park or shopping centre.

Section 5
Organising and Planning Family Support

Choosing a location

When considering a location, first decide why it is needed. If it is required for groups it must:
- suit the purpose
- have adequate facilities, e.g. kitchen, seating, changing facilities, toilets etc
- have sufficient size and space indoors to allow the group's activities to take place
- include outdoor space if necessary
- have the appropriate safety certificate
- be healthy and clean

If it is required for individuals it must be:
- user friendly
- comfortable
- private
- adequately furnished, e.g. seating, toilet facilities, drinks facilities

A location must be:
1. Visible
   - not up an alley
   - sign-posted or labelled in some way that does not discriminate
2. Accessible:
   - to pram users
   - to the disabled
3. Safe:
   - have the appropriate fire certificate
   - contain no hazards e.g. stairs, platforms, thresholds, chemicals etc.
   - have a contained play area for inquisitive and adventurous small children
4. Available:
   - on the right day
   - at the right time
5. Local:
   - within walking distance of prospective users
   - within or near housing
6. Acceptable:
   - not have a local reputation or regular use that may offend group members or other individuals
   - not be graffiti-covered or too run down
7. Welcoming:
   - not forbidding
   - warm and light
   - with a sensible entry system, preferably with a friendly face just inside
8. Affordable:
   - cost-neutral if possible
   - if not, cheap enough to keep charges for members reasonable

The family support handbook

Setting the rules

I like my fags but I know I can't smoke here and that's fine with me. (Parent)

Rules help to provide a working framework. They establish what is expected and what is frowned upon. A person who knows the rules can relax in the knowledge that they will not be suddenly embarrassed by their actions, or by not doing something they should be doing. A large number of confusing rules should be avoided, but there are some which just cannot be left out. Remember that rules should be:

- **Simply stated.** Sometimes a notice will suffice, but a verbal statement of the rules will aid those with literacy difficulties and also add the personal touch.
- **Relevant.** They should cover health and safety, and other practical issues.
- **Reviewed regularly.** They may need to be updated to reflect changes, or be deleted where no longer relevant.
- **Owned by those who keep them.** If a group is operating it may have special rules, only for group times, that have been worked out by members.

Some useful rules might be:

- **No smoking.** Smoking is almost universally frowned on in places where there are children, food or health concerns. Passive smoking can cause ill health.
- **No swearing.** Bad language gives a poor example to young and old. Learning to hold a conversation without swearing is a valuable skill to master.
- **No smacking.** Legal issues are at stake here: European law does not allow smacking. Smacking is an inherently violent approach, which sets a bad example to youngsters. Instead, we need to provide adults with alternative methods to manage their children.
- **Quarantine.** The usual spotty illnesses of childhood can be dangerous for those with particular medical conditions, for some children with disabilities and for many adults who failed to catch them in their own childhood. It is therefore sensible to follow national guidelines on how long a period of quarantine is required. Health visitors are a good source of information for specific illnesses. Tummy bugs can spread like wildfire if not checked by the use of the '24 hours clear' veto before the person is accepted again.
- **Illness.** Surprising numbers of adults send their children to school, playgroup, or family centre when they are patently unwell. Apart from being likely to pass on their illness, it is uncomfortable for the child to be without their personal carers when they feel poorly. Make sure that you have contact details, including a backup person if the main carer is out. There should be clear rules about when a child will need to be taken home. These should be written down and either given or explained to parents or carers on their initial visit. When a child becomes ill during the session, the parents or carers should be contacted immediately and all medical protocols followed exactly.
- **Drugs.** Persons under the influence of drugs should not be in charge of children or cars. This applies to all, whether staff or family members. Certain drugs which have been prescribed preclude driving. Staff who are asked to administer prescribed drugs to children should not do so without a written protocol.

> **Rules reflect the attitudes of the establishment. They should be seen to be applied, fairly and equally, to one and all.**

Parents helping parents

Go to the people. Live amongst them. Start with what they have. Build with them. And when the deed is done, the mission accomplished, of the best leadership, the people will say **'We have done it ourselves'**. (Unknown source)

It was so wonderful to meet someone who had a child who had similar problems. It was good just to talk but we were also able to help each other with tips on what did and didn't work.
(Parent with child who has special needs)

Barriers

> **Barriers**
> - Feeling they are not wanted.
> - Feeling their views are not respected.
> - Believing that others do not think they need or want help.
> - Not knowing what to do.
> - Not knowing how to do it.
> - Having little or no time.
> - Feeling unskilled.
> - Having little confidence.
> - Having low self-esteem.
> - Not knowing what to say.

Figure 11: Barriers to successfully involving parents

So how can we change that?

Breaking down barriers

> A parent may need very little to cross that barrier. You can offer encouragement by:
> - Making people feel welcome.
> - Helping people to build their self-esteem.
> - Treating people with respect.
> - Helping children to treat their parent with respect.
> - Making sure that people know that when help is needed, they need only ask.
> - Where, for example, there are language difficulties, having photographs displayed of what is needed so the parents will not have to ask what equipment or toys to get out.
> - Asking parents for their ideas and advice.
> - Leading by example, explaining clearly what you are doing, and why.
> - Teaching them new skills.
> - Providing interpreters if this will help.
> - Always listening carefully to what parents have to say, and responding clearly and slowly.
> - If parents don't know how to play with their children, by showing them, and helping and guiding them. This will give parents confidence in other areas too.
> - Encouraging parents to organise events or outings amongst themselves.

Figure 12: How to break down barriers

> The best way to learn is often by example. The best teachers may be other parents themselves, or volunteers who are also parents, in which case the organisers become facilitators.

The aims of the groups

For parents, these might be to:
- provide a safe supportive environment for families.
- encourage the inclusion of families within the local community.
- give opportunities for all parents and children to take part in planned activities together in group settings.
- give an opportunity for parents to have access to specialist staff.
- raise parents' confidence in their own parenting skills.
- lessen the isolation sometimes experienced by families.
- give adults and children opportunities to build better relationships.

Ground rules for groups

Groups, whether long running or 'one-offs', large or small, all need to have basic rules, in addition to those mentioned earlier in this chapter, so that everyone knows where they stand before the group commences. Sometimes reminders of the ground rules will need to be repeated at intervals. Some of the more obvious ones are:
- Good timekeeping is essential, both at the beginning and the end of sessions: the facilitator should inform everyone at the outset of start and finish times.
- Confidentiality within groups should be maintained and respected at all times: if someone shares personal experience, only that individual has the right to repeat it in another arena.
- If someone openly criticises the work of a group or organisation, it should not be repeated.
- Individuals must learn and be encouraged to take responsibility for themselves: 'if you don't understand something, then ask!'
- Everyone has the right to challenge statements made by others, but not in a derogatory fashion and never as a personal attack.
- Everyone has the right to defend their opinions but they must recognise that others also have that right.
- Anyone feeling distressed by what is being considered or discussed has the right to take time out. However, they should be encouraged to talk to one of the facilitators, if they wish.

Above all, a facilitator should practise their listening skills by:
- Being considerate of others and giving them time to speak.
- Not interrupting when someone else is speaking.
- Controlling their reactions: you may find yourself responding in unusual ways because of the subject matter.
- Encouraging group members to do the same.

At the end of this section are three examples of planning sheets for different adult and toddler groups. Members and staff sit down informally during a group session to discuss possible ideas, which the staff then write into a plan. In order to remind the members about what has been planned, the details may be published as a leaflet and distributed. In addition, the plan for the week is copied onto card, using clip art symbols as well as words, so that non readers or adults who do not understand English are able to help in preparation etc. rather than feel excluded. Everyone has ownership of the plans. Staff ensure that activities planned are safe and practicable for the venue, and that the equipment is available when required in sufficient quantities.

Planning for groups

In one group parents initially pooh-poohed the idea of swimming due to concerns about their skills, body shape (poor self-esteem) and ability to parent effectively in a dangerous activity. After the first term, the idea was revisited. Several of those who had refused the first time round now felt confident enough to go with support. The group met at the normal venue and were transported by minibus. All the adults went in the water with their children. After the session at the baths, there was a real sense of achievement. (Worker)

I didn't think I could do it, but I did. (Mother)

Adults in the group decided they would like to go out for a meal together, but the cost was prohibitive. They suggested weekly saving with the fund held by staff. When their funds grew, the venue was booked. Group members met at the usual place and travelled to the restaurant together. A great time was had by all and they are already planning their next venture.
(Mother)

...always what they want. (Outreach Co-ordinator)

Setting up groups

Families come in many shapes and sizes. Their level and type of need may depend on the nature of their difficulty, what support they are currently receiving, what is already available but they have chosen not to take up, and what they themselves would like to be offered. Whatever the circumstances, families usually know what their needs are. Family supporters should not presume that they know them better than families do themselves. They should not seek to identify and solve problems about which the family raises no concerns. The family may feel that this is an area in which they are coping well, and will quite rightly resent interference.

The first task in setting up a group should be to ask those who might attend what sort of group would best suit them and respond to their views. After this has been done, perhaps using interviews or questionnaires, it will help to decide clear aims.

The basic function of a group should be to empower its members in some way, not to undermine what might be fragile confidence in their own ability to make choices and to solve problems. There should be a viable number of prospective members. Some groups may start with very small numbers to begin with, perhaps just two or three. Other groups may be larger but numbers should be limited to suit the accommodation used.

Why?
- To bring people within the locality together and promote communication.
- To provide support for particular needs or age groups.
- To enable new people to meet and become friends.
- To promote parenting skills.
- To build adult self confidence.
- To raise self esteem.
- To enable access to new equipment and ideas.
- To raise awareness of local services.
- To have fun in a safe secure environment.
- To develop play skills.
- To develop social awareness and skills.
- To promote cultural awareness and tolerance.

Where?
- Locality: is the venue visible enough? Is it within the neighbourhood rather than away from housing? Is the location within walking distance for the members? Not all have cars: if not, can you supply transport? Do you need transport for yourself?
- Site facilities: overall space, toilets and changing areas, play area, kitchen, child friendly, warm and clean, welcoming rather than forbidding, fire certificate.
- Accessibility: stairs, doorways, hazards such as thresholds.
- Cost: if there is no funding available, 'cost neutral venues' need to be sought. There may be difficulty in retaining members if there is a large charge for attendance, but sometimes a small charge underpins the value of the group. Will there be a need to fundraise? Are there any ideas for this? Remember that if you run several groups of a similar nature, then the charging policy should be the same for all. Members will soon find out and feel aggrieved if one section is treated differently.

Equipment and materials

Will any onsite equipment be suitable, and available? What else will be needed, and how will you get to the venue? Are there storage facilities available?

A basic equipment list for a family session with young children would need to include:
- a good selection of toys, e.g. puzzles, books, table toys, wheeled toys if space is adequate
- art and craft materials and aprons
- domestic play equipment
- small tables and chairs
- spare clothes, rubber gloves, wipes, spare nappies
- drinks and biscuits, cups and beakers, tea towels
- first aid kit
- mobile phone, registers and contact sheets

Staffing
- There should never be less than two members of staff for health and safety reasons.
- Two members of staff can meet more people, provide more activities, support each other, provide different styles of listening, possibly appeal to different age groups.
- Two members of staff can allocate duties between themselves and leave the client group singly to make tea etc. if necessary.
- All staff should be aware of the overall aims and procedures of the service, which should be written.
- Staff should be supplied with a mobile phone for all off-site venues.

Organising and planning family support

- Staff need to be aware of the nature of the groups, and this should form part of their induction training or job description.
- Staff should not be coerced into running groups until they feel confident to do so.

Before you begin
- Contact people who have expressed an interest, preferably by word of mouth. Leaflet drops are useful in the immediate vicinity.
- Advertise to professionals who will know people who might wish to attend.
- Plan and prepare the initial format of the session according to your aims.
- Make up a register to record details of all who attend, and their emergency contact details.
- Prepare health and safety reminders in user-friendly terms, e.g. no smoking, swearing, smacking, no hot drinks near children.
- Organise refreshments, e.g. drinks and biscuits.
- Be ready on time with activities laid out if appropriate.
- Organise name badges on sticky labels; nervous people forget names easily.

When the new members arrive
- Welcome them with a smile and introduce yourselves.
- Wear your name badge.
- Give members their name badges, so they can get to know each other.
- Show them the activities and encourage them to join in, but gently.
- Listen to their concerns and their ideas.
- Don't tell them what to do.
- Point out fire regulations and group rules.
- Fill in the contact sheet and register.
- Keep the drinks and biscuits flowing.
- Have a definite end so that people know when the session is over – for some groups this may be a special song.
- Remind the group of the date of the next session.
- Say goodbye individually, and express your thanks for their attendance and your hopes to see them again.

Until the group 'gels'
- Continue to plan the activities, but increasingly seek members' ideas.
- Continue to listen and encourage but don't pressurise.
- Ask what they think about the activities provided, the venue, etc.

When the group appears to be established
- Encourage ownership of the group by members.
- Involve members in planning activities: make it a joint effort.
- Display and distribute the plan: a leaflet works well, especially in colour.
- Involve members in drawing up rules.
- Maintain contact with any who have attended, so that they may choose to attend again. Home visits may form an important part of this process. Be mindful that some members may have needs that require a non-group or private approach.
- Determine maximum numbers in consultation with members.
- Ask members' prior permission if you intend to bring along visitors.
- Continue to listen and to offer support.
- Refer to other professionals if necessary, but always with the member's support, unless there is a child protection issue.
- Take members' ideas on board.
- Encourage new initiatives by members.
- Aim to empower rather than instruct.

Types of group

The type of group you run will:
- reflect your aims
- vary according to the ages and interests of the members and their children
- be sized to fit the accommodation and needs of the group
- be subsidised or self financing
- be equipped to fulfil its purpose

Support groups run for families may provide for all members or for certain branches of the family only. Most groups for parents tend to be aimed at families with children under five years, or at least for parents who have one child who is under five years of age. However some schools and local further education colleges have introduced groups especially for parents of teenagers. Courses on parenting of teenagers are also proving very popular with particular emphasis being placed on communication. Whatever the age of the child the rules for groups should always apply.

Adult and toddler groups

These need a large enough space to play safely, combined with a welcoming atmosphere. Publicity is crucial to the success of the group, with word of mouth often providing the best return. It is essential to have a regular meeting time. Kitchen and toilets with changing facilities are a must. No family should be isolated, no matter what their difficulty.

Adults should be encouraged to own and run the group themselves, but never forced to do so unless willing. Rules should be enforced with regard to health and safety. Initially staff will need to plan a loose structure, but should involve adults in rule making, planning, setting up and clearing away.

Managing the group will include discouraging gossip, introducing suitable topics, and helping to develop skills in children and adults. It is often difficult to recruit men, so every effort needs to be made to 'hang on' to and interest those who come along. Staff will need to be knowledgeable about local services and sources of help. They will need first aid and child protection training. They should ideally be experienced in working with small children and their families. Running such a group often involves lifting, and energetic play on the floor, so staff must be ready and fit to do so.

Drop-in groups

These also need attention to detail, and all of the suggestions for adult and toddler groups apply.

They are slightly harder to run, in that numbers may vary from nil to capacity. On the other hand, with fewer people about, adults may find opportunities to talk through personal crises more discreetly.

Again, a full range of activities needs to be on offer. It is more difficult to involve adults in setting up, as they may choose to 'drop-in' later in the session. Planning together may need to be scheduled for the time when most members are likely to be in attendance. Structure needs to be applied, but flexibly.

Parent partnership groups

As the name suggests, these groups contain a mix of families and professionals who seek new ideas, clarify current thinking, and plan ways forward to the satisfaction of all.

The venue is usually in a meeting room attached to a school or professional office, but can equally be in a private house or residential common room etc.

There should be an agenda, preferably circulated before the meeting. All attendees, whether family members or professionals, need to feel welcome and valued. Their ideas need to be given equal exposure and respect.

The general aims are to inform, and to enable everyone to have a voice. These meetings are an ideal platform from which to frame future plans, knowing that they have the backing of families rather than being imposed by officials. It is therefore vital to time the meetings so that those who are invited or wish to attend find them convenient and family friendly.

Play days

These groups tend to offer respite to parents and carers by providing a safe play environment for the children or young people to attend, either for part- or full-day sessions. The venue and staff must be registered by social services and inspected as necessary. A fire certificate, trained staff, written procedures (regarding all aspects of the day), adequate premises and equipment are absolutely necessary. See Group Planning Example at the end of this section.

Outings

Outings for children on their own are slightly different from those where parents supervise their children. When staff supervise children, they will need to be trained or experienced in the procedures in place for such activities. See Group Planning Example at the end of this section.

If the children are in the control of their parents, then ground rules should be laid down before you set off as to:
- who is responsible for the children and when
- expected behaviour whilst travelling
- meeting up times at the end of the trip
- how to access staff support if needed
- where to meet in an emergency

As with all trips, someone should go to the venue beforehand and make a risk assessment, see example on page 186. Take spares of everything, drinks, clothes, first aid, nappies, travel sickness pack, etc.

Family learning days

These are usually run by schools. The aim is to encourage parents to help their children to get the best from their school experience.

They usually begin with a general session with adults and children. Later, the children are taken to a different room to work on activities related to literacy or numeracy. The adults are then led through material, which involves both listening and practical activities. At the end of the day the adults and children come together to share activities prepared.

Parents receive a pack full of interesting suggestions to stimulate their child's interest in learning. The ideas are designed to encourage the adult and child to work together. The local adult education department normally provides these days free as part of the Lifelong Learning Scheme.

Adult fun sessions

Adults are given opportunities to try new skills or improve on existing ones in a fun atmosphere. A crèche is provided for the children. The accent is on fun, and having a go. The activities are chosen from suggestions or ideas from staff and group members. No effort goes unrewarded and there is no pressure to achieve a grade or standard. The materials are usually provided by staff. Some sessions afford adults the time to experiment with creative media normally used by their children, e.g. playdough, doughcraft, without embarrassment.

Improving adult skills

Some parents are keen to improve their work-based skills in order to enhance their chances of employment. The local Lifelong Learning Co-ordinator will often fund such groups, including a crèche, if there are eight members wishing to participate.

Groups for teenagers

> ...if you haven't got the group with you in the first five minutes you've had it. (Teacher)

> I'm in trouble for drugs and drinks and look at me. I've been here for two hours and I haven't even had a fag. We ought to have meetings like this all the time.
> (Young person preparing to leave a young offenders institute)

> ...it's the same with all work with young people, you must be prepared. (Carer)

You will need an aim:
- user participation
- research
- decision making
- advisory
- informative
- have fun

Whatever you wish the outcome to be, plan accordingly.

You will need to prepare:
- The place: check it out, what about tables, chairs, access, transport, flip chart, pens, cups, plates etc., room layout?
- The timing: not holiday time, nor during *Neighbours* or *Coronation Street*!
- Making contact: who to invite, how to get access to names and addresses; do not use formal headed paper, use coloured paper, think about language; when to send details out, do you need permission from anyone; follow-up telephone call, both as a reminder and also if no response; handling resistance strategy.
- Whatever you need: refreshments, paper, pens, tape recorder, batteries, tapes, TV, video, leisure equipment, money for expenses.

Organising and planning family support

You will need strategies and procedures:
- A contact person if something goes wrong.
- What to do if there is a disclosure.
- How to ensure confidentiality.
- What to wear.
- Who to work with.
- Have a plan for the group meeting.

The meeting:
- Start and finish on time.
- Welcome, and brief explanation of reason for meeting.
- Introductions: ask them to say their name but also give the opportunity to say something about themselves if they wish.
- Inform of intended outcomes at the beginning.
- Don't make promises you can't keep. If you do make promises, keep to them within a short period and advise if you cannot after all keep them.
- Advise what you will do if you hear anything that may require further action.
- If you wish to make tape recording, ask permission and advise what will happen to tapes.
- If appropriate, advise that they may, if they wish, talk to you privately afterwards.
- Use humour not sarcasm.
- Learn not to show that you are shocked by what you hear (they may be trying you out) but it is acceptable to show disapproval if you wish.
- Listen.
- Be alert.
- Be prepared.
- Use eye contact.
- How will you prevent a few hogging the group?
- Have plenty of alternative material available in case your first or even second plan doesn't work.
- If you plan to have further meetings, ask them for their views on how it should be run and what should be included.
- Ask them what could be done better.
- Advise the group when there are, say, ten minutes to the end.

At the end:
- Thank them for coming.
- Inform them of future outcomes.
- Pay their expenses if appropriate.
- Be prepared if they don't want to leave.

Afterwards:
- Be discreet about what you have heard.
- Have a brief wash-up session with whoever worked with you.
- How will you relax and unwind – group meetings may be stressful?
- Plan for the next meeting based on your experiences of this one.

The family support handbook

Managing groups

Managing groups: what works

You can't buy atmosphere (Worker)

Here are some things which contribute:
- a friendly, welcoming, accepting environment
- support, and sensitive advice, if sought
- willingness to listen
- leaflets to flag up services
- group leaflet and programme
- free facilities
- word-of-mouth publicity
- a gently-gently approach
- no pressure
- member involvement in planning activities, setting up and putting away
- valuing member suggestions
- a follow up home visit if extra support needed

Managing groups: what doesn't work

Here are some things which can detract:
- unfriendly staff
- expecting too much too soon
- too much rigid structure
- insensitivity to individual needs

Managing groups: what prevents them working

Here are some stumbling blocks:
- lack of planning, publicity, canvassing needs
- venue in a building with a reputation; 'I wouldn't go in that block'
- group dynamics; clashing personalities
- gossiping between members going unchecked by staff
- lack of equipment
- rules not owned by members
- members feeling unwelcome, not valued; 'I only went once'
- unplanned visits by professionals who may have a 'history' with members

Helping families to help their children get the most out of school

I hated school and I want my child to like it. (Parent)

When a child starts school, it can be a tense time for all. Parents want answers to their questions:
- Will the child like it?
- Will I like it?
- Will I be able to cope with the routine?
- What do I need to do?
- Will I understand the work they are doing? – It's all different now!

Organising and planning family support

There are certain useful strategies that may help the experience to begin and continue well. Both parents and children need reassurance and general guidelines.

Before the child starts:
- A child's name should be put down for school as soon as possible after their second birthday. A birth certificate will need to be shown.
- Advise the school about any medical condition or other difficulty the child has when you register the child's name. This will help the school to plan.
- Some popular schools may become oversubscribed, so it makes sense to put your child's name down early.
- Parents may appeal to the governors of the school if they are refused a place, whether they live in the catchment area or not.
- There is usually an introductory programme so that both parent and child can see the school layout, meet teachers and other staff and have some taster sessions.
- Many schools have a uniform that will help the child to feel that they belong. Try to ensure that the child has the same uniform as all the other children, or they will feel very different without it. There are grants available to help with purchase for those with limited means.
- Teach the child how to put on and take off coats, shoes, clothing. Make sure that the fastenings on their clothes are those they can manage. Velcro and zips are preferable to buttons and laces.
- Most children attend a nursery, playgroup or pre-school, which helps them to separate from their parent and accept the school routine. If the child has not done this, extra time may be needed in preparing them for school.
- A decision about whether packed lunches or school lunches will best suit the child will need to be made. The child should be prepared for what has been decided.
- Talk to the child about what will happen at school e.g. play and learning, lunch, assembly etc. The more a child understands, the more successful the beginning is likely to be. Stress the positives, and the fun they will have, and that they come home at the end of the day.
- Parents should plan their routine so that they can get the child to school on time. This may entail a lot of organisation, but it is no fun for the child to be missing the start of every session. This is important for children and young people of all ages.

Tips for when a child is at school

- Show interest in what they have done each day and praise their efforts.
- Check their book bag for letters or appointments.
- Attend parent evenings and school concerts etc.
- Check that homework is being done: parents can help if they wish, but mustn't do it for them.
- Ensure that the child gets sufficient sleep.
- Listen if a child reports bullying, and follow it up.
- If you have a concern, don't let it simmer, but make an appointment and take it up with the school, who will normally be only too glad to help. There will also be a complaints procedure in operation if you wish to make a formal complaint.

Parents should try not to lose their temper or shout at staff as this will not achieve anything. They should talk calmly to those involved with the complaint. When a concern is not resolved, a parent has the right to appeal to the school governors.

Older children:
- When a child changes school, there will be a period of adjustment to the new regime. Talk to the child and reassure them if they are anxious.
- Continue to attend concerts and parents evenings.
- Continue to keep an eye on homework and make sure sufficient time is given to it.
- Try to ensure the child has somewhere to do their homework away from distractions such as TV.
- Keep the lines of communication open. The child may be less willing to discuss school during the teen years, but show an interest if they wish to do so.
- Encourage talents and interests, including those outside school.
- Allow the child gradually to take more responsibility for managing their workload, but be there to assist if they wish.

Teenage parents groups

Some groups invite teenage parents along but this does not always work out as many of the girls are often almost children themselves. Sure-Start Plus has been given funding by the government to provide groups especially for teenage mums. Some educational establishments also provide groups for mums so that the girls may continue with their formal education whilst also learning about child care matters.

Most of the suggestions provided in this book are suitable for running groups for teenage parents but it is important that the material used in the groups is age appropriate.

It is also important to encourage the fathers of the children to attend as many may have no, or little experience, of child care matters.

Providing support after visits cease

I could always ask if there was something I was unsure of – the new school is not interested.
(Past parent)

Relationships develop during work with families, and people grow to like and to trust staff to have their best interests at heart. It is natural for there to be a sense of loss when it is time to move on. Families may have developed some dependence on the reliability of help at hand. It may be that there is a real sense of bereavement if measures are not taken to provide follow-on help. This may take the form of:
- Choosing together what the next setting will be.
- Giving all the necessary information about timings, dates, venue etc.
- Helping the family to accept the next setting when there is no choice, e.g. school.
- Going with the family to the next setting and introducing them to a named person.
- Arranging meetings for the family with staff in the next setting.
- Inviting staff and, if appropriate, children, from the next setting to your setting to meet the family, where they feel comfortable and relaxed.
- Checking that the family have all they need to access the next setting, e.g. the correct school uniforms, the right equipment.
- Maintaining contact during the transition phase.

- Contacting the family some time after the change has been made to make sure there are no difficulties.
- Continuing to welcome the family to open sessions.
- Inviting the family to join associations linked to your session.
- Continuing to provide a listening ear until the family no longer need it.
- Getting help for the family from other professionals if necessary.
- Not fobbing the family off with a setting which does not meet their needs.
- Respecting the advice offered to the family by staff in the new setting once the transfer has been made.
- Letting go gracefully when the family have ceased contact.

Further reading

Alexander, T. (1997) *Family Learning: The Foundation of Effective Education*. London: Demos.
Families are one of the most important and influential places of social learning, yet little is invested in them as vehicles for transmitting knowledge about such matters as health, well-being and social skills.

McConville, B. (1999) Teenage Parenting: Stigma Solves Nothing. *Healthlines*. 64 Jul. 10-2.
Teenage parents are not a homogeneous group and support services need to be targeted accordingly.

Mullins, A., and McCluskey, J. (1999) *Teenage Mothers Speak for Themselves*. London, NCH Action for Children.
Report presenting the views of young women who have experienced teenage motherhood between the ages of 13-19.

Phillips, A. (2000) *Working With Family Diversity. A Guidance Pack for Sure Start Projects*. Sure Start Unit.
Advice and practical suggestions for workers dealing with families of all types, and in varied situations such as the transition to parenthood, family breakdown, or the arrival of a new baby in a stepfamily.

Shepherd, A. L., Burrows, R., and McAllister, T. (1999) Parenting Matters Project: A Case Study of a Parenting Group. *Child Care in Practice*. 5:1 Jan. 55-65.
Outlines the background to, and format of, a parenting group initiative in Northern Ireland.

Sure Start Unit (1999) *A Guide to Evidence-based Practice*. 2nd edn. London: DfEE. (Planning Pack).
Sets out examples of good practice, with the aim of helping partnerships plan their services to meet Sure Start targets.

Sure Start Unit (1999) *Sure Start*. London, DfEE.
Briefly summarises the aims of the Sure Start programme, in which local programmes work with parents to improve their children's life chances by better access to family support, advice on nurturing, health services and early learning.

Useful resources and bibliography

Herbert, G. and Napper, R. (2000) *Tips: Tried and Tested Ideas for Parent Education and Support*. Lyme Regis, Russell House Publishing.

Wheal, A. (1997) *Adolescence, Positive Approaches to Working with Young People*. Lyme Regis, Russell House Publishing.

The family support handbook

Model forms and documents

Group planning example

Once a week for seven weeks

Location:				Timings:			
Staff	Date	Activity	Equipment	Method	End Session	Focus	Notes
Danielle Jan Ruth	6.6.01	Paper flower painting and ladybirds.	Paper flowers. Tissue paper. Sugar paper. Scissors. Ladybirds. Paint brushes.	Cut out flower shapes from tissue paper and sugar paper for children to glue and paint. Cut circles from black card and stick onto ladybird shapes.	Candle time and songs.	Creative.	
Danielle Jan Ruth	13.6.01	Library bus. Sticking and glueing.	Glue. Paper and materials.	Children and parents to take turns going out to the library bus. Cover table and floor, put out glue and variety of paper and materials.	Candle time and songs.	Language and literacy. Creative.	Library bus.
Danielle Jan Ruth	20.6.01	Large hands and feet painting.	Large roll of paper. 3 colours of paint. Water. Towels.	Cover floor with large roll of paper. Let children choose paint and explore over the paper using hands and feet.	Candle time and songs.	Creative. Gross motor.	
Danielle Jan	27.6.01	Cornflour and pasta play.	Bowls. Food colouring. Biscuits. Cakes, spoons. Aprons. Floor covering. Table covering.	Cover table and floors. Let children help to mix cornflour and feel the difference, more/less water. Cook pasta. Have cooked and uncooked, let children feel and play.	Candle time and songs.	Sensory.	
Danielle Jan Ruth	4.7.01	Gross motor.	Balls. Bean bags. Hoops. Beams.	Make area safe. Lay equipment out and encourage children to participate. Hold hands where necessary for support. Encourage balance, ball skills and gross motor.	Candle time and songs.	Gross Motor.	
Danielle Jan Ruth	11.7.01	Smell. Tasting and printing.	Variety of fruit and veg. Paper. Aprons. Table covering. Floor covering.	Cover floor and table. Wash hands. Lay out fruit and veg. Encourage children to taste. Talk about smell and taste. Put aprons on, extend to painting.	Candle time and songs.	Sensory.	
Danielle Jan Ruth	18.7.01	Party.	Drinks. Cakes. Sandwiches. Biscuits.	Inform parents of party. Ask them to bring in food.	Candle time and songs.	Personal and social.	

Organising and planning family support

Group planning example

Daily – one week

Location:				Timings:			
Staff	Date	Activity	Equipment	Method	End Session	Focus	Notes
Jan Danielle	18.6.01	CONNOR'S TOY LIBRARY					
Jan Danielle Ruth	19.6.01	LEAP. Crèche.	Sand play.	Lay out sand tray.	Songs.		Cancelled No LEAP.
Jan Danielle Ruth	20.6.01	Hand floor painting.	Large roll of paper. 3 colours of paint. Water. Towels.	Let them choose paint. Hold hands so they don't slip. Let children explore all over the paper, feet and hands.	Candle time and songs.	Creative. Gross motor	
Jan Danielle Ruth	21.6.01	Water play.	Towels, buckets, change of clothes, dolls, jugs, cups, sponges, paint brushes.	Lay out bowls and large plastic box with warm water. Plenty of water toys so children can choose. Towels close by for drying.	Candle time and songs.		Remind parents suncream and hats
Jan Danielle Ruth	22.6.01	ADMIN					

Group planning example

Mornings

Location:				Timings:			
Staff	Date	Activity	Equipment	Method	End Session	Focus	Notes
Danielle Jan	18.6.01	Making pizza.	Pizza base. Tomatoes. Mushrooms. Ham. Sausage.	Cover tables and floor. Wash hands. Put on aprons. Put tomatoes, mushrooms, ham and sausage into dishes. Let parents work with their children and choose which foods to use.	Candle time and songs.	Food tech. Health and safety.	
Danielle Jan Ruth	19.6.01	Individual programmes. Sand play and photos.	Home visiting box. Sand tray and sand. Sand toys.	Work 1:1 with each child working from their individual programmes. Cover floor. Put sand into tray. Let children explore sand. Parents cut out photos.	Songs.	Speech and language.	
Danielle Jan Ruth	20.6.01	Trip out. Large floor painting with squirty bottles.	Bottle. Large roll of paper, tape. Aprons.	Lay out large paper on floor and tape down. Lay out aprons. Fill bottles with paint. Let parents and children choose colours.	Candle time and songs.	Creative.	Trip not possible because of new parents.
Danielle Jan Ruth	21.6.01	Home visiting. Solihull House. Cutting and glueing.	Home visiting box. Paper, material, glue, scissors. Aprons.	Individual programme. Encourage child to co-operate, talk to mum.		Lang/lit. Personal and Social. Creative.	
Danielle Jan Ruth	22.6.01	Home visit.	Home visiting box.	Observe child's PECS programme.		Lang/lit.	

Section 6
Personal Development: All the Family

If

If I had my life to live over, I'd make more mistakes next time.

I would relax.

I would limber up, be sillier than I have been on this trip.

I know of very few things I'd take seriously.

I would worry less about what others thought of me and I would accept myself as I am.

I would climb more mountains, swim more rivers and watch more sunsets.

I would eat more ice cream and fewer beans.

I would watch less TV and have more picnics.

I would have only actual troubles and very few imaginary ones.

I would feel sad, not depressed.

I would be concerned, not anxious.

I would be annoyed, not angry.

I would regret my mistakes, but not spend a lot of time feeling guilty about them.

I would tell more people I like them.

I would touch my friends.

I would forgive others for being human and I would bear no grudges.

I would play with more children and listen to more old people.

I would go after what I wanted without believing that I needed it, and I would not place so much value on money.

You see, I am one of those people who lived cautiously, sensible, sanely, hour after hour, day after day.

Oh, I've had my moments, and if I had it to do over again, I'd have a lot more of them.

In fact, I'd have nothing else, just moments – one after the other – instead of living so many years ahead of each day.

I have been one of those people who never went anywhere without a thermometer, a hot water bottle, a gargle, a raincoat and a parachute.

If I had to do it over, I would go more places, do more things and travel lighter than I have.

I would plant more seeds and make the world more beautiful.

I would express my feelings of love without fear.

If I had my life to live over, I would go barefoot earlier in the Spring and stay that way later in the Fall.

I would play hookey more and wouldn't make such grades, except by accident.

I'd ride more merry-go-rounds.

I'd pick more daisies.

And I would smile because I would be living free.

(Source unknown)

Self-esteem and self-image

We are what we think, and all that we are arises with our thoughts. With our thoughts we make our world.
(Buddha)

He's got two left feet – he'll never be able to do it – that was all I heard in childhood. It took over twenty years for me to start believing that I could succeed.
(Mature student with two degrees who was labelled a failure at school)

Adults and self-esteem

In order to reach one's potential, it is necessary to have a self-image with which we are happy and a level of self-esteem which makes us feel:

- valued
- worthy
- appreciated
- capable
- satisfied
- acceptable

Poor self-image may result from:
- Comparisons with media role models – *myself as I would like others to see me.*
- Comparisons with friends and family – *myself as I am.*
- Perceived attitudes of friends and family – *myself as I think others see me.*
- Adverse comments at your expense – *myself as others see me.*
- Perceived body faults which cannot be changed – *myself as I am.*
- Failed attempts to make changes – *myself as I would like to be.*

Poor self-esteem may result from any of the above, but also from:
- Lack of emotional awareness of one's feelings and their effects.
- Lack of knowledge of one's strengths, limits and capabilities.

In order to raise self-esteem we need to raise self-belief. We must provide opportunities for people to:
- Celebrate success at something new.
- Be praised for a skill or capability they already have.
- Be rewarded for increased competency.
- Take responsibility for their lives.
- State and then work to achieve a goal.
- Share joyful experiences.
- Relax and enjoy being themselves.
- Be proud of themselves, their home and their family.
- Understand how their thinking lowers their self-image.
- Examine the feelings which hold them back.
- Be motivated to change their lives.
- Learn skills which lead to a (better) job.
- Gain motivation and enthusiasm.

There is no quick-fix solution to raising self-esteem, but groups aimed at empowering clients are a very valuable first step, as are honest and trusting relationships. Sometimes counselling is required in order to change a mind-set which is giving rise to low self-esteem. Every small, celebrated step on the way to high esteem will uplift and sustain the effort made to achieve it.

Children, young people and self-esteem

When self-esteem is high, they are likely to be confident, positive, sociable, kind to others and more willing to attempt new tasks. When it is low, children may be negative, withdrawn, socially insecure and can even be quite paranoid.

(Dr Christopher Green, Beyond Toddlerdom)

Low self-esteem in children and young people is every bit as much a bar to progress as it is in adults. Children and young people are also susceptible to perceptions about their:

- body image compared with others
- academic abilities
- social success
- physical prowess

How they deal with these issues will largely depend on their temperament and their ability to bounce back after putdowns.

In response to research linking esteem and achievement, schools place importance on increasing self-esteem as a way to boost achievement. Many schools use a version of 'Quality Circle Time', which was developed by Jenny Mosley in Wiltshire in 1987. It follows a set pattern of systems that allow children and young people to discuss issues that concern them in a safe environment.

They agree golden rules which can lead to extra choice or 'golden time' if kept, or a reduction in this time if they are broken. During the actual circle time there are:
- Meeting up games.
- Open forum discussions of any issue.
- Cheering up games.
- Closing down ritual which prepares for a return to normal school working.

Helping to raise self-esteem
In order to be sensitive to children's and young people's needs we must:

- Respect their feelings.
- Handle their feelings with care.
- Accept that they may make mistakes and not humiliate them for it.
- Praise positive achievement.
- Allow some privacy.
- Resist comparisons with their peers.
- Have sensible rules which are kept.
- Listen to what they say.
- Explain our own feelings.
- Teach coping and surviving skills.

Feeling down?
Feelings follow actions
Change your actions to change your feelings!

- Do something new.
- Indulge yourself.
- Take a walk.
- Call a friend – talk about it.
- Write down your feelings; keep a diary.
- Exercise.
- Have a massage.
- Get outdoors in the fresh air and sunshine.
- Read a funny book.
- See a funny film.
- Watch or do your favourite sport.
- Meditate.
- Eat well; get plenty of rest.

What else works for you?

The family support handbook

> **Tips**
>
> - Give yourself a treat
>   – Stroke a cat, watch the sunset, have a bath, draw a picture, read a good book, watch a favourite video.
> - Remind yourself how nice you are
>   – Make a list entitled 'things I can do' and 'nice things I know about me'.
> - Look after your body and your brain
>   – Go swimming, eat fruit, solve a puzzle, learn a song.
> - Start a praise box
>   – When someone says something nice about you write it on paper and put it in the box. Open it often to remind yourself how nice you are.
> - Play the difference game
>   – With a friend outline the ways you are different and tell each other the things you like about each other.
>
> Produced by Jacqueline Coulby, Head teacher of Batheaston Primary School, Bath, for children to use to cheer themselves up. It could work for parents too!

Figure 13: Tips to help children cheer themselves up

Contraception and choices

There are at least ten methods of contraception available at present. Family planning clinics, doctors' surgeries and health centres give advice and guidance as to which method is best for an individual and on how to use the particular form of contraception.

If contraception is used to prevent pregnancy, people will be:
- Free to make choices in their lives.
- Free to enjoy themselves and take on responsibilities without the worry of unwanted pregnancies.
- Able to go where and when they please.
- Able to live with whom they wish.
- Able to have children when **they and their partner** want and are ready.
- Given time to learn about relationships.
- In a position to decide with whom they would like to have a child.
- Able to say yes or no to sex, which will give them confidence and freedom.

Note: Using a condom is an effective form of birth control if applied carefully, ensuring it does not split. Using a condom is also an effective way of preventing the spread of disease from infected semen. When having anal sex, a strong condom should **always** be used.

Using contraception is beneficial in most cases. However, there may be circumstances when this may not be the case. For example:
- Girls and women with learning difficulties may have their rights infringed if they are not given choices.
- Non-articulate families are sometimes not offered a full choice of contraception. They may receive contraception that may have side-effects.
- Religious barriers.

Coping strategies

Stress and pressure are part of modern living, but excess stress can lead to:
- Increased anxiety and irritability.
- Increased smoking or drinking – or both.
- Loss of interest and motivation.
- Reduced concentration.
- Poor performance levels.
- Increased anger and frustration.
- Inability to ask for help or delegate to others.

When stress builds up and is not dealt with it can lead to:
- physical illness
- depression
- loss of vocation
- low self-esteem
- extreme fatigue

Stress may result from:
- Pressure of work.
- Lack of recognition.
- Low pay.
- Adverse environments or conditions.
- Lack of privacy.
- Lack of training or instruction.
- Bullying or harassment by staff or family members including children and teenagers.
- Combined personal and work pressures, or personal and family pressures.

What can we do about it?

Support systems act as an outlet for stress by supplying:
- A forum for letting off steam.
- Other ideas on how to solve problems.
- A listening ear.
- Mutual support – sometimes stress can be lessened by trying to help colleagues or other family members deal with their own crises.
- An acknowledgement of feelings.
- Time out to cool off or relax for a few moments after stressful situations.

Everyone has to find and develop their own support systems. These may be family, friends or close work colleagues. No matter how lonely or isolated they are feeling, parents should avoid using their child to unburden their troubles upon as this will cause anxiety and may give them undue and unnecessary responsibilities.

If you are at work, your employer may offer a formal staff support scheme which may or may not be helpful.

Developing ways of coping

We all experience stress to varying degrees. When it won't go away, we need to develop strategies to cope with it in order to lessen its detrimental effects.

In the Emergency Coping Strategies at the end of this section, there are a variety of useful strategies to try. Some will work better for you than others, but all will be useful for someone. Go on, try them!

Learning to play: the family

The irresistible urge in young children to be active, to investigate and discover, to imitate and pretend, to plan and construct, finds its outlet in what we call play. (E. Mellor, 1950)

Play has been described variously as:
- Preparation for life.
- The integrating mechanism in children's experiences.
- An intrinsic pleasure.
- Recreation.
- An outlet for surplus energy.

Babies begin to play in their earliest months by reaching out to investigate the world around them. Children use play as both a private and a social experience. Adults play through hobbies, joining interest groups and social events, and through sport. The world would be sadder but not wiser should we all give up play, so what can it do for us?

For children, play can:
- Provide opportunities to revisit life experiences which may have worried them.
- Enable practise of skills which are new or emerging, including:
    - physical skills
    - emotional skills
    - social skills
    - intellectual skills
- Allow a safe forum in which to try, to make mistakes and try again.
- Help bodies and minds to develop and increase in health and strength.
- Enable the growth of talents, life interests and leisure pursuits.
- Encourage the development of social awareness.
- Foster the ability to share and work together with others.
- Give endless pleasure and satisfaction.

Young children are enthusiastic and active learners, passing by degrees through developmental play stages, which include:
- **Solitary play** – the child plays alone and may be unaware of others.
- **Parallel play** – the child plays alongside and may watch others.
- **Joint play** – the child will connect with one other child in shared endeavours.
- **Group play** – the child joins several others and begins to follow rules.
- **Imaginary play** – this transcends several stages and involves make-believe.

During different stages of play, children focus on various repeatable and generalised activities, which are called schemas. For example, for young children this might be:
- Banging – not just drums, but everything they come across.
- Infilling – putting things inside others to see how they fit.
- Lines – investigating lines in the environment, with drawing materials, toys, etc.
- Trajectories – everything from throwing toys to flying planes.
- Enveloping – practising wrapping things up, from sweets to trees.

The schemas in play help children to make sense of what they are experiencing and to develop ideas about how the world works. Play enriches children's lives.

What hinders play?

- **Lack of opportunity** – if a child is encouraged to sit in front of a TV or video all day, or is marshalled constantly from pillar to post, they have no time to play.
- **Lack of play materials** – these do not, contrary to popular opinion, have to be those bought as a result of 'pester power'. Such toys often pall quickly, leave no room for imagination and may lack possibilities for sharing amicably. Many of us have experienced the situation where we spend oodles of money on something expensive which is supposed to be the most popular and developmentally correct thing for children. The young child takes endless pleasure in playing with the wrapper, but ignores our apparently 'well-chosen' offering. A box of old clothes, bricks, or even a large cardboard box, sustain hours of play at little expense.
- **Adult interference** – we all know the one about the dad who buys his son a train set and plays with it himself, but what about the adults who constantly direct and limit play to their ideas?
- **Lack of support and encouragement** – this is the other end of the scale when play is sterile because supporting adults show no interest or enthusiasm for the game.
- **Lack of room** – a child indoors cannot express joy in large physical movements, or set out a mammoth play scene in a tiny area.
- **Gender** – boys and girls need different sorts of play opportunities to develop their strengths, so we need to provide opportunities for both sexes.

    A selection of toys was put on a table in a room. A group of girls were put in the room for fifteen minutes, then a group of boys for the same amount of time. At the end of their allotted time, the girls had made friends, knew each others' names, family members, schools, hobbies, likes and dislikes, but the toys were barely investigated. The boys had put together the train set, made towers of bricks, laid out the farm and tried the cars, but none of them knew the others' names. (Group leader)

What is the adult's role in play?

The sensible adult will support play in the following ways:

- Follow the SOUL process before joining in –
    - **S**ilence
    - **O**bservation
    - **U**nderstanding
    - **Li**stening
- Move around the children, helping them in their activities.
- Take the children's lead rather than directing them.
- Notice which children need help to get started.
- Talk to the children about what they want to do or are doing.
- Join in with the play, trying the child's ideas rather than imposing your own.
- Help to extend the play by asking a question to spark new ideas:
    - What if…?
    - Would you like more…?
    - Would it help if…?
- Encourage exploration and discovery.
- Avoid doing things for children, but don't leave them struggling if they have tried repeatedly, failed and are getting distressed or frustrated.
- Help the child to think of their own solutions to problems.
- Introduce new materials.
- Let the children choose what they want to play with.
- Ask questions which relate to concepts, e.g. colour, size, shape, strength, number.

- Be prepared to play the same game again next time, and the time after that.
- Take on the role assigned to you, e.g. you may be the baby, the child or the adult.
- Offer comfort and contact.
- Be a chauffeur – some forms of play involve trips to the playing place, e.g. football.
- Give a warning when the play needs to stop, then help to clear up, but don't do it for them.
- In games where there are winners and losers, play fairly but don't insist on always winning just because you are the grown up. Letting them win a little will foster their interest, whereas feeling that they have no chance of doing so will destroy it.

Play for adults

The students we have this year won't play with the children. They spend all their time playing with the toys themselves. (Playgroup leader)

We all know the old adage 'All work and no play makes Jack a dull boy'. This is also true for adults and for teenagers, who sometimes feel that they should not be caught playing. The students in the playgroup were still at an age where they were unable to resist the toys in front of them. They may have been reflecting on the fact that in their childhood they were unable to play sufficiently, so are filling gaps in their experience. In the adult world, work tends to be rewarded more often than play, but adults still have a basic need to relax and unwind. Adult or teenage play may take the form of:
- Pursuing a hobby.
- Learning a skill – individually or in a group.
- Practising leisure activities such as painting, hairdressing, carpentry.
- Physical games – sports, the gym or dancing.
- Social games – pubs and clubs, visits to relatives and friends.
- Educational games – evening classes, courses, quizzes or reading.
- Relaxation activities – TV, chat, sex, food, music.

Adults and teenagers should be encouraged to play in order to:
- relax the body
- rest the mind
- reduce stress
- engage in pleasurable activities
- experience joy in achievement
- enjoy socialising
- stimulate new ideas and approaches to life
- learn new skills or revisit those previously learned

What hinders adult play?
- Guilt at engaging in pleasant activities when work is outstanding.
- Inability to relax due to a life overburdened with stress.
- Poor self-esteem.
- Poor social skills.
- Fear of ridicule.
- Lack of money to follow some ideas, e.g. to buy a racing car or go to the gym.
- The lack of value society places on play compared to work.
- Sparse or no information about opportunities.
- Absence of transport to play places.
- Ignoring the need to play and using all available time to work.

Adults need to accept that play is just as important for them as for their children, as their 'recharged batteries' afterwards will enable them to enhance their:
- parenting skills
- work skills
- social skills

Above all, when we provide activities aimed at adults or teenagers, we need to reassure them that it is OK to play.

Behaviour management

Challenging behaviour can cause distress in the most well organised families or the establishments which support them. It has been a subject of discussion between parents and carers, teachers and other professionals throughout the centuries. Many books have been written and many experts have put forward theories.

The theory suggested here is one of many that you may come across. It is based on a system called 'Strategies for Crisis Intervention and Prevention' which was compiled by Hampshire Educational Psychology Department in the mid-nineties, from the teachings of Gary La Vigna. It is based on positive intervention and can be used with all ages, including children with disabilities.

So what do we look for from behaviour management? Tradition says 'spare the rod and spoil the child' but the law says that no physical punishment is allowed.

What we really want is:
- To reduce or minimise the unwanted behaviour.
- To change the behaviour without harming the child or young person.
- To provide lasting solutions rather than quick fixes.
- To raise the child or young person's self-esteem.

The golden rules to remember are:
- Everyone who deals with the child or young person must be consistent – plan together.
- Behaviour is learned.
- Unwanted behaviours may be due to a mismatch between what the child or young person is trying to communicate and what they actually do.
- Responses to behaviour should be age-appropriate.
- A child or young person cannot behave better than the example they are set.
- A child learns controls gradually throughout childhood.
- A child or young person who lacks positive attention will try for negative attention.
- Don't discuss the child or young person's behaviour in their presence. This is awarding negative attention that they may come to seek. Remember 'give a dog a bad name'.

The over-riding principles of behaviour modification are:
- Behaviour is learned and maintained because of what happens afterwards.
- Behaviour that leads to the child or young person seeing or feeling it to be rewarding is more likely to be repeated.

There are four parts to this management system:
1. Looking at environmental factors.
2. Teaching new skills.
3. Reinforcing positive behaviour.
4. Reacting appropriately to unwanted behaviours.

The family support handbook

1. Looking at environmental factors

When the child or young person's feels conflict with the environment, friction may occur. Look at their needs and examine the context in which the behaviours occur. Is there a difficulty that a change to the environment may solve? Use the checklist to do an audit.

Environmental factors checklist

Physical characteristics
- size
- space
- lighting
- noise
- temperature
- room layout
- access to materials
- appropriateness of equipment
- access to outside areas

Personal feelings
- anxiety
- self-esteem
- sadness
- hunger
- feelings of loss
- frustration
- tiredness
- physical health
- confidence

Social relationships
- expectations
- quality of relationships
- respect
- dignity
- grouping arrangements
- opportunities for interaction
- time available for the child
- peer group
- ability to express needs

What is on offer
- activities
- task difficulty
- make up of the day
- proportion of time on activities
- stimulus overload or deprivation
- interest level
- predictability
- relevance
- variety of materials
- transition times
- availability of attention
- communication style
- consistency between staff
- appropriate goals
- ability to exercise choice

When you find a problem, make sure you include it in your behaviour plan, preferably with an idea that solves it.

Example:
My toddler keeps taking chocolate from the fridge.
My 13 year-old keeps taking money from my purse.

Solution:
Don't keep chocolate in the fridge or your purse lying around.

2. Teaching new skills

A child or young person may use an unwanted behaviour because they do not know how to communicate their intentions in a more conventional way. We have to consider:

- What the child or young person is trying to tell us – keep asking yourself 'Why' if they are unable to voice their intentions. You will eventually get to a difficulty which can be solved practically.

> **Example:**
> A teenager says of his teacher 'She's stupid, she doesn't know what she is talking about'. What he actually means is that he doesn't understand and doesn't want to admit it so disrupts the class.

- The skills the child needs to use a better way to have their needs met.
- How we will teach the skills.

If the child does not have the skills, you will need to teach them. Remember, the skills you teach should be those which:

- Provide the child or young person with an acceptable way of behaving.
- Include all the skills needed to make up the new behaviour.
- Include coping and tolerance skills.

> **Example:**
> James grabs the best toys and won't let any of the other children play with them.
>
> **Solution:**
> James needs to learn:
> - The toys are not for him exclusively.
> - If he asks for a toy another child will give him a turn.
> - Grabbing is not acceptable.
> - Sometimes he has to wait for a turn.
>
> We might teach James by:
> - Involving him in sharing the toys out fairly.
> - Playing games which involve give and take.
> - Teaching him the words to ask for a turn (and all the other children if necessary).
> - Helping him to share with one child only to begin with, then extending to others.
> - Using timers to help him wait for his turn.

3. Reinforcing positive behaviour

When a child or young person learns a new behaviour, they do not always produce it consistently. It may be:

- patchy and irregular
- shaping towards the behaviour we want, but not quite right
- used tentatively, as if they are trying it out

We all enjoy the feeling that we are doing the right thing. Reinforcement is all about praising and encouraging the new behaviour as it appears.

There are all sorts of ways of reinforcing – many people will be able to add to the list below, which provides a starting point for ideas. No two people will respond in the same way to rewards, so you need to find the one that suits the child or young person you are teaching.

Social rewards include:
- attention
- praise
- touch
- smiles
- body language
- tone of voice

Material rewards include:
- toys
- money
- trips out
- extra TV
- choice of activity

Sensory rewards include:
- food
- edible treats (but beware of the dental fraternity)
- hugs and touches
- favourite music

Secondary rewards include:
- star charts
- stickers
- smiley stamps
- gold stars
- tokens
- leisure centre tickets
- extra use of the computers or sports equipment
- a mention in front of others (this may, of course, have the opposite effect so you have to know who you are dealing with!)

Whatever reward or reinforcement we choose, there are some basic principles to remember:
- There should be a clear link between the behaviour and the reward; young children in particular live in the 'here and now' so a reward half an hour later will not lead to a repetition of the wanted behaviour and may even confuse.
- Initial rewards should be tangible, but eventually the child or young person's self-esteem in producing the right behaviour will be an intrinsic reward.
- Reward behaviours which are 'nearly right' in the initial stages of learning.
- Reward every time to begin with, but gradually reduce the rewards as the behaviour becomes more fixed.
- Make the rewards age-appropriate. What suits a six year-old may profoundly embarrass a thirteen year-old.

The relationship you have with the child or young person is important to the success of the plan.

4. Reacting appropriately to unwanted behaviours

The three sections above are about changing the unwanted behaviour. The fourth section of the system is about how to deal with the unwanted behaviour while the child or young person is still producing it. You will need to decide what your reaction is going to be, and ensure that all who deal with the child follow the plan.

There are a variety of ways in which you might react to the child. The golden rules are:
- Use the least intrusive strategy to stop the behaviour.
- Don't come out with your guns blazing; decide on a range of strategies and their order of use with the least intrusive first.

Useful strategies include:
- Non-verbal signals, e.g. body language, 'the look'.
- Close proximity; just by you moving closer the child or young person may change their behaviour.
- Redirection; remind them what they are doing and praise them for what they have achieved so far.
- Praising someone near to them who is behaving correctly.
- Active listening; do not always assume you know what led to the behaviour. Listen to those involved.
- Humour; laugh with a child or young person but not at them. Don't use sarcasm as this is not humour.
- Relocation; move them away from the scene of the 'crime'. Some children or young people may need to go to a place for 'time out'. For small children, this time should not exceed a minute for each year of life.
- Distraction; produce something interesting to look at, or point to something, taking the attention away from the behaviour.
- Tactical ignoring; some behaviours disappear if ignored. Think about the child or young person who swears loudly. Everyone gasps and pays attention, so the behaviour is rewarded, albeit negatively. If you ignore the swearing, they get no pay off and hopefully the behaviour ceases.

Making a plan

In order to use this form of behaviour plan, it is necessary for all involved to:
- Design the plan as a team.
- Know what the plan is.
- Stick to the plan until it is reviewed.

Children or young people who get a 'No' from one parent or carer may go to another to try their luck. It is vital that everyone presents a united front if the plan is not to be undermined. One dissenter may cause the plan to fail by not adhering to it completely. In order to ensure that everyone knows the plan, it is useful to have a proforma that can be copied for all, or put on a wall. Older children and young people should be given a copy of the plan.

The behaviour plan sheet at the end of the section is simple and effective. It has been kept deliberately short. We all lead busy lives and do not always have time to read pages of instructions, but a single sheet of A4 paper is manageable.

Use the form as follows:
- Gather the people involved with the child or young person.
- Choose the worst behaviour to plan for. You cannot fix everything at once, but by choosing the worst first, some of the lesser behaviours may disappear with this one.
- Put the child or young person's name on the sheet. If the sheet is to go on the wall in a staff establishment, a code may be needed to avoid embarrassment to them or their family. Confidentiality should also be considered.
- Observe the behaviour and write it in exactly under 'Behaviour we do not want'.
- Decide what you would like them to do instead and write it in under 'Behaviour we do want'.
- Consider which environmental factors increase the behaviour and write them in.
- Decide what the child or young person is trying to achieve or communicate.
- Write in which new skills you need to teach the child or young person, who will do this and when and how they will be taught.
- Choose and write in what reinforcement will be used as the new behaviour appears.
- Choose the response strategies and write them in order with the least intrusive first.
- Decide on a review date.

Cooking, menus and diets

Who can resist the tempting waft of freshly fried chips and burgers or the intoxicating aroma of a succulent lamb biryani? OK so it's about as healthy as being run over by a bus and probably makes my insides look like an explosion in a treacle factory, but that's entirely missing the point. Fast food is quick, cheap and convenient.

(Self-confessed junk food addict, aged 31)

There are many experts only too ready to say what you should or should not eat as an adult or as a child, but food can give rise to tensions for many reasons other than its nutritional value. There may be concerns about time and cost, etc. Advice about food needs to be carefully given but should not be too prescriptive. Care should be taken that the advice:
- Suggests options which are reasonably within budget for the family.
- Allows for diets, whether these are for medical or cultural reasons.
- Is simple enough to follow, backed by pictures and instructions.
- Allows for personal choice.
- Allows for lifestyle.
- Allows a broad range of options within the main food groups.

Food and babies

Babies are given much the best start in life by breast-feeding, but if this is not possible or desired by the mother, then advice should be given on how much milk and how often. If reading is an issue, this advice should be in pictorial form. Hungry crying babies may need to be offered:
- An overall increase in milk throughout the day.
- Water instead of milk on some occasions.
- Water only at night in order to develop good habits.

The best person to advise on milk, weaning and diet for babies is either:
- the midwife or
- the health visitor or
- the GP

Food and children

Children are remarkably quick to cotton on to the fact that food is an incredibly useful weapon. Parents desperately want their children to thrive and they cannot do this if they won't eat. Therefore they have parents over a barrel. Refusal to eat which gains attention for the child will result in further refusals. Attempts to encourage and cajole encourage negative behaviour and may result in stress and distress all round.

Every mealtime was a struggle. Her father would try to get her to eat just one more mouthful, playing aeroplanes with the food. She would take the mouthful eventually, swallow it, and then spectacularly throw up everything she had eaten all over the table. After that, no-one fancied any more.

(Frustrated mother)

There are a few tips to remember with children who won't eat:
- Praise them for what they have eaten, rather than castigate for what they have not.
- Disguise the food – make it into a picture or a pattern, change the colour.
- Give small portions – too much will produce the 'I can't eat all that' response.
- Introduce new foods one at a time and little by little.
- Give them a set amount of time to eat, then take the food away without comment on what they have left.
- Do not be led by misguided emotions into providing snacks between meals.
- Provide sufficient variety for boredom not to be the cause of the refusal.

I once met a mother whose child woke at midnight every night and demanded a full dinner, which she cooked with loving care and which they ate cosily together. She was, of course, shattered, and the child refused food all through the day. Once she followed my advice, stopped cooking at night and offered only water, the child began to get hungry and to eat during the day. And he slept through the night!

Children and diets

No child should be on a diet unless a doctor has suggested it. If a child is unable to digest particular foods, or has diabetes or some such medical condition, parents should be encouraged to ensure that the child:
- Eats no food which is not allowed – the parent may need reminders.
- Takes medication if necessary.
- Is encouraged to eat special foods necessary to their wellbeing, disguised if needed.
- Avoids foods which cause allergic reaction. It is essential that all who deal with the child know about the allergy.

We live in a society where food is freely available. This has led to obesity in some children. In order to reduce obesity, children should be encouraged to:
- Eat sensible amounts from all the major food groups.
- Reduce the amount of junk food in their diets, as this is often high in fat and salt.
- Take sufficient exercise.
- Reduce and preferably stop eating sweets and snacks between meals.

If this regime does not help reduce obesity, medical advice should be sought. The child should not be put on a diet designed for adults, as children need different proportions and combinations of food groups to maintain healthy growth of tissue and bones.

Older children who will not eat should be monitored and medical advice sought if there is weight loss. The child or young person may:
- Have a physical or medical condition.
- Be trying to emulate media images of ultra thinness.
- Have low self-esteem.
- Be a victim of bullying or harassment.
- Need emotional support or counselling.

Food and adults – cooking and meals

Some of the popularly perceived feelings about food and mealtimes are:
- We are bombarded by media images, which suggest that we are less than perfect if we cannot rustle up a banquet for 40, in half-an-hour.
- There are many programmes about cooking which provide instruction in the exotic and unaffordable rather than the basic.
- These days people watch cooking programmes but are not motivated by them to try out the dishes.
- Convenience foods do it all for us.
- One magazine says *'eat this'*, another says *'eat this'*, and the government says *'eat this'*. It's all too confusing.
- There is no time to cook, given the busy lives we lead.
- Families all arrive home at different times and eat different things; the family meal where everyone eats together is obsolete for some.

Whatever the arguments for and against, cooking a meal is a basic skill, which can lead to adult confidence and satisfaction when successfully accomplished. In order to foster skills in cooking, we need to:

- Make suggestions for affordable menus.
- Encourage interest in nutrition, e.g. the benefits of fruit.
- Provide information about the merits of different food groups; proteins, carbohydrates, vegetables, fats, etc.
- Provide a suitable forum in which ideas can be exchanged and recipes attempted together which are within budget, simple to remember, fun to eat and nutritionally sound.
- Practice the same recipe again if the parents wish.
- Go to the supermarket together to select ingredients, or get a week's shopping within an agreed budget.
- Select recipes which can be given out in pictorial form so that those who are unable to read or speak English can join in.
- Encourage experimentation and diversity – try a new vegetable together.
- Ask members from different ethnic groups to hold tasting and cooking sessions.
- Compare home cooked and convenience foods for taste, price and nutritional value.
- Enjoy a meal together in a restaurant as part of a group outing.
- Put the fun back into food – it may be a chore, but it can be enjoyable.
- Praise and respect all attempts to improve the family diet.

> **Our society expects adults to provide suitable food for the family. It is one of the basic rules by which we live. Any help we can give to empower adults to be comfortable in this role will raise their self-esteem and benefit the whole family.**

Hygiene

Modern media implies that we are living in a germ-infested state and that we must use the latest product in order to protect ourselves and our family. The *Good Housekeeping* magazine recently suggested that washing-up liquid and household bleach will, in most cases, offer similar protection at a fraction of the cost.

What is important is:

- The cloths used for wiping worktops are clean.
- The cloths don't need to be replaced but soaked overnight in washing-up liquid and a small amount of bleach or put in the washing machine.
- Chopping boards only need to be thrown away if they are scored.
- Glass, melamine or wooden boards can be cleaned thoroughly using the same two products.
- Kitchen floors don't need to be washed every day unless there are pets or young children crawling on the floor.
- Fridges should be kept clean and wiped out in the same way.
- Food in fridges should be kept covered, especially cooked and uncooked meats which should always be stored separately.

- Bathroom and kitchen sinks can also be cleaned with these products as can cookers, provided they are not allowed to get too dirty.
- Toilets can be kept sterile with bleach – but don't use this with other products as the two together may cause a chemical action that will remove the glaze from the pan.

Warning: care needs to be taken when using bleach as it can damage clothes, carpets and other goods.

Mentoring

Mentoring is about:
- **companionship**   • **support**   • **friendship**

Mentors are usually:
- people from the local community
- different from the person whom they are mentoring
- different from other adults the mentored usually meets
- good listeners and communicators
- good community role models
- multi-talented individuals
- high integrity individuals
- open-minded
- kind and down-to-earth
- strong personalities
- not easily influenced or 'taken-in'
- people with a broad experience of life

The three stages of mentoring are:
1. Building a relationship of trust and getting to grips with the issues of the person concerned.
2. Helping the person to understand the basis of these issues and develop strategies to cope with the situation.
3. Evaluating the strategies the person uses; recognising what does and doesn't work and helping the person to develop a new plan.

Mentors are usually volunteers but may occasionally be paid workers. They may work with one person only or have several clients. The mentoring may last a short time, say a few weeks, or may last for a year. Either party may stop the mentoring if they feel it is not working or they have achieved their goals. Mentoring should be time-limited and extended only if all parties agree.

Mentors:
- Have an awareness of themselves and how they function.
- Must be able to challenge their own strengths and weakness and areas for development.
- Should be able to relate to their own experiences objectively.
- Must understand that the relationship is task orientated.
- Must be suitably checked, trained, supervised, supported and monitored.

The family support handbook

Mediation

Mediation is a structured process in which both parties to a dispute meet voluntarily with one or more impartial people known as mediators. Mediators help those in dispute to explore possibilities of reaching an agreement. They do not have the power to impose a settlement or the responsibility to advise either party individually.

When thinking of mediation most people think of family mediation for separated parents discussing issues relating to children. Family mediation may also include negotiating agreements concerning matters of property and finance.

For direct mediation work with children:
- Both parents must agree to the children being seen.
- The children should be brought to the session by a parent but then seen alone.
- Confidentiality must be maintained, with the exception of child protection issues.
- Children will agree what information is to be given to their parents.
- Mediators must remain neutral.
- Children must be told that, although their parents will be given their views as agreed, parents remain the decision-makers.
- Sessions with children are for the purpose of consultation, not therapy.

There are usually nine stages in the mediation process:
1. recognising the problem
2. choosing the arena
3. selecting the mediator
4. gathering the data (fact finding)
5. defining the problem
6. developing options
7. redefining positions
8. bargaining
9. drafting the agreement

Mediation may also be used in other circumstances such as:
- Victim/offender situations.
- Community/neighbourhood mediation, where conflict may have arisen over children's behaviour.
- Schools' conflict resolution, where children are taught mediation skills as an alternative form of solving dispute.
- Medical mediation, enabling people to make complaints about their doctors or hospital treatment.
- Environmental mediation, which may help resolve disputes over planning issues.
- Elder mediation, helps to resolve disputes concerning older members of the family which may be proving stressful for all generations.

Brief therapy

This is sometimes known as a solution-focused approach.

We are working with a person with a problem, rather than a problem person. (Professional)

Brief therapy is a positive way of looking at problems and finding solutions to difficult situations or unacceptable behaviour. It is equally valuable for work with adults as well as children and young people.

Brief therapy has respect for and works with, not only the ethnic and socio-economic culture of the client but also their unique, individual family culture.

When a problem has been identified questions such as the following may be asked of all concerned, parents, social workers or teachers, for example. Each person concerned will be asked:
- *Are there times when the problem isn't happening?*
- *Are there times when you cope better? Why?*
- *What's happening differently at these times when you cope better?*
- *Who is doing what differently?*

The aim is:
- To talk about the future rather than only about the past.
- To talk about when the problem is solved rather than only when it began.
- To highlight what was done right not what has gone wrong.

In this way the possibility of solving the problem becomes a distinct possibility.

Brief Therapy is a non-damaging therapeutic method of resolving problems. It is suitable for use by social care professionals from many fields including those in education and social work who are usually trained in its use.

Counselling and therapy

The relationship between the helper and the one to be helped must be such that, if one shall really succeed in leading a person to a certain place, one first has to make sure one finds where the other person is, and start there. This is the secret art of helping.
(Soren Kierkegaard, 1948)

I was sitting on the train, crying my eyes out.
(Teenage boy who had just received counselling)

Just as I felt it was doing me good the money ran out and it stopped.
(Young girl who had been sexually abused and who had been to counselling sessions)

Counselling may best be described as a helping relationship within which the client is helped by the counsellor to make changes in themselves or their behaviour. It is usually offered after trauma, for example, changes in personal or family life, bereavement, or to clients with depression, but can be used solely as a vehicle for self-discovery. It enables clients to move past a worrying or upsetting phase and enjoy their future. Counselling is usually accessed through a GP.

Certain organisations offer free counselling for particular groups, e.g. teenagers (Off the Record), Samaritans, some family centres and outreach services. There may be a wait for an appointment with the counsellor attached to the surgery. Private counselling may also be arranged with the help of a GP.

Barriers to effective counselling are:
- The context and scene in which the counselling takes place (seating, privacy, etc.).
- The timing and frequency of sessions.
- The ability of the helper.
- The responsibility of the helper.
- Confidentiality.
- The relationship between helper and client.

The counsellor is trained in the art of listening and responding to the client. They will generally subscribe to either one or several of the three main strands of counselling: psychodynamic, behaviourist and humanist.

Psychodynamic

The **psychoanalytical theory** is now more usually termed the **psychodynamic approach**. It is largely based on the work of Sigmund Freud in the early 1900s. It is essentially a pessimistic view of humanity.

Freud believed that personality is fixed in childhood, and that people experience conflict in expressing internal drives and feelings. The therapist strives to be neutral and to seek out blocked drives, helping clients to overcome them. There are three main beliefs in this type of counselling:

1. **Relating** – people respond to situations according to both past and present experiences.
2. **Transference** – the therapist may be experienced as part of the past rather than the present during counselling, as clients transfer their feelings about the past to the present.
3. **Regression** – people can experience the therapist in terms of their earliest ways of being or life experiences.

Behaviourist

The **behaviourist approach** is based on a view of personality as a collection of learned behaviours. It is a mechanistic approach, which ignores the concept of free will or choice.

Behaviour that is rewarded continues, but behaviour that is not rewarded ceases. When a person cannot find a response that is rewarded in some way, anxiety and distress may occur. Behaviour that is unwanted or non-conforming will continue if it is rewarded in some way – usually by attention. Thus you have the scenario of the child who is seen as the 'bad' one living up to their name, providing a scapegoat for all that goes wrong, so that the parent does not have to look for other reasons. The focus of this type of therapy is using a range of techniques in order to:

- Define the problem clearly.
- Analyse what is maintaining the behaviour.
- Interrupt the client's stimulus/response routine.

Humanist

The **humanist therapist** sees people as unique in personality and constantly aiming for fulfilment. It is an optimistic view. Carl Rogers, one of its main proponents, believes that the concept of self develops slowly throughout life and that other peoples' attitudes and positive or negative regard affect its development. This method uses:

- Unconditional positive regard of the whole person of the client.
- Assisting the client to gain self-awareness.

- Total acceptance as a vehicle to free the client from the need to use defences, thus allowing personal growth.
- The 'whole counsellor' as part of the counselling process. The counsellor may require extensive regular support in order to deal with their own issues arising from such close involvement with the client.

From these three strands, several types of counselling have emerged and are available, usually via the client's GP or privately.

Person-centred counselling
This is based on the work of Carl Rogers. It uses the following precepts:
- The client knows best – their experiences are highly valuable.
- Counsellors must be aware of their own thoughts, feelings and intuitions.
- The quality of the client/counsellor environment and relationship is fundamental to success.
- The environment is best created by:
  - genuineness
  - unconditional positive regard
  - empathic understanding

Transactional analysis
This type of counselling is behaviourist, and is based on the work of Eric Berne. It relies on determining interactions between people as relying on three ego states, which we all have present in us – parent, adult, child. At any given point, we will be operating in one of these ego states:
- **Parent** – this state can be critical, restraining and authoritarian or nurturing, caring and supportive.
- **Adult** – this is the voice of reason, logic and realism. It updates the other states to determine valid feelings and behaviour.
- **Child** – can be complying, procrastinating or ashamed. May also be creative and inventive, mischievous and manipulating. It may also be the voice of the 'free child', which is the spontaneous, curious, fun-loving and rebellious part of us.

When two people are in the same ego state, their transactions are successful and mutually satisfying. When there are opposing ego states, the transactions cause dissatisfaction, emotional reactions and prolonged ill feeling.

> **Example:**
> *A boss demands angrily that a person stays to finish a job. The employee meekly concurs, even though he has promised to get home early for his child's party.*
>
> The boss is in his 'critical parent' state and the employee is in his 'compliant child' state. Were both to have been in the 'adult state', a reasoned compromise may have led to a satisfactory outcome for both.

The object of this type of counselling is to:
- Develop awareness of ego states.
- Use knowledge of ego states to make better transactions.
- Analyse what caused or causes difficulties in particular communications.

Cognitive therapy

This type of therapy relies on challenging the thinking styles of clients, which are believed to influence how we feel and how we behave. This is a time-limited approach consisting of a number of sessions, with 'homework' for the client in between. The counsellor will:

- Collaborate with the client to work on the thinking, rather than be seen as the expert.
- Challenge 'automatic' thoughts which do not arise from reasoned reflection, but are usually the result of a faulty interpretation of past experience.
- Have highly developed skills.
- Form a good relationship with the client.
- Use guided discovery methods to support the process.

Gestalt therapy

This form of counselling originates from Maslow. It relies on the theory that the cognitive and experiential wholeness of every person, moment and event is central to counselling. It is sometimes referred to as 'psychodrama'. There are three basic principles:

1. **Figure and ground** – the ground is our experience and the figure is our focus of thought. We should be able to move between the two.
2. **Closure** – we tend to perceive whole items, even when there is some information missing. Looking back at an experience can tell us what this is and on filling in the gap by an action or communication we can achieve closure.
3. **Clear figure** – we need to construct a clear figure from our available field of impressions. Muddied or unclear thoughts are counter productive.

The Gestalt therapist uses a 'cycle of formation and destruction' with the client as follows:

- Withdrawal – a calm resting phase.
- Sensation – new ideas arise in the client and gradually become clear.
- Awareness – the client gets in contact with the most important event in the field of consciousness.
- Mobilisation – images become clearer and trigger energy and possibilities for satisfaction.
- Action – the client chooses and implements actions.
- Final contact – implementation is followed by contact, which takes place at the boundary of self and environment.

> *I do my thing and you do your thing,*
> *I am not in the world to live up to your expectation,*
> *And you are not in the world to live up to mine.*
> *You are you and I am I.*
> *If by chance we find each other, it's beautiful.*
> *If not, it can't be helped.*
> (Gestalt Prayer by Perls 1969)

Counselling or therapy will not help everyone. It may also be used as an excuse for other behaviour. People receiving counselling or therapy must be patient. It is not a 'quick fix'. It should be time-limited and the client should be told at the onset how many sessions they can expect. These may be extended by mutual agreement.

Counselling and therapy may also stir up all sorts of emotions so it is a good idea to have someone available to talk to after a session – not like the lad in the second quote above.

Anger management

Anger is a natural emotion that we all feel from time to time. It can be a barrier to effective communication and working if not recognised and expressed. Unexpressed anger may build up and eventually lead to an outburst. Assertiveness and aggression are behaviours which may result from angry feelings. Bruce Fisher quotes three stages of anger:
1. Learning to accept that it is alright to feel anger.
2. Expressing anger in a positive way.
3. Learning to forgive the other person and yourself – healing the verbal wounds.

The positive way to deal with your own anger is to use the four part response of:
1. **When you say or do...** Tell the person exactly what they do which makes you angry, using simple words.
2. **I feel...** State your feelings clearly, e.g. I feel let down, I feel uncomfortable, I feel unloved.
3. **Because...** State your reasons for not liking the person's actions – this may be expanding on your feelings or saying why you think the comments or actions are unfair or unjustified.
4. **I would rather you...** Provide a possible solution to the problem, which will be effective for both of you. You need to deal with the situation in the present and stick to the facts. There is then room for negotiation.

> Mr Brown gives out work at four o'clock and expects it done before Mary goes home. He complains about the quality of the work and questions Mary's commitment. The dialogue may go:
> Mr Brown: *Mary, this work is just not good enough. You obviously don't care about how things look when we send them out.*
> Mary: *When you say I don't care about this firm I feel angry and undervalued, because I put every effort into my work. When I have time to do it, what I produce is a credit to my skills. I would rather you gave me the work early enough so we have time to discuss it and enable me to do it as we would both wish.*

What we hope for is that people will be assertive. What most of us dread is aggression, particularly when it involves violence. So what is the difference?

Assertiveness is:
- being able to voice feelings in a positive way
- being able to stand up for your rights
- refusing to be treated badly
- thinking well of yourself and others
- listening to other opinions
- recognising that it is OK to have a different opinion
- asking for what you want calmly
- using positive body language

Aggression is:
- a mask for fear.
- thinking others are less important than you.
- thinking other people are unable to do things you can.
- not listening to other opinions.
- using negative body language such as foot stamping and arm waving or finger stabbing.
- using negative words and tone of voice such as shouting and swearing.

Sometimes aggression is hidden and expressed as:
- making others feel guilty
- not co-operating
- withdrawing communication or walking out
- sabotaging the efforts of others
- subtly despising the tastes of others or trying to make them feel inferior
- sarcasm
- helplessness
- repeating behaviour which offends.

What should one do when confronted with an angry person?
- The first thing to remember is not to join in. Be assertive but not aggressive.
- Keep enough distance to be socially polite; arm's length is a useful guide and you are far enough away to take avoiding action if necessary.
- Be careful not to be backed into a corner – an escape route is essential.
- Acknowledge their anger. Say 'I can see that you are angry' It may be necessary to repeat this several times while the aggression is at its height.
- Match their body language, e.g. posture and weight distribution, then gradually slow down the speed of gestures, blinking, etc.
- Match the tone, pitch and speed of voice, then gradually slow it down and lower the pitch. If you find this too difficult, then talk in a strong, steady voice.
- Show that you are listening by using nods, 'uhuhs' etc.
- Respond using compatible language and avoid jargon.
- Use co-operative words like 'Let's...' to begin to negotiate a solution.
- Deal with the problem first, not the person.
- Try to see both sides of the argument.
- Refer back to the parts you are agreed on.
- When the person calms down, offer refreshment and a chance to chat.
- Ensure that the cause of their anger is dealt with adequately, using normal complaints procedures if appropriate.

Conflict resolution

Any time two people are together, there is room for conflict, so:

Define the problem:
- What's the history?
- What's the current cause?
- Who is involved?
- What's been tried to resolve it?
- What are the obstacles to resolution?

FOCUS on solutions, not on the problem or the person:
- List three possible options.
- Look for win-win solutions.
- Decide on the least explosive option.

Take action:
- Bring parties together.
- Remain calm.

- Think, think, think, listen, and then do.
- Listen, listen, listen, and then talk.
- Define conflict as a mutual problem to be solved, not a win-lose struggle.
- Resist the impulse to take sides.
- Show concern and let everyone put their points of view.
- Is this a battle or a war?
- Assess the consequences.
- Be specific about your expectations after the conflict has been resolved.

Common pitfalls:
- Ignoring the conflict; hoping it will go away.
- Jumping in too impulsively.
- Taking it personally.
- Minimising complaints. If it's a crisis to them it will soon become a crisis for you.
- Making assumptions.

If all else fails, is there a mediator who might help?

Parents' factor 85

Children spend 85% of their time at home. (Researcher)

Mums and dads sharing and learning together to bring the best out of our children.
(Parent's view of the course)

This is a co-ordinated initiative in Portsmouth to help parents increase their skills in parenting and behaviour management. The system could be used equally well, or adapted for use, nation-wide.

It consists of six two-hour sessions, delivered by trained facilitators. A crèche or facility for looking after children is always provided. The sessions are most likely to be based in a local school, possibly that attended by their child, though any parent can ask to take part. There are courses tailored differently for parents/carers with children in the age ranges three to four, five to seven and eight to eleven. The sessions are practical and activity based. Video is used to show situations and there is time for discussion. Parents leave each session with a positive message and raised esteem.

They learn to:
- Help and support each other.
- Have fun.
- Share information and good ideas that work.
- Improve their confidence and skills.
- Understand, deal with and reduce difficult behaviour.
- Recognise the importance of play, praise and rewards.
- Know their children.
- Increase personal safety.
- Relax and deal with stress.

More information about the courses may be obtained from The Primary Behaviour Support Team in Portsmouth, telephone: 023 9281 8547.

The family support handbook

Language, words and praise

> **The things we say and the words we use can have a huge effect on the people around us.**

If a young person or an adult uses any of the terms or actions (or similar ones) to those shown in the left-hand column below, what they usually mean **are** any of the terms shown in the right-hand column.

For example, if someone says 'It's stupid' in a somewhat aggressive tone, they may mean they don't understand or equally they may be worried about something else.

refuses to do something	*can't do something*
says it's stupid	*doesn't understand*
won't speak	*doesn't know what to say*
rants and raves	*is embarrassed*
acts the fool	*is unsure*
gets angry	*needs attention*
shows off	*is worried*

> **Look out for the signs!**
> **Don't just hear what is said but think about how it is said.**

Many people find it hard to give praise. Others do it all the time, when it becomes meaningless. However, positive praise rather than negative criticism makes us all feel better. Encourage parents, children and young people to get into the habit of saying good things to each other, such as:

That's great	It's looking good	Hip, hip, hooray
Good for you	Well done	You're important
I'm proud of you	Nice work	That was nice
Excellent	Terrific	I liked that

Say 'yes' as often as possible.

Further reading

Gavazzi, S.M. (1995) The Growing Up FAST: Families and Adolescents Surviving and Thriving Program. *Journal of Adolescence*. 18:1, 31-47.

Sutton, C. (1995) Educating Parents to Cope With Difficult Children. *Health Visitor*. 68:7 Jul. 284-5. Studies have linked poor parenting with children's subsequent anti-social behaviour continuing into adulthood. Sutton summarises the evidence, and describes a study to test the effectiveness of intensive training and support in helping parents to cope with their child's disruptive behaviour.

Useful resouces and bibliography

Berne, E. (1964) *Games People Play*. Penguin.

Bruce, T. (1991) Time to Play. in *Early Childhood Education*. London, Hodder and Stoughton.

Clarkson, P. (1989) *Gestalt Counselling in Action*. Sage.

Cohen, D. (1987) *The Development of Play*. London, Croom Helm.

Cooper, C. et al. (1988) *Living with Stress*. Penguin.

Egan, G. (1986) *The Skilled Helper*. Brookes Cole.

Foggo-Pays, E. (1983) *An Introductory Guide to Counselling*. Ravenswood.

Gilbert, P. (1992) *Counselling for Depression*. Sage.

Green, Dr. C. (1992) *Beyond Tollerdom*. London: Vermillion.

Harris, T. (1973) *I'm OK You're OK*. Pan.

Heron, J. (1986) *Six Category Intervention Analysis*. University of Surrey.

Heron, J. (1990) *Helping the Client*. Sage.

Isaacs, S. (1968) *The Nursery Years*. London, Routledge.

Jacobs, M. (1985) *Presenting the Past*. OUP.

Klein, J. (1987) *Our Need for Others and its Roots in Infancy*. Routledge.

Mellor, E. (1950) *Education Through Experience in the Infant Years*. Oxford, Blackwell.

Munro, A. et al. (1989) *Counselling: the skills of problem solving*. Routledge.

Nelson-Jones, R. (1992) *Personal Responsibility: An Integrated Approach to Counselling*. Sage.

Penn Green Centre for Under-fives and Their Families (1990) A schema booklet for Parents.

Piaget, J. (1962) *Play, Dreams and Imitation in Childhood*. London, Routledge.

Pugh, G. and De'ath, E. (1984) *The Needs of Parents*. London, Macmillan.

Rogers, C. (1955) *Client Centred Therapy*. Houghton Mifflin.

Rogers, C. (1961) *On Becoming a Person*. Constable.

Russell, J. (1993) *Out of Bounds*. Sage.

Tizard, B. (1984) *Young Children Learning*. London, Collins.

Weikart, D. P. (1988) A Perspective on High Scope. *Early Education Research*. 33, 29-40.

Wheal, A. (1997) *Adolescence, Positive Approaches to Working with Young People*. Lyme Regis, Russell House Publishing.

Wheal, A. (Ed.) (2000) *Working with Parents, Learning from Other People's Experiences*. Lyme Regis, Russell House Publishing.

Wheal, A. (2000) *The Foster Carer's Handbook*. Lyme Regis, Russell House Publishing.

Model forms and documents

Behaviour plan for ....

The behaviour we don't want:

The behaviour we do want:

Environment – what factors might cause behaviour	New skills – what we need to teach so the new behaviour can be used.
Reinforcement – what we will do to reward/promote the new behaviour.	Plan for immediate action when these don't work.

Emergency coping strategies

1.	Humour	Laugh it off outwardly or inwardly. See the funny side. Talk very seriously but wear a huge grin. Threaten to do something ridiculous, e.g. 'If you do that again, I'll pull your ears off'.
2.	Reason with yourself	Tell yourself that this is not the life crisis you are making it out to be. In a week or month or year it will be a memory.
3.	Distancing	Mentally step outside a circle, leaving the problem and the people inside the circle. Look at it from a distance and look at your participation in it.
4.	100 S.Rs	Imagine you have only 100 stress responses left. If this were so, wouldn't you use them wisely? Is this person or situation worth using one up for? Say to yourself, 'You are not important enough in my life for anger and a rise in my blood pressure'.
5.	Mr Shiftit	Move the problem to a later time. Suggest discussion at the end of the day or after the meeting. Be determined to calm down before that time and know what you are going to say.
6.	Calming	Repeat softly to yourself, 'Calm down, calm down'. At the same time, make a conscious effort to relax your facial, shoulder and neck muscles. Count backwards from ten to one.
7.	Breathe it away	Breathe in deeply and say, 'Peace in'. Breathe out deeply and say, 'Problem gone'. With **practice**, this can reduce tension in twenty seconds.
8.	Reason with others	Someone who stays calm calms others. Mentally stand above the situation and guide your behaviour as if using a puppet.
9.	Compartmentalise	When a problem is worrying you, but you are unable to act immediately, mentally place the problem in a box or room, close the lid or door and walk away. Promise yourself that you will come back to it and **deal** with it when first able to do so.
10.	Worry session	Develop a worry session. Store up the problems for a special worrying time that is allowed to last for a short specific time. All worries must be dealt with at this time only.
11.	'Beam me up Scottie'	Saying this phrase to yourself often lightens your approach to a stupid or intolerable situation, and helps you to see the funny or pathetic side of your work.
12.	Thanks for small mercies	Feel thankful that you do not behave like the person causing the problem. Reduce your anger to a sense of gratitude that you are not as irate as the offender.

→

13. Karma	A Hindu remedy is to try to accept that everything is 'Karma' – a little bit like 'That's Life' but deeper. It is more of an acceptance of life events **after** they have occurred. You cannot put the clock back and change the past, therefore you must accept that it has happened.
14. Reverting	Pulling faces and using silly noises can work wonders. Make sure there are no witnesses!
15. Feign pain	Appear to be deeply hurt and cut to the quick by a remark or by someone's behaviour. Play to a sense of compassion and honour.
16. Imagery	While the person is 'in action', imagine their face turning purple or a load of custard (or worse) dropping on them.
17. Pause for thought	Engage brain before putting mouth into action. A pause of only seconds can avert a crisis or an unpleasant scene.
18. Perspective	Ask yourself what the real priorities are in your life. *Are they these people or this place?* Your priorities are your own wellbeing and that of your loved ones. These problems are on the periphery of your life.
19. Looking forward	Bring your mind off your anger. Think of the nicer parts of your life. What are you going to do that evening, that weekend? Focus your mind on the **real** part of your life.
20. Break the spell	Look for reasons behind the other person's actions or words. Recognise when they are under stress or appreciate that they could be. Try being a tower of strength!
21. Moaning deadline	When at home, set a deadline (e.g. 7 p.m.) for moaning about work and the problems you are facing there. And make your partner stick to the deadline too.
22. Be tough	Be tough on yourself. Tell yourself to snap out of this anger or mood. There are so many people worse off than you. No-one forces you to do anything – it is your choice.
23. Unlock	Never get locked into disagreements. They have a tendency to spiral and draw you in. Better to stand away. Your opponent will think better of you when they have cooled off.
24. Cutting off	As you leave work or whatever you are doing (angry or annoyed) have your favourite music or an amusing tape to listen to on the way home. Set landmarks after which you promise yourself not to think about or dwell on the issues. If alone in a car, have a good scream or curse time after which say, 'That's it! No more! My real life now begins'.

Note: the above strategies are taken from notes included in 'SCIP' course run by Hampshire County Council

Section 7
Cultural, Disability and Family Issues

Respecting race, creed, culture and disability

There are acts of parliament in force, which endeavour to prevent discrimination:
- The Equal Opportunities Act 1993
- The Education Acts 1993, 2002
- The Disability Discrimination Act 2000
- The SEN and Disability Act 2001
- The Human Rights Act 1998

However, acts of parliament may not prevent every unthinking racist comment:
An incident is a racist incident if one person believes it to be so. (Gbedebo, 2000)

Acts of parliament set the rules, by making it unlawful to discriminate because of:
- race
- gender
- disability
- creed
- ethnicity
- sexual orientation
- age

The act on SEN and Disability in education for example:
- Strengthens the rights of children with Special Educational Needs (SENs) to be educated in mainstream schools.
- Gives a new duty to the Local Education Authority (LEA) to provide:
  - information and support to parents
  - pupil participation in decisions made
  - parent partnership systems which are independent of the LEA

In practice, there are several strategies, which may be used to prevent discrimination.

Cultural backgrounds and family beliefs

Learning about the cultural backgrounds and beliefs of families may prevent insult and embarrassment on both sides by providing guidelines on:
- dress for males and females
- social and cultural rules for males and females
- acceptable diet
- proximity to animals
- greetings and farewells
- photographs or images
- alcohol
- food
- religious beliefs
- things held sacred, e.g. hair, medallions etc.
- methods of child rearing
- marriage

The family support handbook

Disability

Learning about disability and its causes and effects may prevent insult and embarrassment on both sides by providing guidelines on:

- Talking to a disabled person, not at them.
- Asking if help is required before giving it.
- Treating people as individuals.
- Asking if your dress code, etc. is acceptable: most people of other ethnic groups are only too happy to explain the rules. You may need to cover your arms or legs.
- Allowing dress codes to be kept by members of other cultures, e.g. covered legs for females above a certain age.
- Inviting groups from other cultures to share their way of life by showing others:
  - what they wear
  - providing cooking lessons or food samples
  - talking about people who are famous or special to them because of their achievements.
- Acting on advice given – if a child is not allowed to be near pigs, then don't let them when a farm visit is made.
- Refraining from making remarks or jokes at the expense of different cultures or disabilities.
- Providing what is culturally necessary e.g. separate rooms for males and females, praying places during Ramadan.
- Discouraging children and young people from breaking the tenets of their faith, e.g. the eating of forbidden foods via friends.
- Talking to children, young people and families about their way of life.
- Welcoming others no matter what their disability, beliefs or sexual orientation.
- Taking care not to insult them or their faith, e.g. a cup of tea is not always acceptable to vegetarians unless without milk.
- When visiting a family from another cultural or religious background, politely accept any hospitality offered and strive not to cause offence by behaviour or dress.
- Ensuring disabled persons have good access both to the building and to the place of meeting, e.g.
  - ramps
  - lifts
  - wide doorways
  - low thresholds
  - adequate toilet facilities
- Providing own language speakers or interpreters if English is not spoken well enough to understand what is being said or to participate in conversations.
- Placing equal value on the contribution of others of all races, genders, disabilities and sexuality during meetings, seminars, discussions, etc.

Discrimination

Parents, professionals and children and young people may all have different ethnic origins and different cultural expectations. This should always be borne in mind.

When working with parents one's own views and beliefs should take second place to that of the family.

The Disability Discrimination Act 2001 has made discrimination of many sorts a legal offence. However, all the laws in the world will not change the way people behave unless they think about situations from their own perspectives. Here are a few examples:

- How would you feel if your own child was being described in a derogatory way?
- How would you feel if you were the only black, Asian or white person in the group?
- How would you feel if you were blind and walked into a room knowing everyone could see you but you couldn't see them?

Pretty angry – shy – embarrassed?

As individuals it is often not possible to change other people's behaviour or certain situations. However, by providing information and knowledge it should help individuals learn to cope with a situation. It should also be possible by using open discussion, scenarios and direct situational work with parents and children, to heighten their awareness, understanding and tolerance.

Direct discrimination happens when someone is treated worse than others or segregated from them because of their race, colour, nationality, gender, sexual orientation or ethnic or national origins.

Indirect discrimination happens when everyone seems to be treated in the same way but, in practice, people from a certain ethnic group are put at a greater disadvantage.

Victimisation: if someone is victimised because they have complained about discrimination, or because they have supported someone else's complaint, this too is unlawful discrimination.

Impairment is a loss of function caused by physical, mental or sensory impairment.

Disability is the loss or limitation of opportunities to take part in the mainstream of the community on an equal level with others due to physical and social barriers.

Working with people with disabilities

Many adults and children experience some form of impairment that can range from a minor condition such as myopia to a major dysfunction such as paraplegia. The extent to which the disability is seen by the person as a handicap will vary enormously. This may depend on a number of factors such as their background, available support, understanding and knowledge.

> **It is vitally important to remember that adults and children with disabilities are people first, they have the same physical, sexual, emotional and social needs. However, the way that these needs are fulfilled may not necessarily be quite the same as for able-bodied people.**

People use different terms to suit the occasion or sometimes to prevent embarrassment, often to themselves. The chart on the next page (Figure 14) is some guidance of the currently acceptable terms.

When working with individuals or groups, emphasise the uniqueness and worth rather than individual differences. Your efforts can do much to eliminate the 'them' and 'us' attitude that hampers the integration of disabled people. It is also important to remember disabled people come from all communities, they may also be black or lesbian. The whole person should be considered, their culture and community. Consult them in the planning for their time with you.

Working with people with disabilities

Terms to avoid	Use
victim of	person who has or person with or person who experienced
crippled by	person who has or person with
suffering from	person who has or person with
afflicted by	person who has or person with
wheelchair bound	wheelchair user
invalid (means not valid)	disabled person
mental	disabled person
spastic	person who has cerebral palsy

Offensive	Preferred
handicap	disability
handicapped person	disabled person
spastic	cerebal palsy
deaf and dumb, deaf mute	deaf or partial hearing
Mongoloid	Downs Syndrome
cripple	disabled person or mobility impaired or ambulatory disabled
blind	blind person, partially sighted, person with visual impairment
deaf	deaf people
mentally handicapped, backward/dull	learning difficulty
retarded, idiot, imbecile	developmental disability
mute, dummy	speech difficulty
crazy, maniac, insane	emotional disability
abnormal	exceptional, different

Figure 14: Working with people with disabilities

Practical suggestions for working with disabled children or parents

Generally:
- Do offer help, but don't get upset if it is rejected – sometimes it will be welcome, but sometimes it won't be needed or may hinder the disabled person doing it in their own, possibly slower but efficient way.
- Sometimes people who are disabled may become angry or aggressive as they try to come to terms with their disability or want to learn to become independent.
- Do not make assumptions – many people have invisible disabilities such as epilepsy.

- Don't make comments like 'I don't know how you manage.' or 'I'd die if I was blind or deaf or couldn't walk.'
- Speak directly to the person, not to whoever may be with them. People still say 'Does he take sugar?'
- Obtain as much knowledge regarding the person's or the child's special needs or disability as soon as possible.
- Have high but realistic expectations.

Wheelchair users

- Don't lean on wheelchairs, the chair is part of someone's body space and it is extremely annoying.
- Do not grab the back of someone's wheelchair to push them along. Always ask first if help is required and do not be offended if it is refused.
- Never grab a person's wheelchair when they are manoeuvring it, such well meant help is dangerous and may hurt the disabled person's arm or wrists.
- If you have to negotiate a chair up or down steps, get the advice of the wheelchair user on how best to do it.
- Try to seat or situate yourself at eye level with the person as much as possible. It is extremely difficult to join in and hear conversations that are going on over one's head. Try not to stand too near, causing the wheelchair user to have to crane their neck to keep eye contact.
- Reserve head patting for animals even though a wheelchair user's head may be temptingly at the same height. Disabled people find this sign of affection patronising and inappropriate.

People with speech impairments

- Wait and do not jump in to finish what you think they might be saying.
- Don't pretend to understand if you don't. Ask the person to say it again, and repeat what you understand to gain confirmation.
- If there is a facilitator, use that person **only** as an interpreter, i.e. do not engage in conversation directly with the facilitator.

Meeting and communicating with deaf people

- Don't talk with something in your mouth such as a pen or a sweet and try to remember to keep your hand away from your mouth.
- Do not stand against a window or bright light as it hinders lip reading. Stand where your face is best lit.
- Don't talk away from the deaf person, e.g. to a blackboard or other people.
- Don't use sign language unless you know the deaf person uses it. Deaf people who do use sign language prefer this, however, so provide interpreters for meetings, interviews, etc.
- If you are not understood by the deaf person, rephrase a sentence, keeping it brief. Repeat or rephrase a whole sentence not just a single word. If you don't understand, don't pretend that you do.
- If you are with a deaf person when some audible warning, or announcement is made, explain or write down what is happening, e.g. a fire alarm.

Working with people who are blind or have visual impairment

- Don't be afraid to offer help, but speak first and ask if they want assistance. Don't be upset if they say they don't need help.
- If guiding a blind person, go first, i.e. slightly ahead of them, with their hand holding you under your elbow. Get into trains, buses before them, and if entering a car, guide their hand to the roof over the car door.
- Give verbal warnings, say when you are approaching steps and whether these go up or down, and if helping a blind person into a car, say which way it is facing. Guess and say the distance if you can.
- Indoors, describe furniture as you move past it and mention head and body level hazards. To help someone to a chair, guide their arm to the back or armrest so that they can seat themselves.
- Do not leave doors half open or chairs sticking out.
- Meals; describe what is on the plate and where – relate the food position to the clock; e.g. potatoes at twelve o'clock. Don't fill cups, glasses to the brim.
- When talking to a blind person always introduce yourself and the people with you including their relative positions to you. It may help to go over to them and touch them on the arm as you first speak or enter the room and say 'Hallo'.
- If in a group, say the name of the other people to whom you are speaking or get them to introduce or announce themselves so that the blind person can keep track of the conversation. If you are directing a question or remark to them in particular, use the person's name first in a sentence.

> **The worst betrayal of intelligence is to leave things as they are!**
> **Disabled people, as do all people, have the right to privacy, dignity,**
> **independence and fulfilment. Make it happen!**

Families and friends

We all have had families at some point in our lives. Families may have different meanings to different people. It may mean:
A couple living alone
- A couple and children.
- An extended family such as grandparents, uncles and aunts.
- A single parent, possibly with visiting partner.
- One parent and a step-parent plus parents' child.
- One parent and a step-parent plus both parents' children.
- One or two parents plus fostered children.
- Two parents plus adopted children.

Some families are very close in terms of relationships, others quite the opposite. Some people would like a close family but this is not possible, others find their close family stifling. Some people rely very heavily on their friends whereas other people have hardly any friends. Sometimes, close family friends are thought of as relations and have as much, or more, influence than related family members.

We are all different and need and want different things from our family and friends who in turn want different things from us. No two families are the same. There will be differences in:

- customs and traditions
- values
- atmosphere – formal or informal
- expectations
- attitudes to noise, shouting, playing
- religion
- acceptable standards of behaviour

What is important is that we respect other people's families and their values even if we don't always agree with them. For example, when looking for a solution to a family problem, we must **not** look for middle class solutions for working class families; they may work, but in most cases they will be a waste of time. We should work with the families, including the extended families, to find a solution to a particular situation.

Another point to remember is that sometimes one member of a family who has a problem will not want other family members to know of the difficulty. This may be because they are ashamed, embarrassed or blaming of the family. This wish should, of course, be respected unless there are safety issues involved.

Developing positive approaches

Children and young people learn by imitation and example. They quickly pick up on hostility or lack of respect. Prejudice is learned behaviour, which can be prevented by:

- Learning about other cultures; provide artefacts, clothing and stories so that they can immerse themselves in what may feel strange or different to begin with.
- Learning about disability; let them try hands over ears, blindfolds, wheelchairs and crutches so that they gain some insight into how disability affects in different ways.
- Learning about other faiths and beliefs; the Qu'uran, for example, as well as the bible. There are religious articles which may be held, examined and looked at without offence.
- Adults and older children showing acceptance and respect for others in their behaviour and responses; using the correct form of greeting, for example.
- Talking to children about the diversity of backgrounds of children they know; this may be accomplished during group discussions about what happens at home.
- Celebrating the differences as well as the similarities in people; everyone has something different at which they shine, or in which they believe.
- Showing interest in others and their ways of life by using TV and video representation. In some regions there is not enough cultural mixing to make first-hand experience of other cultures available, though this is always preferable. There are, however, usually older people who are only too willing to come to talk to children or teenagers – replacing the skills which would have been offered were they in closer contact with grandparents, for example.
- Using Persona dolls, for example, which are ethnically correct dolls to use with stories and scenarios about other faiths and beliefs.
- A child who is taught acceptance and celebration of the diversity of life at a young age is less likely to grow up with ingrained prejudices.

Further reading

Barn, R. (1999) White Mothers, Mixed-parentage Children and Child Welfare. *British Journal of Social Work* 29:2 Apr. 269-84.
Explores some of the underlying factors which increase the vulnerability of mixed-parentage children in relation to the care system.

Bignall, T. and Nair, C. (2000) *Directory 2000 of Black Voluntary Organisations Working With Black Children and Families*. Race Equality Unit.
Covers London and the surrounding areas, regional groups and national groups. Includes an index of the commnunities.

Butt, J. and Box, L. (1998) Engage and Provide. *Community Care*. 1230. Jul. 22-3.
Looks at what family centres can do to make themselves more accessible to the wishes and needs of black people.

Butt, J., and Box, L. (1998) *Family Centred: A Study of the Use of Family Centres by Black Families*. London, Race Equality Unit.
Examines the debates that have informed policy and practice in the development of social care to support families, including looking at changes in family life and parenting, before focusing specifically on Black family life.

Evans, G. and Grant, L. (1995) *Moyenda Project Report 1991-1994*. London, Exploring Parenthood.
Describes the development and progress of a project set up to consider the specific needs of Black parents for information and support.

Hylton, C. (1999) *Family Survival Strategies: Black Families Talking. Moyenda Project*. London, Exploring Parenthood.
Examines the various coping mechanisms and parenting styles used by minority ethnic families in the United Kingdom.

Qureshi, T., Berridge, D. and Wenman, H. (2000) *Where to Turn? Family Support for South Asian Communities: A Case Study*. London, National Children's Bureau.
Report based on a research study evaluating the availability and perceived effectiveness of family support services for a particular section of the community – South Asians, those originating from India, Pakistan, Kashmir, Bangladesh or Sri Lanka.

Useful resources and bibliography

Brown, B. (2001) *Combatting Discrimination: Persona Dolls in Action*. London, Trentham.

Race Relations Act 2000. The Stationery Office.

Wheal, A. (1998) *Adolescence, Positive Approaches for Working with Young People*. Lyme Regis, Russell House Publishing.

Section 8
Inter-agency working

Who's who in helping families

Beware of too many 'experts'. (Parent)

He's my baby and I'm going to do what I think is best. They all tell me something different.
(Parent)

Communication within professions is not always as good as it should be. It is important we all strive to improve so that important information is exchanged sooner rather than when it is too late. We must also consider, and respect, the views and wishes of the parent and child.

Whilst inter-agency working has improved in recent years, there is still urgently needed a considerable amount of:
- re-education
- development of trust
- discussions on shared understandings about boundaries of responsibility between agencies

Groups who work with or support families vary; the police, teachers, social workers, health visitors, mental health workers, children's guardians, therapists, counsellors, youth and community workers and also palliative care workers. The list is endless and the task of ensuring good communication between groups is enormous. However, if the child and their parents are to be protected and the best interests of the child ensured then ways must be found to disseminate information within groups.

One dilemma is the fact that these same groups of people whom we are encouraging to work together may be the very people who may report abuse or impending difficulties. This may cause, or be seen as causing, a conflict of interest. So who are these people?

The key worker

Key workers solve some of the problems arising from poor communication within groups of professionals involved with the same family.

Key workers may act as a:
- Funnel for information between professionals.
- Central person who will be able to contact any named professional on behalf of the family.
- Support for the family's strengths and weaknesses.
- Voice to disseminate the family's thoughts, feelings and wishes.
- Preventer of duplicated assessments.

The main feature of key working should be an open and honest relationship with the family, working with, and for them, as opposed to any agency. Key working ceases to be effective if the worker fails to take on the role identified for them, or feels uncomfortable or inadequately trained to do so. Key workers should be impartial.

Child Development Team

This is a multi-disciplinary team of health, social services and education personnel who meet on a regular basis to discuss referrals from any professional involved with a preschool child who is causing concern in any area of development. The referral has to be agreed and signed by the parent. When a child is discussed, the team will refer the family to individual, or a range of appropriate, professionals who will arrange to assess the child's needs and put in progress systems which meet them. The team is a funnel for those children who develop difficulties, which were not apparent at birth and have therefore not been seen at the Child Development Centre (CDC) as a matter of course. The team may decide that a referral to the CDC is appropriate.

Connexions

Connexions is a centrally funded service to look after the interests of young people aged between thirteen and twenty-five. It aims to ensure that young people are not prevented from taking up life options because of problems due to their disability, being in public care or other institutions, or social exclusion. In partnership with others, Connexions looks to:
- Provide each 13-19 year-old (up to 25 years if the need is apparent) with the help and support they need through the services of a personal adviser.
- Offer advice and guidance on careers, learning and personal development.
- Help to motivate and raise aspirations.
- Identify and address issues as they arise and before they become barriers to learning.
- Help young people overcome the barriers which prevent them from participating in life experiences that other young people enjoy.

Personal advisers are trained for this role and come from a variety of backgrounds, e.g. social work, education, health, careers or youth work.

The children's guardian

Formerly known as the 'guardian ad litem', this person is appointed by the court to look after the interests of the child if someone has applied for a court order relating to them. Their task is always to help the child and they:
- Are independent and work alone.
- Look at what has happened by visiting the child, talking and listening to the family and every involved professional and reading relevant reports.
- Try to find ways to keep the child safe and well.
- Write a report for the court saying what they think is best for the child, which includes the child's wishes and feelings.
- Choose a solicitor to explain what is best to the court.

Social service workers

Social worker

Families may require the support of a social worker because:
- They are in short-term crisis.
- They are unable to cope because of trauma or life experiences.
- They have a child who is looked after.
- They have a child or adult with a disability or special needs.
- Abuse of any kind has been suspected or identified.

The social worker is based in the office of the area in which the family lives. Generally their job is to keep in touch with them, to make plans with them, and to make sure these plans are carried out, with a view to improving the lives of family members. The social worker will often be able to find funding for respite care of various kinds to ease the pressure on the family if this is appropriate. They have statutory child protection duties, which involve investigation of the facts, setting up multidisciplinary case conferences or planning groups, and court work.

Team manager, area manager or director of social services

Most social service departments are organised like pyramids, with team managers, area managers, deputy directors and finally the director. Each level is responsible for the level below. It is a good idea to find out how social services are organised, as occasionally a family member might need the help of someone senior. If there are difficulties with a social worker families should contact any of these people.

Children's rights officer

Some areas have a children's' rights officer (CRO) who is usually independent of social workers. Children in residential and foster care should be able to telephone the CRO and discuss privately anything that is bothering them. If they have a problem, children should also be able to contact Childline or similar organisations.

Family centre or family resource centre worker

Many areas have a family centre, run by the social services department, where parents are helped and supported in caring for their children. The support may take place at the centre, or in the family home as part of an outreach scheme. Help is usually centred round:
- parenting skills
- health matters
- managing budgets
- home organisation

The strong, trusting relationship the family and support worker build enables their advice to be more readily accepted. Help is practical and enables families to move past a point of crisis, whether this is by learning to manage a budget or increasing parenting skills. Family workers are usually trained in basic counselling skills.

Complaints officer

Each local authority must have a person appointed to handle complaints from children, families and carers. If a disagreement cannot be sorted out informally with the social worker, team manager or residential staff, families should contact the complaints officer and ask for the local authority's leaflet on how the make a complaint.

Education workers

Educational welfare officer/educational social worker

Their job is to be a link between the school and the home. They talk to the school about any problem a child may be having at school, for example, bullying and are also involved when a child is playing truant. They can usually be contacted through the school. Part of their job is to work with the child on any difficulties within their education.

Educational psychologist

If a child is having significant difficulties in learning or concentrating at school, the headteacher may ask for an educational psychologist to see the him/her. An educational psychologist is not a psychiatrist, but someone who has special knowledge about how children learn and what may be causing them to have difficulties. Educational psychologists are involved with families when children need specific educational help to overcome difficulties. They may set programmes for the child, or recommend a change of schooling, if the parent is in agreement. They always work in close partnership with the parents and child.

Portage home worker

Portage is an early intervention programme for children under five with special needs. It involves a weekly home visit from a worker who, together with the parent, will assess the child's developmental progress on a comprehensive set of checklists. These lists cover six areas of skills:

- infant responses
- fine motor
- speech, language and communication
- social
- physical
- cognitive

When the assessment is complete, the worker and the parent will choose a set of targets for the child. The worker will show the parent how to teach each skill. The parent will then teach the skill daily and record progress on a chart. This will be examined at the next visit and adjusted to ensure that the child is successful.

Portage is based on empowering parents and children and builds on the success of activities. Portage workers and families make strong relationships, which sometimes endure long after the child has moved on. When a child is diagnosed with a condition at birth, Portage may start as early as six weeks of age. Portage generally ceases when the child attends school or nursery for 50 per cent of the week, or when the child's development reaches normal limits.

Health workers

Child Development Centre (CDC)

This is an establishment which aims to bring together a team who can diagnose problems with a child's development in any area. The idea is to produce a 'one-stop shop' and thus avoid parents having to 'do the rounds' in order to find out what might best help their child. The team normally includes:

- a paediatrician who will assess and make a diagnosis if appropriate
- a social worker
- a speech and language therapist

- an occupational therapist
- a physiotherapist

It may also include education personnel. Once assessments have been made by all involved, a meeting is held to discuss plans for the child, which the parents attend. The team may refer the child for child guidance or educational psychology.

Child guidance worker, child and family therapy worker

Child guidance workers help children who may have an emotional or behavioural problem perhaps because of some earlier unhappy experience. A child psychiatrist will be part of the team, which includes psychologists and specialist social workers. With the help of the child, their carer or their family, the child guidance worker draws up a plan to overcome the difficulties.

Health visitor

This person is attached to the local GP surgery or health centre. They work with children under five years-old and with families who may need extra help with children over five years. Health visitors are qualified nurses and some are qualified midwives. Carers and parents can contact them at any time at the surgery or health centre. They will make visits to the home if required. They perform developmental checks on children under five at specific ages, which may vary from region to region.

General practitioner

The general practitioner looks after the health of the family, sending out reminders for specific health checks ,e.g.

- ante-natal
- post-natal
- immunisations
- well women checks

They hold surgeries to deal with illness and keep careful records. Some doctors run appointment systems, while others hold open surgeries. They are called upon to take part in case conferences where there is suspicion of abuse.

Community midwife

Community midwives oversees the health of the expectant mother, run preparation for parenthood classes, supervise at the birth of a child and visits the home for the first two weeks of life. They complete checks for specific conditions which may threaten a child's development and are an excellent source of advice for problems related to feeding or birth recovery.

Speech and language therapist (SALT)

Children may be referred to a SALT when their language or communication skills fall behind what would be expected for their age. The general rule is that development must lag by at least six months. The health visitor, school or social worker, among others, may refer a child for therapy. The child will be assessed and programmes set if necessary. Sometimes the SALT decides to monitor progress rather than intervene. Programmes are usually made available to the school or early years setting so that everyone knows what should be done and how. SALTs use a variety of programmes to effect progress in both receptive and expressive language. There is sometimes a waiting list for therapy.

Occupational therapist (OT)

Occupational therapists are experts in seating and all aspects of hand function. They will see the child regularly to advise on specialist exercises and equipment the child may need. They advise both school and home about adaptations needed to accommodate a person with a disability.

Physiotherapist

A physiotherapist may be involved with a family from birth when there is a physical problem with a child. They are trained to improve physical skills by the use of specialist programmes and massage. A physiotherapist may also be involved with older members of the family who are disabled or who have suffered an injury.

Mental health team

The mental health team workers look after all aspects of mental health. They are usually trained psychiatric nurses. They visit the mentally ill and those whose medical conditions cause behaviour or emotional changes. They may be involved when there is a suicide attempt. As well as for the patient, they will provide support for other family members and frequently run groups for them, where they can talk about their experiences with similar families.

Other referrers

Family, friends and neighbours usually know the children, young people and parents better than anyone. Sometimes someone from one of these groups has concerns about an event, family matters, drug abuse or the development of a child, for example. After a good deal of soul searching they may find it necessary to refer their concerns to others such as social services or to a health visitor. Alternatively, they may just appear at a group hoping to find someone to talk to about their concerns.

It has shown a lot of courage and genuine concern for them to make the decision to tell so you should listen carefully to what they have to say and keep them informed of developments.

Sometimes they could act as a go-between, sometimes they could share the care of the child or young person whilst the difficulty is resolved and sometimes they may become the main carer. Whatever is decided they should be offered all the services that a parent might be offered although sometimes in a different form as many may have been parents themselves already so may be a little sensitive.

There are many voluntary groups around; Barnardos, NCH Action for Children, NSPCC. Sometimes a parent needing help will contact one of these groups because they have heard the name rather than making contact with social services, erroneously believing that social services will take their child into care. Sometimes these groups may be able to help the family directly but at other times they may refer them to another group or organisation. For example, if a young parent was suffering from depression they may think that a Home-Start volunteer visiting the parent in their home would be the best solution so, with the parent's permission, they would suggest a Home-Start worker contacts the family.

For parents of children with special needs different parts of the country have different organisations that may be able to help. One such organisation is the Parent Partnership Service which was set up to develop and improve communication between families, schools, voluntary agencies and the local education authority. They aim to support families by:

- Listening, talking through problems and worries that families have.
- Giving practical support to families going through the statutory assessment process.
- Giving information about local and national voluntary and support groups, activities and other sources of help.
- Ensuring special educational needs information is relevant and accessible to all families.
- Keeping other agencies and groups informed and networking with them.
- Holding regular drop-in coffee sessions for families and linking them up with existing groups.
- Holding workshop sessions for parents on issues that are important to them, allowing them to share their experiences and skills.
- Recruiting, training and supporting volunteers and others who are in contact with families whose child has been identified as having special needs.
- Responding to requests promptly and treating families with respect, sensitivity and understanding.
- Respecting families' confidentiality and gaining permission to share any information or contact with other professionals unless there are issues of child protection in which case the advice of social services will be sought.

Further reading

Integrated Services Initiative (1997) *Common Goals Unmet Needs: Meaningful Collaboration in Tackling Exclusion in Dublin's North East Inner City*.
Evaluates the work of the Integrated Services Initiative (ISI) whose primary objectives are to examine models of provision in the education, health, justice and social services systems as they operate in the Dublin's north-east district.

McGlone, F. (1999) A New Role for Grandparents. *Family Policy*. Spring, 8.
Briefly looks at the role of grandparents in family support.

McGrath, P. (2001) Trained Volunteers for Families Coping With a Child With a Life-limiting Condition. *Child and Family Social Work*. 6:1. Feb. 23-9.
This Australian study surveyed families with children mainly suffering from cystic fibrosis and muscular dystrophy. Many families welcomed the idea of trained volunteers to help with a range of activities from practical assistance, such as baby-sitting and help with household chores, to emotional support.

Reid, C. and McDermott, B. (1996) The Family Support Worker Scheme: Its Role in Prevention to Children and Families in Need. *Child Care in Practice*. 2, (Special issue), 55-61.
Family Support Workers assist and enable parents with a range of parenting and household skills. Reid and McDermott argue that the Family Support Work model is a highly cost effective and flexible scheme that can be adapted to meet a wide spectrum of family problems which children in need will experience.

Sinclair, R., Hearn, B. and Pugh, G. (1997) *Preventive Work With Families: The Role of Mainstream Services*. London, National Children's Bureau.
All families need family-friendly and child-centred environments to promote the welfare of their children, with some requiring additional support. Sinclair et al. discuss the role of mainstream services in preventive and family support work and set out an agenda for future research and development.

Bibliography

Wheal A. (2001) *The Foster Carers Handbook*. Lyme Regis, Russell House Publishing.

Section 9
Management Issues

This is not a management training manual so we have not gone into the theories of management nor given detailed guidance on what you should or should not do. However, this chapter is a series of checklists and guidelines to help those involved in employing staff, or utilising volunteers to make judgements about their team and to help to develop them as people working with, and supporting, families.

Recruiting staff and volunteers

You are who you hire! (Kaufmann, 1994)

Before the interview:
- Develop a job description that lists all skills necessary to do the job exceptionally well.
- Review the job application to match the person with the job skills required. Check details including gaps in dates, if the job requires qualifications obtain proof, assess medical openness.
- Develop a list of interviewing questions that elicit skill-specific information.
- Check references and read between the lines.
- Check with the applicants whether any require special access or other requirements.

During the interview:
- Develop an easy opening, also ask about the need for toilets and check whether any expenses are required.
- Say how long you anticipate the interview will last.
- Gain rapport.
- Use applicant's name frequently, and ask easy questions at first.
- Listen more than you talk. Don't let interviewees interview you. Give them time to answer – silence is OK, check their understanding.
- Briefly describe the job and job expectations. 'Let me outline…etc' so they know when it is their turn.
- Ask open-ended questions who, what, when, where, why. Good general questions are best, e.g. 'What would you like me to know about you?', ' Why are you leaving your present job?', 'Why do you want this job?', 'What is most important to you in a job?'
- Observe dress, grooming, health, disposition, punctuality, movement, alertness, hearing, communication skills and body language.
- Present a hypothetical situation and ask how the interviewee would handle it.
- If skills are demonstrable ask for a demonstration or samples of work.
- Ask non-related questions, for example, 'Who do you admire most?', 'Who has most influenced your career?', 'Describe your best and worst work day ever?', 'Who has been your favourite boss and why?'
- As far as possible, ask every interviewee the same questions.

- Topics that are best avoided unless they have a bearing on the job being offered are:
  - age, or date of graduation
  - marital status
  - religion
  - military service or discharge status
  - race or national origin
  - children
  - political beliefs
- Give applicants time to ask questions.
- Thank applicants for their time.
- Let them know when a decision will be made and how they will be informed.

Deciding:
- Select the top two or three applicants and interview them again if you wish. You don't have to hire on one impression.
- Don't get caught in the need for a new person.
- Ask yourself: *'How would I feel about working with this person?'*
- Be cautious of the tendency to hire a clone of yourself. Hire for a balanced staff.
- Hire from within whenever possible – hire the known rather than the unknown.
- Don't ignore your gut feeling. Ask yourself: *'Do I like and trust this person?'*
- In making your decision, remember, past behaviour is the best predictor of future behaviour.

> **References (and police checks if appropriate) must be taken up *before* anyone starts working regardless of circumstances.**

Most of this will apply whether you are recruiting a volunteer or a paid employee. It is important that volunteers are treated with equal respect and that they receive appraisals and training in the same way as the other staff.

A person specification

Being a parent is a good starter but certainly not a necessity for working with parents.

To work with parents it is important to:
- Have a positive attitude to working with people of any gender, family status or sexual identity, or with people who are from any ethnic origin, culture or religion, or who may have a disability.
- Demonstrate a sensitive and caring attitude towards others.
- Have a non-judgemental attitude.
- Value the contribution of parents.
- Be clear about confidentiality – to understand:
  - When what has been told in confidence remains so, or
  - When what has been told should be passed on sensitively in order to protect the child.
- Be reliable – for many parents reliability is of paramount importance.
- Have good communication skills.
- Be a good listener.
- Understand the need for support.
- Have a warm and open personality.
- Have a sense of humour.
- Be enthusiastic.
- Work as a member of a team.
- Keep records sensitively but clearly, regularly and well.

The family support handbook

The new worker or volunteer

Things usually are how they begin. (Worker)

- Be prepared for the new person's arrival; have the work area set up.
- Inform all members of staff about the new person and their starting date.
- Don't leave a new person on their own on their first day.
- Assign someone to show them around.
- Assign someone to take them to lunch and generally look out for them during the first week.
- Much of what the person hears on the first day will be forgotten. Tell the person it's OK to take notes.
- Clearly state performance expectations within the first few days.
- Orient the new person to both the formal and the informal rules.
- Make it clear who will be training them and to whom to go for guidance.
- Set a time at the end of the week to talk to them and review the week's experiences.

Volunteers

Volunteers are a godsend to many organisations. They supplement staff and their talents and enthusiasm often brightens the day. Most establishments take a management decision, or are bound by rules, about who they may take as volunteers. People who give their time freely need to feel both safe and valued in their chosen activity. It is therefore wise to follow some basic guidelines:

- Volunteers should be checked by police if they are working with children. This should be explained sensitively and the relevant forms filled in. Police checks should be initiated before they start working. The process usually takes some time, during which it is at the discretion of the manager or leader whether they begin work immediately, or wait until checks are complete. Should they begin before checks are completed, then it is obvious that they should not be left alone with families until cleared.
- Volunteers need an established time. Whilst it is nearly always useful to have an extra pair of hands, it is more efficient to be able to plan for them. Most volunteers prefer to agree a set time to attend which suits the establishment and themselves. They have other commitments too, so it is not wise to presume that they are willing to be always on call. Prearrangement avoids embarrassment and awkwardness all round.
- Volunteers need to feel valued. Sometimes they are people who are making a slow return to the world of work, but need to develop confidence. Sometimes their qualifications may vastly outstrip those of staff. Apart from the courtesy of regular thanks, they need to feel part of the team, which means that they should have:
  - Proper induction as for a staff member, including staff names and hierarchy, rules and protocols, particularly regarding confidentiality. Some volunteers may be relatives or friends of families attending, which will require discreet handling so that the family feels suitably secure.
  - The same respect and treatment as other members of staff.
  - Opportunities to take part in training so they can increase their skills.
  - Invitations to social events.
  - Information about prospective job openings. They may not get the job, but may feel slighted if overlooked when it is advertised.

- Volunteers need variety or to be given a specific task to do such as visiting a family in their own home to give support. They are not there just to do the menial tasks which no-one else fancies unless that is their clear choice. They would need to be very enthusiastic indeed if they were to continue on such a level alone.
- Volunteers need to know when they are getting it right. Some folk learn more quickly than others, but praise is often a spur. Remember that we repeat behaviour that is rewarded.
- Volunteers who prove unsuitable need to be told honestly, but gently. On the odd occasion when a volunteer really does not suit they need to be taken aside and the facts explained. Provided that there is no child protection issue, it may be possible to suggest another outlet for their talents.

Volunteers who are properly trained and valued quite often develop into highly regarded staff members if afforded due consideration by the team. Those who feel underused or put upon will simply give up. It is worth time and effort to smooth the way and make your volunteers feel welcome and part of the team.

Gloria's view

Gloria is the organiser for Home-Start Meon Valley. When recruiting volunteers she always:
- Visits them in their own home. This gives her an idea of the sort of person they are and what their values are so that she can better match the volunteer with a family.
- Looks for evidence of strong religious convictions and will talk to the volunteer about this. She will emphasise that it is important that their beliefs are not imposed on the family they are visiting. Occasionally, if she feels that the volunteer will not be able or willing to do this then they will not be accepted. Conversely, sometimes families try to impose their beliefs on the volunteers so they are advised to be aware of this and plan their response accordingly.
- Talks to the volunteers about their skills and experience and also about their previous professional life if they had one, asking them what they feel they might have to offer a family.
- Tries to ascertain their motive for volunteering.
- Discusses with the volunteers what they are willing to do or not do – not change nappies, not drive the family in their car, for example.
- Explains that some families will expect more of, or a different, service than they are able to offer and they may have to be firm with the family (in the nicest possible way, of course!). The need for clear boundaries cannot be over-emphasised.

Gloria explains to the volunteers:
- That there is absolutely no need to give their personal telephone number to a family unless they so wish. By dialling 141 before the family telephone number their own number remains secret. Home addresses should not be given, again unless the volunteer wishes to do this.
- That volunteers must never make promises they can't keep.
- About the difficulties of becoming too emotionally involved with the family and gives advice on how to avoid this.
- That the Home-Start officers are always available to discuss any concerns the volunteers might have.
- That even when a volunteer has been visiting a family for many months the family may not say 'Thank you' and that they should not be discouraged by this.
- That on the first, and sometimes second, visit to a family they will be accompanied by a member of staff.

Gloria and her staff send the volunteers birthday cards, invite them to social functions and generally treat them as though they were paid members of staff.

It is also explained to the volunteers that they should complete an eight-week preparation course before they are introduced to a family and visit them in their home. The Volunteer Training Plan at the end of this Section outlines a typical course.

Characteristics of a team

- A definable membership.
- A shared sense of purpose.
- Group pride.
- A clearly visible interdependence.
- Much interaction between the members.
- The group works as a single organisation.
- Members want the team to succeed.

There are usually five stages in the team building process:

1. **Forming** – where members get to know each other and their likes and dislikes.
2. **Norming** – the group works out rules and standards for operation.
3. **Storming** – the group tests new ideas and sounds out theories.
4. **Performing** – the group are at their peak level of output and work well together.
5. **Mourning** – there is a sense of loss as parting is planned. The output slows down and ceases as the group splinters.

In order to work effectively during the performing stage, the group needs time to master the preceding stages.

Planning should also take place so that replacement staff/volunteers are recruited to prevent the mourning process lasting too long or being too powerful.

Training

This part of this section provides some simple guidelines for developing a training plan for staff and volunteers. At the end of the section you will find checklists for *Staff and Volunteer Training Needs Assessment* and *Staff and Volunteer Training Priorities*, as well as examples of a *Volunteer Training Plan* and *Keeping Records of Training*.

Information needed to devise a training plan

- Who has had training?
- What training have they had?
- Who needs what training (team and individual) **now**?
- Future needs – for both the organisation and the staff and volunteers.
- Plan and audit.
- Evaluation strategies and feedback.

Devising a training plan

- Skills and knowledge team will need for for the future
- Where we want to go
- Present skills and knowledge of individuals
- Training needs
- Training needs of team to meet future plans
- Individual's training needs

Figure 15: Devising a training plan

Appraisals

We all like to know how we are getting on. We also like to be given an opportunity to say what we think. Appraisals are a good way of ensuring this happens.

Appraisals may be brief informal chats that happen from time to time, monthly get-togethers, or formal annual appraisals. Whatever scheme is used the information should be recorded, acted upon and future plans made for changes and improvements.

Delegation

Delegation does not mean working harder, it means working smarter! (Trainer)

The ten steps to effective delegation:
1. Clarify and prioritise all activities that need to be done.
2. Decide what you need to handle personally.
3. Decide what you can delegate.
4. Match the task to the person (Beware: don't always give tasks to the same person. They may be best at them but they will get overloaded and the others will not learn or develop and may become disillusioned or even jealous.)
5. Provide adequate information and the overall picture, i.e. why, how, what.
6. Give authority along with responsibility.
7. Get their agreement and commitment – are they happy and keen to do it?
8. Check for understanding – not just 'Do you understand?'
9. Share results.
10. Give feedback and praise.

Goals

Your values determine your goals. Your goals determine your priorities.

Set **SMARTER** goals:
- **S**pecific
- **M**easurable
- **A**ttainable a
- **R**ealistic
- **T**imely
- **E**valuated
- **R**eviewed

- **Write** down your goals – writing goals down will dramatically increase the likelihood of achieving them.
- **Review** your written goals weekly and keep them in view.
- **Set both short-term and long-term goals** – make sure your short-term goals are compatible with your long-term goals.
- **Limit** your number of goals.
- **Prioritise** them.
- **Break down** goals into easy steps.
- **Ask yourself**: who, what, when, how, and why not?
- **Evaluate** your progress at each step
- **Modify** the steps as necessary to achieve the goal.
- **Reward** yourself (and your team) at the completion of each step; doing so will help you all stay committed to your goals.

Using time effectively

Using time effectively is critical to good stress management at work. Try the following guidelines:
- Make a 'to do' list and prioritise tasks. One way to do this is to use the 'Swiss Cheese' theory to get things done. When you have a free moment, always do a little of a top priority task, thus making a small hole in it. Like a Swiss cheese, it will soon have so many holes that it will take very little time to complete.
- Set realistic deadlines for delivery of each of these objectives.
- Break up the various tasks into smaller bite-sized units, with time deadlines for each.
- Prioritise phone calls, letters, e-mails; deal with the most important ones first.
- Don't juggle paper; read it, act on it, file it or bin it.
- Once a decision is reached, forget it. Don't waste time thinking about whether it is a good decision or not.
- Stick to one task at a time and finish it.
- Decide on what time of day is good for you and use it for important tasks.
- Use your 'low point' time for routine or less important tasks.
- Keep meetings short and to the point.
- Manage meeting times if you are in a position to so do.
- Keep to the deadlines on appointments you make with other people.

Communication

Good communication for anyone working with people is essential. If we don't give it thought we may give out the wrong message. It may be:
- what we say
- what we don't say
- how we say something
- when we say it
- in what we wear

Our body language is another important form of communication.

The environment in which we operate, the use of colours, background music, even the condition of the toilets will tell others about ourselves.

> **Good communication is about thinking, preparing and doing in the most appropriate way for the situation and the people concerned.**

Listening and responding to adults (also adolescents)

Question: *Do you know why you have two ears and one mouth?*
Answer: *Because you should listen twice as much as you talk!* (Source unknown)

The Chinese characters that make up the verb 'to listen' include those that mean:

you   eyes   undivided attention   heart   ears

This suggests the Chinese understand listening very well.

Some simple listening rules:

- Listening is an extremely powerful skill. People will accept your ideas more readily when they feel you have truly listened to them.
- Concentrate and focus your attention solely on the talker. Don't stare.
- It's OK to take brief notes in most circumstances – you could ask if you are not sure.
- Listen with your eyes and ears. Listen for what's not being said.
- Don't interrupt. Listen to people all the way through to make sure you could repeat their point of view.
- Maintain neutral body language. Avoid grimacing or shaking your head, and other gestures that will deter the talker. Encourage the speaker with head nods, uh-huhs, etc.
- Suspend judgement about the person and issue. New good ideas often come from the unexpected.
- You may want to summarise briefly what the speaker has said. Don't mind-read. If needed, ask for clarification.
- Good leaders are good learners. You're learning when you're listening.

Active listening consists of:
- Looking at the person who is talking.
- Sitting quietly.
- Doing nothing else but listening.
- Responding naturally with your own gestures and expressions.
- Reflecting back the essence of what you have just heard.
- Asking no questions.
- Making no comments of your own.

> **Active listening is**
> *observing, reflecting on what you hear, summarising, reflecting feelings.*

It only occurs in an atmosphere of trust and acceptance.

The benefits are that:
- The speaker feels understood.
- The speaker has opportunities to express their thoughts more clearly and concisely.
- The speaker has opportunities to correct misunderstandings.

Not listening is much more common in our society than listening. When was the last time someone:
- Interrupted you?
- Took over the conversation you had started?
- Switched off while you were talking?
- Fidgeted around, looked at their watch, edged towards the door?
- Changed the subject?
- Answered with an inappropriate response?
- Could hardly wait for you to finish so they could speak again?

How did you feel?

Barriers to effective listening

Developing the skills of effective listening requires attention to these barriers. This will enable the listener to recognise the barriers and find ways to control them:

- *What you want to say* – it is possible to be so busy deciding what you will say next and thinking about this that attention is not given to the sender's message.
- *Triggered responses* – something the other person says may trigger a strong thought or feeling within you, or a person may remind you of someone or something in the past, triggering fantasies. Attention is diverted and effective listening ceases.
- *Defence of self* – if there is a strong need to defend yourself due to a perceived threat you will not attend to this threatening person, but do whatever seems best to protect yourself.
- *Ignoring cues and clues* – because you are busy, tired, feel inadequate, or just do not wish to know, cues and clues may be ignored. The facial expression, tone of voice, body posture and words which hint at strong feelings are not picked up.
- *Assumptions and judgements* – when made hastily, these may prevent effective listening either by diverting your attention from the person or by provoking you to evaluate statements, thus preventing acceptance of the person. Accepting another person without judgement does not mean agreeing with them. You may choose to act quite differently, but you are able to accept their right to act as they see fit, even their right to be wrong and make mistakes.

- *Patronising and placating* – these remarks are addressed at a perceived inadequacy of the other person. Reassurance of the 'There, there, don't worry. I'll look after you' kind is an example.
- *Clichés* – these are offered as support for yourself rather than hearing and offering support for the other person's needs. They are meant to reassure. It is of value to stop and ask 'Who am I trying to reassure; me or the person I am attempting to help?' 'The grass is greener on the other side of the fence' is not necessarily a helpful cliché to a person struggling to decide between several difficult paths.
- *Inadequate response* – responding to content and ignoring how it is said may be fine for ordinary everyday interactions. However, sometimes a strong clue may be provided but response is made only to the content; 'the music' of the message is ignored. This is inadequate when the person has high feelings that they wish to share.
- *Lack of empathy and incongruence* – if a discrepancy exists between what you say and how you say it, then empathy is not expressed. If in response to a cue you say 'You sound worried' in a cross voice, whilst bustling about, it will leave the person feeling put down and judged, despite the fact you have picked up the correct message. Your voice and actions are incongruent.
- *Sympathy and loss of person boundary* – your own reaction to the exchange interferes with your ability to listen effectively and to reflect back what you hear.

> **Attention from a good listener does wonders for people, helping them off-load negative feelings and experiences which get in the way of clear thinking and effective, efficient functioning.**

Meetings

They seem to have meetings to justify having meeting and this prevents them doing their job properly. (Worker)

Meetings can be:
- one to one
- in a small group
- a large group
- formal
- informal
- just a meeting place for people

A meeting should only occur if that is the best form of communication. Whatever type or whatever the purpose the following guidelines should be used to ensure success.

Aims
- To provide a safe supportive environment for families.
- To encourage the inclusion of families within the local community.
- To give opportunities for all parents and children to take part in planned activities together in a group setting.
- To give an opportunity for parents to have access to a variety of staff and volunteers.
- To raise parents' confidence in their own parenting skills.
- To lessen the isolation sometimes experienced by families.
- To give adults and children relationship building opportunities.

Why?
Work out what you wish the outcome of your meeting to be and plan accordingly. Is it for:
- decision making?
- imparting and receiving the information?
- making new contacts?
- imparting advice?
- teaching and learning new skills?

The family support handbook

Preparation
Good preparation is vital, so think about:
1. The place – check:
   - the room layout
   - any necessary equipment
   - is there room for a crèche?
   - nappy changing facilities
   - transport facilities
   - table and chairs
   - cups, plates, etc.
   - toilets
   - access
2. Timing – ensure it is:
   - not school holiday time and
   - during *Neighbours* or *Coronation Street*
3. Making contact:
   - Who to invite?
   - What is the criteria for attendance?
   - How to get access to names and addresses?
   - If writing, think about language.
   - When to make contact?
   - Do you need permission from anyone?
   - Make follow-up telephone calls, both as reminders and if no initial response.
   - Have strategies for handling resistance; make contact if a parent fails to turn up or suddenly stops coming without a reason.
4. What do you need?
   - refreshments
   - paper and pens
   - materials
   - register
   - contact forms
   - money for expenses
5. Strategies and procedures
   - a contact person if something goes wrong
   - what to do if there is a disclosure
   - how to ensure confidentiality
6. What to wear.
7. Who to work with.
8. A plan for the group meeting.

The meeting
- Start and finish on time.
- Welcome and give a brief explanation of the reason for meeting.
- Introductions.
- Address issues of confidentiality.
- Inform of intended outcomes at the beginning.
- Don't make promises you can't keep. If you do make promises, carry them out within a short period and advise if you cannot after all keep them.
- Advise what you will do if you hear anything that may require further action.
- If you wish to make a tape recording, take photographs or have visitors or researchers, ask permission from the parents, and, if appropriate, the young people, and advise them what will happen to tapes and snaps, etc.
- If appropriate advise that they may, if they wish, talk to you, or someone you tell them about, privately afterwards.
- Use humour not sarcasm.

- Learn not to show that you are shocked by what you hear – they may be trying you out – but it is acceptable to show disapproval if you wish.
- Listen.
- Be alert.
- Be prepared.
- Use eye contact.
- How will you prevent a few hogging the group?
- Advise the group when there is, say, 10 minutes to the end.

> **Have plenty of alternative ideas and material available in case the first or even second plan doesn't work.**

At the end
- Thank them for coming.
- Inform them of future outcomes.
- Pay their expenses if appropriate.
- Be prepared if they don't want to leave.

Afterwards
- Be discreet about what you hear.
- Have a brief wash-up session with whoever worked with you.
- How will you relax and unwind – group meetings may be stressful.

Telephoning

Message from a professional left on an answerphone:
I want to know, I don't know if you can help me, maybe it's not to do with you, but I'm hoping it will be, now let me see where was I…I'm all of a muddle ummm well, the thing is you may be just the person I need…by the way it's…from…

Nothing is more guaranteed to annoy busy people than messages that are incomplete, unless it is someone discourteous on the end of the line.

Telephones are used constantly to share information and to plan ahead. We use them so often that we sometimes forget the simple rules that make telephone communication so much easier. In order not to alienate those to whom we wish to speak, we should remember the following:
- Telephone conversation relies heavily on warmth and tone of voice – there is no visual clue from expression or body language to help tease out meaning, so we need to speak clearly, without aggression or bored-sounding pauses.
- Give your name and title first – it helps the listener to tune into you.
- Check that you and your listener have understood what is being said or arranged by repeating it back.
- Make notes and keep them, dated and signed.
- Keep messages simple if not speaking to the person you need, particularly if you speak to a child.
- Some answerphones take only short messages, so don't ramble.
- Give a time to ring again if your contact is out and remember to do it.
- Do not speak to others whilst on the phone unless you have a secrecy button to press – a hand over the phone is not good enough.
- Follow up your messages as soon as you can – generally within 24 to 48 hours.
- Plan what to say if a call may be difficult – make a list of the points you want to get across or the questions you want to ask.
- Keep relevant information to hand, e.g. the family file.

Feedback

If you can manage to criticise and praise you can manage! (Consultant)

- Frequent, brief, immediate praise or criticism is more effective than infrequent lengthy, delayed praise or criticism.
- Think of criticism as helpful advice to help people improve and succeed.
- Don't procrastinate. Give immediate feedback at the time a negative situation occurs.
- Focus on the problem and the solution to it not the person or their attitude.
- Ask for, and listen to, ideas for solutions and improvement.
- Listen at length to a response without defending your position. The person may need to vent pent-up feelings and you may learn something you didn't know.
- Stay calm. Adjourn your meeting and schedule a follow-up one if either party becomes too upset or agitated to discuss or listen effectively.
- Be clear and specific about what went wrong and your expectations and hopes for change.
- Get the person or group to buy into the idea and commit to change.
- Offer support and guidance for desired change.
- Ask yourself, is it important or am I 'nit picking'?
- Think about the language to use.
- Praise in public, criticise in private.

The four 'Fs' of feedback are:

- factual
- fair
- firm
- follow-up

> **How you say it is as important as what you say.**

Refusing requests

If you never say 'no' what is your 'yes' worth? (Counsellor)

- If you can buy yourself time to do so, try not to agree straight away.
- Ask for clarification or more information, 'What detail does this entail?'
- Ask for more time to decide on requests if necessary. 'I need time to think this through' or 'I need to consult my diary, I will get back to you.' Or 'I need to talk to my staff or manager. I will get back to you.'
- Keep your reply short. If you have to give a reason for refusing then give the real reason rather than inventing an excuse.
- With short replies you need to slow down, speak steadily and with warmth, otherwise replies can sound abrupt.
- Don't apologise profusely.
- Avoid 'I can't' phrases and say 'I'd rather not' or 'I'm not happy to.'
- Acknowledge the requester, e.g. 'Thank you…but I'm not ready at present to change the system to enable this to happen.'
- Identify yourself with the decision, e.g. 'I'm not prepared to bend the rules on this' rather than, 'My staff wouldn't want it.'

If the requester becomes persistent repeat your refusal adding the reason if you didn't give it first time. Don't search for better reasons.

Record keeping

Normal organisational records will need to be kept, such as:
- Staff records including mobile 'phone details if staff are out and about.
- Volunteers' details.
- Visitors and reasons for visits.
- Student records.
- Training.
- Buildings.
- Services.
- Vehicles.
- Toys and equipment – including dates of regular safety checks.
- Evaluation and monitoring records to help forward planning and to make improvements.

In addition, you will need to keep records of:
- Parents' names, addresses and telephone numbers.
- Emergency telephone numbers.
- Names and details of children – you may need those attending the groups or being visited at home plus all other children or you may only need details of the ones for whom you are concerned.
- Next of kin.
- Special dietary requirements, allergies, etc.
- Other professionals involved with the family.

If you are running groups you will need a record of:
- Attendance.
- Reasons given for non-attendance, as these may be pertinent too.
- General observations regarding parents or children.
- Causes for concern.
- Programmes of events and plans for the future.
- Successes and failures.
- Visitors to the group – be sure to tell the parents and young people about who the visitor is and why they are attending. Sometimes it is necessary to keep control of the number of visitors – a successful group may excite interest in a wide variety of professionals, students and other interested people which may be to the detriment of the group.
- Any other relevant information.

If you are organising home visits you will need a record of:
- When, how often and for how long the visits are to take place.
- Who the visitor will be.
- The reason for the visit.
- The aim of the visit and what it is hoped to achieve.
- How the visit went and plans for the next visit.
- Any other relevant information.

Good record keeping is essential for any organisation. It ensures the groups or visits are well run and planned and when things go wrong the records can easily be referred to or information gleaned. Records should be kept safely. Confidentiality rules must apply, e.g. files about a client should not be left lying around even if you are going to use them again shortly.

Visitors – pain or pleasure?

There were more visitors than staff. The staff and the children missed out because staff were kept so busy by the visitors that they had no time to play with the children.

(Staff member)

Visitors may sometimes alter a meeting or session to the extent that both family and professionals feel dissatisfied. Where there are many visitors, the pressure can be intolerable. A little forethought may pave the way for more useful outcomes. In the first instance, the type of visitor you welcome may depend on what sort of establishment you are running.

When working with a single family, the rules differ to those when working with a group of families away from their homes. You would not expect to welcome visitors to a family home without the express permission of the family members or without some discussion around the reasons for visiting.

In a group situation, especially where your success has become known either locally or nationally, some visitors are likely to have less pressing reasons to look you over apart from professional interest. It is up to you to establish rules, both for the type and number of visitors you will welcome. Hospitality may increase your good name, but if not properly organised may alienate your staff or families. So who are these visitors?

Possible categories of visitor might be:
- professionals attending arranged meetings
- students on placements
- interested extended family members or supporters
- interested professionals
- volunteers
- inspecting or regulatory officers
- disgruntled clients

Numbers are important. Visitors should be allocated so that:
- Families present have prior warning and are consulted.
- Staff are consulted about who arrives, when, and how many. Lots of visitors all asking questions while you are trying to work on a programme with a child or family is the stuff of nightmares.
- Staff know when to expect them – a chart or information board reduces stress and aids proper planning.
- Confidentiality is not breached.
- The numbers are manageable and do not disrupt normal working.
- There is time to welcome them and to brief them on what to do or not do.

Names are vital. As they arrive, visitors should be:
- Welcomed promptly and not kept waiting.
- Asked to sign in, including the time of arrival – this is important for health and safety.
- Allocated a name badge.
- Given any relevant information about their visit, e.g. leaflet about work at the venue or the agenda for the meeting.
- Introduced to who will look after them, or taken to the meeting place.
- Given a brief outline of the plan of the visit.
- Informed about general rules, e.g. smoking, etc. Visitors who are not told the rules may be embarrassed by accidentally breaking them.
- Reminded about the working nature of the establishment and confidentiality.
- Asked to keep questions to a prearranged time, if appropriate.

Before they leave, visitors should be:
- Given time to ask questions.
- Asked what further help they need.
- Informed about who else might help them.
- Asked to sign out and return name badges.
- Thanked for their visit and accompanied to the door to ensure security.

A disgruntled visitor should be afforded:
- A courteous welcome, including normal tone of voice.
- Acknowledgement of their anger or distress.
- An unbiased ear to hear their concern.
- An opportunity to record their complaint.
- A follow up appointment to check outcomes.
- An explanation of how the establishment deals with complaints

A planned approach to visitors will be part of policy making decisions:
- A 'Visitors Policy' provides a framework. See example on page 177. It will ensure that visits and visitors are managed effectively.
- Visits are recorded efficiently and statistics kept.
- Staff and families are least disrupted and stressed.
- Visitors are given relevant information.
- Visitors are monitored and regularly canvassed for their opinions, both formally by questionnaire samples and by recording of anecdotal comments and testimonials.

Complaints

No one is perfect. We may strive to please everyone by putting systems into place that would appear to be failsafe, but every so often a glitch will occur. When a complaint is made, however trivial it may seem to you, it is important to the person who made it to have answers that satisfy their concerns. It may have taken them days to muster the courage to make the complaint in the first place. If it is dealt with superficially or in a condescending way, their self-esteem may take an unfair slide. They may refuse to attend further sessions or withdraw their children

The wisest rule about complaints is always to listen carefully to what is said. Check that you have understood the nature of the complaint and make notes which should be kept. Show the person what you have written and allow them to write their feelings if they wish. Keep expression and body language open and positive and do not be drawn into angry exchanges.

There should be a complaints procedure (see example on pages 178-185) which is adhered to. This will set out the route for dealing with concerns. Remember that:

- Complaints may be verbal or written – they should be taken equally seriously, whether from an adult or from a child. What you may think is scurrilous may be vital to the other person.
- Complaints should be numbered and all actions recorded, signed and dated.
- Thanks should be offered for bringing the matter to light.
- Apologies restore confidence in the complainers if given sincerely.
- There should be plans for independent investigation of those complaints which cannot be readily settled.
- Complaints may trigger changes to working practices which need to be publicised to staff and to user families.
- Confidentiality should be observed and others told only on a 'need to know' basis.
- Complaints are not always from client to staff. Staff may have grievances about other staff or working practices which should be dealt with just as carefully as other types of complaint.
- The complaints file should be regularly reviewed and overall types of grievance evaluated. It may be that there is a fault in the system which needs correction.
- Some complaints result from human error. If this is on the part of the complainer, then explanations should be offered. If the error is by staff, then training needs should be reviewed. Staff may need reminders to read protocols and guidelines regularly.
- People are diverse. Occasionally you will meet a person who is a serial complainer by disposition. If this happens, you must still treat each concern as valid, no matter how much paperwork it engenders. Smile sweetly and button your lips, for some of their concerns may also be a problem to other families who do not have the communication skills needed to state their worries.
- When a complaint has been dealt with satisfactorily and all necessary changes have been made, it should not be used against the family or staff at future times.

Complaints are not a mark of failure. They are necessary to a healthy establishment to avoid complacency. Practices which upset those people you seek to serve and empower should not be allowed to continue because *'That's the way we do things here'*. Nothing should be set in stone.

What happens if things go wrong?

Despite having the best laid plans things will sometimes go wrong. In order to avoid 'things going wrong' becoming a disaster, it is important not just to plan and organise your group or visit as efficiently as possible, but also to have contingency plans in place. These should cover such things as:

- Child protection issues.
- Health and safety issues including when home visiting.
- Child, young person, mother, staff or volunteer sickness.
- An accident to staff, volunteers, parents, children or young people.
- Arguments.
- Problems with the buildings such as heating breakdown or flooding.
- Building evacuation.
- Insufficient staff in attendance.
- Someone arriving under the influence of drugs or alcohol.
- A child with head lice.
- The aggressive arrival of someone demanding to see a child or young person.
- A home visitor arriving to find the person they are meant to see is not there but someone else opening the door in a less than friendly way.
- Someone arriving who the worker or volunteer knows is not meant to see the child or young person.
- Staff safety from aggressive parents and/or child or young person.
- Stealing.
- The group not gelling or the session not going well.
- The parent not getting on with one member of staff or volunteer.
- Plus any others that may be specific to your organisation.

Either everyone involved should know the procedures or there should always be a named person in place who knows them, who is frequently reminded of them and has the authority and confidence to implement them.

After an event has occurred staff or volunteers and, if appropriate, parents should meet to discuss the situation and consider:

- How it was handled.
- What could have been done better.
- Whether any changes to procedures are required.

It is also important to focus on the good points as well.

Useful resources and bibliography

Blanchard, K. and Johnson, S. (1984) *The One Minute Manager*. London, Fontana Books.

Hillyard-Parker, H., Mabon, G., Payne, C., Phillipson, J. and Riley, M. (1993) *How to Manage Your Training*. London, NISWE.

Kaufman, P. and Wetmore, C. (1994) *The Bullet Manager, Getting down to What Really Counts in the Workplace*. London, Arrow Business Books.

Walsh, J. (1989) *The Manager's Problem Solver, Practical Solutions to Managers' Questions*. London, Sphere Books.

Young, A. (1986) *The Manager's Handbook*. London, Sphere References.

Model forms and documents

Volunteer training plan

Session 1
Why is a volunteer needed by families?
What is the approach?
What is a volunteer?
How can **you** help a family?

Session 2
How are relationships established and what can go wrong.
Confidentiality, commitment, boundaries.
Listening and communicating.

Session 3
Child development and 'the Importance of play'.
Learning through play.
Family therapy and behavioural difficulties.
Language development.

Session 4
What do we mean by 'special needs'.
Helping children with 'special needs' – the 'Portage' service.
How we can help.
Equal opportunities.

Session 5
Working with mums with depression and anxiety.
Being a volunteer.
Bereavement and loss.

Session 6
The role of the health visitor and other professionals
Hormones.
Sexual health and family planning.
Personal safety.

Session 7
What is child abuse?
Issues and Child Protection Practice.
The Children Act.

Session 8
Benefits available to families.
Endings.
Admin.
Meet the management committee.

Adapted from Home-Start Training Plan

The family support handbook

Staff and volunteer training needs assessment checklist

	Yes/no	When	Details
1. Have you had induction training?			
2. Have you qualifications: – relevant to this post (specify)? – other?			
3. Have you attended any short courses or workshops: – put on by us? – put on by the agency? – put on by others?			
4. Have you had any specific training to help you with your job?			
5. Have you any other sources of help with your development, e.g. places, people, hobbies, friends, evening classes?			
6. Have you any places booked on courses or workshops in the future?			
7. Please list any future training you would like.			

Note: all existing and new members of staff and volunteers should ensure this form is kept up-to-date which will enable training plans to be made.

Staff and volunteer training priorities: checklist

Framework for training	What kind of training do we need?
Developing criteria and determining priorities	How do we decide what sort of training?
Linking training needs to priority criteria	Whose/which needs should receive the greatest priority?
Assessing the resource implications	How much will it cost in money and staff time?
Taking a decision	Factors to be considered in decision taking

Types of training:
- Necessary planned routine training, i.e. induction.
- Planned continuing training, i.e. personal development.
- Responsive training, i.e. changes in the law.
- Responsive training, i.e. training for change in practice.
- Unplanned responsive training, i.e. problem-solving, crisis resolution.

Developing a positive training climate:
- Is training seen as a positive opportunity that is essential for everyone?
- Is training clearly seen as improving the attitude and skills of staff?
- Have definite changes in individual and/or general practice resulted from training?
- Is there a genuine thirst for further learning and development over a wide range of subjects?
- Are training plans subject to regular appraisal and review?

Keeping records of training

Programme	Who attended	Who responsible	Date	Comments/ assessment	Employee/ volunteer	Staff

Section 10
Policies, Procedures, Evaluation and Monitoring

Evaluation needs to be built in from the start of any initiative and to be based on the resident's (user's) views of what outcomes they want from the intervention in terms of both tasks and processes.
(Taylor, 1995)

In addition to external assessments we continually monitor our work internally. We use questionnaires extensively, for example to parents. We have been asking the advice of parents of new children, and those recently left, about the time of transition. Can we do better?
(Mann, 2000)

Evaluation and monitoring carried out well with the commitment of all concerned will encourage the development of good practice, improve morale and provide tangible benefits for children and families. Most people like to know how they are getting on. Evaluation and monitoring enables realistic assessments to be made.

In order to be able to evaluate and monitor what is being done it is necessary to have clear policies and procedures in place as a yardstick by which to measure success.

Policies and procedures

These should be concise and to the point and show clearly what it is hoped to achieve. They should show:

- The overall aim of the work.
- How this will be achieved.
- Principles by which the work will be undertaken.
- Success criteria.

The model forms at the end of this section may be photocopied for use elsewhere or adapted to suit different situations but please acknowledge the source.

Evaluation and monitoring

Evaluation and monitoring should be seen as a necessary tool and not as something negative which 'must be done'. It should:
- Contribute to the development of good practice.
- Produce data that accurately reflects the impact of the work being undertaken.
- Encourage a high profile for routine tasks carried out within an organisation.
- Place emphasis on the role, values and interests of key players.
- Consider the dynamics of communities and the interpersonal relations and aspirations of the group or individual.
- Consider qualitative data – stories, case-studies, etc.
- Promote learning and development through an organisation.
- Validate accurately the impact and contributions of the people in organisations.

As a secondary aim evaluation and monitoring may be used as:

- A method of enabling control to be maintained on expenditure.
- A way of providing greater accountability.
- A type of inspection and quality control.
- As a means of meeting the criteria set by funders.

Young people, and children when they are old enough, should all be part of the evaluation procedure. In this way it will ensure that the service is in the best interests of the child or young person and meets their needs. They often have very good ideas as to how things can be improved.

The work and ethos of any organisation should be around striving to continue to monitor, evaluate and thus improve their quality standards which in turn will benefit both children and parents as well as staff. To do this, Willows Nursery School in Portsmouth ask:

1. **Their old customers:**
   - Whether their child went to the school the parent wanted when they left the Willows.
   - If they listened and talked about the move to the parents' satisfaction.
   - Did they help with visits to the new school?
   - Could they have done better?

2. **A selection of new parents:**
   - If the initial home visit was helpful.
   - About the user-friendliness (or otherwise) of the parents booklet.
   - About their first visit to see the school.
   - If they like home books and newsletters.
   - If they know about 'Friends of Willows' meetings.
   - If they feel worries and concerns are listened.

3. **College students:**
Students who are at the Willows for two weeks or more are asked to complete an evaluation pro forma. This information is collated by a classroom assistant who regularly reports to a staff meeting and to governors.

4. **Professional colleagues:**
Visiting professionals judge Willows performance via questionnaires.

5. **Fellow early years workers:**
Willows teachers have produced a training pack for a wide variety of early years workers wanting to know more about working with children with special educational needs. Evaluation sheets (collected after each training day) are analysed and used to inform future training.

As part of their In-house Evaluation the Willows have:

- A suggestion box – one suggestion made was 'Please will staff wear name badges'. They now have badges and fine themselves 10p if they forget.
- A 'problem' sheet on which to record minor problems.
- Improved monitoring of the curriculum. Staff have developed a monitoring pro forma and agreed a consistent frequency of use including an effective reporting system. This will evidence their strengths, inform planning and highlight training needs.
- Curriculum co-ordinators, report to a full staff meeting offering support and advice as appropriate.
- Continued to commission the inspection service to comment on their expertise.
- Tried to ensure value for money quality training for staff and volunteers. Requests for training are made on a pro forma. A short presentation is made to a full staff meeting by the person trained.
- A whole school development day. The aim is to develop a strategy for the next five years. All Willows staff complete a questionnaire evaluating effectiveness both as trainers and in communicating the values of the school.
- Agreement by staff of whole school targets.
- A fact finding mission – what other services do parents need? e.g. more play schemes, Saturday clubs, babysitting service.

Evaluation tools

It is vitally important that the material used should be:

- Easy to read.
- Easy to understand.
- Easy to use.
- Have an even number of options (most people will choose the middle one if there is an odd number).
- Easy to collate.

Outcomes should:

- Be recorded for future use.
- Be reported back to all concerned within a reasonable time.
- Ensure that all points are actioned.
- Ensure that all improvements are made where necessary.
- Ensure that success is celebrated.

Evaluation and monitoring is not new. Most good organisations already carry it out, in some cases, without realising they are doing it as it is just part of their good practice. What is important is that needed changes are made within a reasonable time framework, success celebrated and plans for the future are informed by the existing good practice. Everyone should be kept in touch with the outcomes.

Further reading and bibliography

Dixon, J. (1995) Community Stories and Indicators for Evaluating Community Development. *Community Development Journal*, Vol.30, No. 4.

Edmonds, J. (Ed.) (1999) *Health Promotion with Young People: An Introductory Guide to Evaluation*, London, Health Education Authority.

Everitt, A. and Hardike, R. P. (1996) *Evaluating for Good Practice*, London, Macmillan.

Factor, Chauhan and Pitts (2001) *RHP Companion to Working with Young People*, Lyme Regis, Russell House Publishing.

Guba, E. and Lincoln Y. S. (1989) *Fourth Generation Evaluation*, London, Sage.

Home-Start (2001) *Annual Report, Supporting Families*, Home-Start Meon Valley.

Mann, M. (2000) in Wheal, A. (2000) (Ed.) *Working with Parents*. Lyme Regis, Russell House Publishing. Ch. 4.17.

Taylor (1995) in Dixon, J. (1995)

Model forms and documents

Beacon Policy

Our overall aim for Beacon work is:
- To disseminate ……………… good practice throughout the city.
- To enhance teaching and learning for young children with special needs.
- To promote inclusion.

To achieve this we will:
- Offer help and support to year R and KS1 staff.
- Develop a range of services for colleagues.
- Respond to consultations.
- Offer advice and support for special needs issues to mainstream colleagues.
- Offer training for SEN to mainstream KS1 colleagues.

Principles are that:
- Confidentiality will be respected.
- Methods of working will be consistent with ……………… standards.
- Staff will keep comprehensive records and assist in evaluations.
- Staff will be offered regular appraisals.
- We will seek to continue and develop Beacon initiatives.
- Our staff will be offered suitable training and support.
- We will liaise with colleagues to foster consistency of practice and co-operation.
- Financial accounts will be available.
- Contributions towards supply cover costs will be made when possible.

Success criteria:
- Evidence from regular evaluations will be analysed to improve our service.
- Training for ……………… staff will be appropriate.
- A variety of Beacon initiatives will be offered to clients.
- Allocation of visitors to ……………… will be fair and manageable.

Date:

Discussion with chair:

Modifications:

Discussed with full governing body:

Passed:

Review date:

Policy for outreach work

Our overall aim for outreach work is to disseminate ……………… good practice throughout the city to enhance learning opportunities for young children with special needs. To achieve this we will:

- Offer help and support to parents and carers of young children with special needs.
- Train and support our outreach staff.
- Develop a range of services for parents and colleagues.
- Offer outreach services in a variety of convenient settings across the city.
- Respond to consultations with all user groups.
- Provide special needs training to other early years workers in the city.
- Offer advice and support for special needs issues to mainstream colleagues.
- Offer training and support for SEN to mainstream KS1 colleagues.
- Offer respite care to special needs and community children on Saturdays (excluding bank holidays).
- Offer holiday playschemes to ……………… and community children.
- Evaluate all aspects of outreach initiatives.

Principles are that:

- Confidentiality will be respected – excepting child protection issues.
- Agreed procedures will be followed (available in school).
- Methods of working will be consistent with ……………… standards.
- Cost neutral venues will be sought throughout the city.
- Regular management meetings will be held.
- Termly newsletters will be circulated to all involved in the services.
- Staff will keep comprehensive records and assist in evaluations.
- Staff will be offered regular appraisals.
- We will seek to continue and develop outreach initiatives.
- Our staff will be offered suitable training and support.
- Transport to ……………… for the summer playscheme will be offered if practical.
- Free or reduced cost places on playdays may be available.
- Health and safety requirements are met for all.
- We will liaise with other EY providers (statutory and non-statutory) to foster consistency of practice and co-operation.
- Financial accounts will be available.

Success criteria:

- Evidence from regular evaluations will be analysed to improve our service.
- Training for ……………… staff will be appropriate.
- A variety of outreach initiatives will be offered to clients.
- Termly newsletters will be circulated.
- Saturday Playdays and summer playschemes will be available.
- Allocation of visitors to ……………… will be fair and manageable.

Home/outreach agreement

We promise that we will:
- Provide daily/weekly/monthly visits for .... at an agreed time in your home for .... hours.
- Notify you of any personnel problems, e.g. sickness when cancellation is necessary as soon as possible.
- Agree areas of concern.
- Agree strategies for help.
- Offer advice and support.
- Offer referral to other agencies if necessary or wanted.
- Provide toys where necessary.
- Offer hands-on help.
- Offer accompanied visit to a local drop-in group, playgroup or toy library of your choice if you wish.

It will help us if you will:
- Be at home at agreed time or notify us by .... on day of appointment at latest.
- Turn off TV, radio or CD player during visit.
- Not entertain visitors during visit.
- Be ready to share areas of concern.
- Be ready to try suggested ideas.
- Be ready to ask questions if idea is not clear.
- Make sure child is at home.
- Be ready to work with staff for the agreed period of the appointment.

The family support handbook

Outreach monitoring

Group:	Date:
Venue:	Author:

Staff:

Overview:

Observations:

Climate:	
Adult/child involvement:	
Team effectiveness:	
Planning:	

Outreach monitoring – Record of feedback

Date of feedback:	To whom?
By whom?	About what?

Focus of discussions:

Suggestions:

Future plans:

Playscheme procedures

Structure of the sessions:
- Free play, choices.
- Suggested activities, e.g. craft.
- Drinks time (ringing of a bell will signal).
- Free play.
- End Session (songs, stories).
- Home time (member of staff to stand by the door to stop escapees!)

Packed lunches:
- Packed lunches to be kept in kitchen during the morning.
- Children to wash hands before and after lunch.
- Children and one member of staff **per table** together in a play room.
- After lunch a changeover of staff.
- Children move to carpet room for quiet time and TV.
- For children needing a nap beanbags are available.

Activities:
Variety and range of equipment and toys on offer daily, e.g.

- sand
- water
- craft activities
- ball pool
- light room
- garden
- home corner
- quiet area
- books
- computers
- songs
- stories

A minibus is also available if required.

Equal opportunities:
- A range of toys and equipment reflecting the diverse culture we live in are present in the nursery.
- Providing 1:1 support allows children to access the playscheme who have more specific needs than the higher ratio of staff could practically cope with.
- A minibus will pick up children from the .... area whose parents are not able to bring them to the playscheme.

Minibus drivers are: ....
Children attending by minibus will be picked up and dropped off at the prearranged time and stop as arranged with individual parents. A mobile phone will be used as a link with staff in the case of an emergency. Supervisor to ring emergency contact numbers for children.

Minibus trips out:
- The ratio of staff will be one adult to two children.
- Only approved drivers to drive the minibus.
- All staff on the outing will carry a list of children plus our contact number.
- A list of children will be left in the office.
- Only children whose parents have signed a consent form will be taken offsite.

Policies, procedures, evaluation and monitoring

First Aid:
Named first aiders are: ……………………………………………………………………………………………………..........

All accidents/incidents to be recorded in the accident or incident emergency book. These are kept on a shelf in the …………………............... area.

Inform relevant staff when a child or member of staff is in need of first aid. Ensure that information is passed on to Supervisor or Deputy Supervisor so that parents or carers can be informed.

Behaviour strategies:
Staff prefer to use positive reinforcement of good behaviour rather than focusing on negative behaviour. The staff approach to negative behaviour is:
- **Ignore it** (usually in the case of attention seeking behaviour).
- **Distract** (encourage appropriate behaviour by distracting the child, e.g. another toy, book, game, someone else to play with, etc.).
- **Removal or withdrawal** (take the child away from the source of the incident and tell or show them you are not happy with their behaviour).
- **Time out** (usually the ………………. for two or three minutes only to be used for biting or something equally harmful to another child or adult).

If you are not sure what to do ask for assistance from another member of staff.

Bathroom:
Toiletting/nappies to be changed as and when appropriate, e.g. when soiled, mid-morning, after lunch, mid-afternoon, before home time.
- All staff must wear gloves when changing or attending to a child's toiletting needs.
- Nappies to be disposed of in nappy bin provided.
- Potties to be emptied down the toilet and flushed.
- Potties to be cleaned with tissues and disinfectant provided in toilet area.

Fire alarm:
In the case of a fire, staff will gather up the children and proceed to ……………..……………..........

Last member of staff out of the room/garden to check for hidden children and close doors if possible.

Nominated staff to phone emergency services. Supervisor to check building for children or staff and collect register.

Once all assembled at the ……………………..……….. the register will be taken. Parents and carers will be informed through contact numbers.

Questionnaire for 'new' parents

Now that your child has started at ………………………………….. we would like to find out if you are happy with the way it was managed. By answering these questions we will be able to find out how to improve – so please be honest!

Did you come to look around?

If not, would you have liked to?

Was the person showing you round helpful?

Were they courteous?

Did you feel welcome?

Did you see the work/play rooms?

Was your visit useful?

Is the Parent's booklet helpful? User friendly? Yes/No/OK

Have we missed anything?

Any way it could be improved?

Questionnaire for parents

1. Roughly, how many times have you visited the group? ☐

2. What do you think about our work?

3. What do you think about the building?

4. Are there any parts you think are not appropriate? If yes, please detail.

5. What do you think is needed? What would you like to see changed?

Any other comments?

Name: ....

You may return this anonymously but if I need to ask for more detail it would be helpful to know who you are.

The family support handbook

Questionnaire for visiting professionals

Date:

Dear

Helping to Improve Quality at ………..............…………

We are continually trying to monitor and improve the service we offer to professionals visiting ……….....................……. We would appreciate it if you would kindly complete the questionnaire below so that we can objectively measure our performance and maintain and strengthen our standards:

Professional category:

S.A.L.T. ❏   Physiotherapist ❏   O.T. ❏   Dietician ❏   E.P. ❏

Health Visitor ❏   Social Worker ❏   Tutor ❏   Teacher ❏   Doctor ❏

Other ❏ (Please specify) ……………………………………………

When did you last visit us?……………………………………

Please tell us your opinion of the following if they apply to you:

	v.good	good	average	poor
The prior arrangements and administration for the appointment	❏	❏	❏	❏
The accommodation provided	❏	❏	❏	❏
The environment and ambience of the place	❏	❏	❏	❏

The staff:	agree	tend to agree	tend to disagree	disagree
Were friendly and co-operative	❏	❏	❏	❏
Had carried out previous recommendations appropriately	❏	❏	❏	❏
Had the necessary documentation to support this	❏	❏	❏	❏
Were able to understand any suggestions or proposed help for the child	❏	❏	❏	❏
Were willing to implement this programme	❏	❏	❏	❏

Did you feel you were allocated sufficient time with the member of staff?   Yes/No

Was all the information you needed made available to you, e.g. case history, developmental charts etc.   Yes/No

We would very much appreciate any other comments you may like to make overleaf to help us in our quest for excellence. Thank you very much

Questionnaire on our outreach service

1. What services have you used from our outreach services?

2. Have you visited us here? Yes/No What were your first impressions of the building and of the work?

3. What do you think about the service you received?

4. What do you think about where you received the service?

5. How did this affect you?

6. How could things be done differently/better?

Any other comments? (Please continue on reverse if necessary)

Name: ………………………………..…………………

You may return this anonymously but if I need to ask for more details it would be helpful to know who you are.

The family support handbook

Questionnaire for parenting groups

As you know we have .... meetings every ..... weeks, between ....
and ....

We want to know what you think about them so please would you spend a minute or two to answer these questions for us? Thanks!

Do you think meetings are a good idea?	Yes	Ok	No
Do you come along sometimes?	Yes	Ok	No
Is the room OK?	Yes	Ok	No
Is it hard for you to get here?	Yes	Ok	No
Would a lift help?	Yes		No
Would a crèche help?	Yes		No
There are always jobs needing to be done – like cutting tokens off crisp packets and covering books. Would you like to help out while we chat over a cuppa?	Yes		No

Any other ideas?

If you have some ideas or can give me a hand it will help me a lot. Please let me know.

Please return this as soon as possible.

Name: ....

Students and professional visitors policy

Students, potential parents of new pupils and professional visitors attend .... to learn something about our way of working.

The Headteacher (or in her absence, the Deputy) will be responsible for introducing visitors and supply staff on initial visit to:
- The pupils and admission procedures.
- The operation of the day.
- Curriculum and checklists leading to reporting to parents, including the mock-up review.
- The contribution of speech, physio and occupational therapists.
- Team composition and operation.
- The .... leaflet.

Longer term students, e.g. N.N.E.B. students (and supply staff) will need the same introduction, but additional information on:
- Confidentiality.
- Responsibility to group and absence procedure with the stress put on the two-way responsibility.
- Clarification of projects expected and needed for inspection by class teacher.
- Issue of job description and clarification including times, duties and identification of a nominated S.S.A. on .... leaflet.

Professional Pack including:
- sample curriculum checklists
- explanation of scoring
- mock-up report
- staff structure
- description of language problems
- aims
- aims and explanation of home-based projects

These will be given to:
- County personnel with a responsibility for early years' development.
- Out-county visitors who are partaking in some particular early years' project.
- Advanced study students involved in early years' projects.
- New personnel with long-term connection with ....
- Others who request where appropriate.

After an introductory talk, visitors will be given a geographic tour with a minimum introduction (their presence will have been already mentioned at staff meeting and added to chart (unless a short-notice visit).

Timing of one-off visits, if at all possible, will be at 10-10.15 am or 1.15 pm, as these are the most settled times for classes. Wherever possible Fridays will be avoided.

Geographic tours for parents will aim to end up with the group which their child will join to allow an in-depth time with the staff. Other visitors will be offered the opportunity to join in with a group as appropriate: one visitor per group.

Passed by full governing body:

Reviewed:

Review date:

Complaints

Stages for handling complaints

Stage One: Informal

Member of staff hears about concern
↓
Satisfactory outcome reached?
↙ ↘
No   Yes → **No further action**

Stage Two: Investigation

Organisation receives written complaint
↓
Investigation conducted and reported
↓
Satisfactory outcome reached?
↙ ↘
No   Yes → **No further action**

Stage Three: Review

Formal complaint to complaints panel
↓
Panel meeting of governors/trustees
(Complainant and senior person may attend)
↓
Satisfactory outcome reached?
↙ ↘
No   Yes → **No further action**

Stage Four: Review by LA (Where applicable)

Complainant refers matters to Local Authority
↓
Satisfactory outcome reached?
↙ ↘
No   Yes → **No further action**

Stage Five: Beyond the LA

Appeals to:
Secretary of State or to Ombudsman

Policies, procedures, evaluation and monitoring

Complaints

How to listen to complaints
(Developed from a Hertfordshire County Council guide)

As soon as you realise that you are listening to a complaint, remember these points:

Don't pass the buck.	Do not keep transferring an angry person from one place or person to another. Make sure you know the contact person for anything you cannot deal with yourself.
Don't be flippant.	First impressions count. You and the organisation may be judged on your immediate reaction.
Treat all complaints seriously.	However small or trivial it may seem to you, the complaints will be an important problem for anyone who takes the trouble to complain.
Treat every complaint individually.	Even if you have already received several similar complaints the same day, it is probably the person's first chance to have their say.
Be courteous and patient.	Be sympathetic and helpful, but do not blame other colleagues.
Say who you are.	If you are unknown to the person, introduce yourself.
Ask them their name and use it.	Anonymous complaints are acceptable only where there are special circumstances.
Take time to find out exactly what the problem is.	It is easy for someone to forget to tell you an important detail, particularly if they are upset or annoyed.
Don't take the complaint personally.	To an angry or upset person, you are the only one they can put their feelings to right now.
Stay cool and calm.	Do not argue with the person – be polite and try to find out exactly what the person thinks is going wrong, or has gone wrong.
Check you are being understood.	Make sure that the person understands what you are saying. Don't use jargon: it can cause confusion and annoyance to someone 'not in the know'.
Don't rush.	Take your time. Let people have their say and let off steam if they need to. Listen carefully and sympathetically to their problems before replying and attempting to find a solution or offer a next step.

Complaints

Complaint policy: guidelines for parents

If you have any worries or concerns please talk to us. Your child's teacher will always make time to listen. If you prefer to talk to the Headteacher please telephone to be sure of an appointment. Complaints can be referred to the school's governors.

If the matter cannot be resolved by informal discussion, then an appointment with the Headteacher or Chair of Governors should be made, or the matter put in writing to the Headteacher or Chair of Governors of which the Headteacher or Chair of Governors will acknowledge receipt and advise the next stage.

At the start of this meeting the parent will be shown a pro forma which will be explained.

If at the end of the meeting the matter has not been resolved the parent will be asked to complete the pro forma detailing the nature of the complaint. They will be advised of the action the school will take and kept informed regularly of any developments throughout.

At this stage parents who remain dissatisfied may be advised to contact the Chair of Governors and/or the CEO at ………………………

During the investigation the Chair of Governors will decide which of the governors will form a sub-committee to handle the complaint. Parents will be advised of the outcomes.

Outcomes will be reported to all concerned as appropriate and action taken as necessary.

If complaints are about the Headteacher then parents should speak or write to the Headteacher or if they feel they cannot then they should speak to the Chair of Governors.

If still dissatisfied parents may contact the Chair of Governors as in the parents' booklet and/or the CEO as detailed in the parents' booklet.

Records of complaints and notes of action taken will be kept in the locked drawer of the Headteacher's desk.

If complaints are made to the LEA the school will be informed and whoever has had an official complaint made against them will be entitled to union and legal representation. These representatives will attend meetings with parents, governors and the LEA regarding the complaint.

We strongly encourage parents to contact the school in the first instance.

Complaints

Complaints policy: guidelines for staff

All staff must be aware of the complaints procedure and be reminded of them termly. Training on handling complaints and difficult situations will be included as part of the induction process and skills/refresher courses provided annually.

When a member of staff raises concerns with outside agencies a note is made of the time and date and brief details of the consultation, initiated by the Headteacher if appropriate and placed on the child's file.

When a member of staff believes that a parent has a cause for concern, this should be reported to the Headteacher and a course of action agreed. This should be recorded, dated and agreed by both parties.

Informal complaints
Complaints regarding head lice, lost clothing, etc. will be dealt with positively by informing all parents of the complaint and the action to be taken in response in the weekly newsletter.

Formal complaints
When a formal complaint is made, staff should put nothing in writing in response without it being checked by the legal department. At least 24 hours notice, maximum 2 working days should be required for all written responses.

Staff are entitled to union, legal or other representations at meetings about complaints.

Staff must be vigilant in maintaining confidentiality when complaints arise, to protect all parties.

The School/Home Book remains the property of the school. It is an informal two-way contact document and cannot be used as legal evidence. It is confidential to the parent and staff team.

Staff complaints
Individual staff grievances will be dealt with by the Headteacher and governing body following the procedures in the Manual of Personnel and Practice.

Records of complaints and notes of action taken will be kept in the locked drawer of the Headteacher's desk.

Complaints

Complaints policy: guidelines for governors

Governors must be given the freedom to investigate complaints independently.

When a satisfactory outcome to a complaint cannot be reached after Stage 2 Headteacher's investigation, Chairman of Governors on receiving written complaints will convene a panel of governors to investigate. Any changes of policy and procedure necessary as a result of the complaint will be notified to the Headteacher.

Stages for handling complaints
} Induction pack/governors
How to handle complaints

Stages for handling complaints   Parents/carers

Records of complaints and notes of action taken will be kept in the locked drawer of the Headteacher's desk. Who has access?

Only the Head and Chair of Governors will hold keys. At an agreed point all documents related to the complaint should be filed in this locked drawer.

Should the complaint be specifically about the Headteacher then appropriate recorded action will be taken.

Complaints

Complaints procedure

Parents wishing to complain about the actions of .... staff may do so by:

- Speaking to that person.
- Making an appointment to see the Headteacher or Parent Governor (details in parents booklet).
- Writing to the Headteacher.
- The Headteacher will speak to the staff in an attempt to mediate the situation.
- If sufficiently serious the Headteacher will follow LEA complaints procedures as laid down in the Personnel Manual.
- If complaints are about the Headteacher then Parents should speak/write to the Headteacher.
- If still dissatisfied parents may contact the Parent Governor or the Chair of Governors as in the parents' booklet and/or the CEO at .... as detailed in the parents' booklet.
- Individual staff grievances will be dealt with by the Headteacher and Governing Body following the procedures in the Manual of Personnel and Practice.
- Parents or staff may nominate an independent person to advise, support and accompany them.
- In the event that this procedure is bypassed and a complaint is made directly to the CEO at ...., or others, we will act as follows:
    - Inform the Governing Body.
    - Governors will instigate the formal complaints procedure.

All complaints will be dealt with according to the stages laid out in the policy.

All complaints will be numbered and recorded.

Date: ....

Discussed with Chair: ....

Modifications: ....

Discussed with Full Governing Body: ....

Passed: ....

Review date: ....

Last review: ....

Note: This may be adapted or individual need

Complaints

Record of complaint

No:

Stage 1: Informal

Name of complainant :   Date:

Description of complaint:

Action taken:

Satisfactory outcome:

Changes to policies/procedures: Staff informed:

Complainant informed of next steps:

Stage 2: Investigation

Date written complaint received:

Description of complaint (if additional to Stage 1):

Action taken:

Changes made to policy/procedures:

Complainant informed:

Trustees/governors informed: Staff informed:

→

Complaints

Stage 3: Review

Date formal complaint received:

Panel convened on:

Names of trustees/governors on panel:

Action taken:

Changes made to policy/procedures:

Complainant informed:

Trustees/governors informed: Staff informed:

Stage 4: LA Review

Date complaint received by LA:

Date organisation informed of decision by LA:

Changes to policy/procedures:

Complainant informed:

Trustees/governors informed: Staff informed:

Stage 5: Beyond the LA

Date complaint referred to Secretary of State or Ombudsman:

Date organisation informed of decision by Secretary of State or Ombudsman:

Changes to policy/procedures made:

Complainant informed:

LA informed:

Trustees/governors informed: Staff informed:

Summer school for teenagers: risk assessment

Activity	Associated risk	Management of risk
Coach travel to and from summer school	• Accident en route. • Participant goes missing during comfort stop or at handover between. organisation and parents • Parents fail to materialise to pick up participants. • Participant misses outward or return coach.	• Use reputable coach companies. Ensure coaches have seat belts. Brief student helpers on emergency procedures • Employ sufficient student helpers/staff for one to stay behind. Check mobile phones are operable. Brief students on procedures, including contacting police and parents or carers. • Employ sufficient student helpers for one to remain with uncollected child. Ensure mobile phones are operable and telephone numbers are available. • Ensure mobile phones are operable and telephone numbers are available at all times. Provide information in joining instructions so parents, carers and helpers know procedures.
Train travel to and from summer school	• Accident en route. • Participant goes missing during unescorted phase of journey.	• Ensure at least one person is first aid trained and that mobile phones and contact details are available. Brief student helpers on emergency procedures. • Ensure that joining instructions make it clear that this phase of the journey is unescorted and that handover is at collection point. Reserve seats for all participants travelling by train.
Halls of Residence	• Fire in hall. • Serious illness of participants. • Misconduct on the part of participants – could be drink, drugs or sexually related. • Theft or damage to participants property.	• Normal hall emergency and evacuation procedures apply. Hold a fire drill in hall shortly after arrival. Ensure that student helpers and staff are briefed about hall evacuation procedures. • Ensure that student helpers are briefed on action to take. Site health service consulted. Complete accident/illness form. • All participants to complete and sign code of conduct; all incidents to be referred to summer school office and records kept. Procedures in place to send a participant home if in breach of code conduct. • Joining instructions to advise against bringing valuables and advise that participants do so at own risk. All participants to be issued with individual key giving access of their own room and corridor only.
Visits	• Accident en route to employer visits.	• Use reputable coach companies. Ensure coaches have seatbelts. Brief student helpers and staff on emergency procedures. →

Policies, procedures, evaluation and monitoring

Activity	Associated risk	Management of risk
Visits – contd.	• Participant goes missing en route to visit.	• Employ sufficient student helpers/staff for one to stay behind, and brief them prior to visit on set procedures, including contacting police and parents/carers.
	• Participant misses outward or return coach.	• Ensure mobile phones are operable and telephone numbers are available at all times. Provide information in joining instructions so parents, carers and helpers know procedures.
	• Fire during visit.	• Site to be asked to brief visitors on arrival.
	• Hazards specific to nature of the activity observed e.g. boating.	• Ditto.
	• Incident related to unauthorised use of equipment or access to restricted area.	• Site to be asked to ensure that visitors are briefed on arrival and are escorted at all times during visit.
	• Accident or injury linked to inappropriate dress for activity concerned.	• Summer School organisers to check on any specific dress requirements with site; ensure that any participants affected by this are informed before the visit. Student helpers to be asked to check dress of those involved when boarding buses.
General	• Participant fails to attend activity.	• Registers to be taken at start of each session. Completed registers to be delivered to summer school office within 30 minutes of start of session by someone who is not responsible for supervision of young people during the specific session.
	• Incident associated with unauthorised access to restricted areas.	• Warning about access to restricted areas to be included in summer school programme. Information on this to be included in briefing at start of event for young people, student helpers and staff.
Social programme		
Humanities group		• Each group to produce their own risk assessment for the week.
Engineering group		• Staff and student helpers to be briefed and records kept in summer school office.
Science group		
Social science group		

Note: All student helpers and staff should be fully trained and conversant with emergency procedures and risk assessment information before the start of the summer school.

Confidential staff questionnaire

	Negative Unhappy				Positive Happy

1. Do you think ……………….…. is an effective leader? 1 2 3 4 5 6

2. Do you think ……………….…. supports your own development and training? 1 2 3 4 5 6

3. Do you think ……………….…. is approachable
   a) on professional matters? 1 2 3 4 5 6
   b) on personal matters? 1 2 3 4 5 6

4. Do you think ……………….…. runs an effective organisation? 1 2 3 4 5 6

5. Do you feel valued as a member of the team? 1 2 3 4 5 6

6. How important do you think ……………….…. has been in the development of your organisation? 1 2 3 4 5 6

7. How important to you think ……………….…. is in the continuing development of the organisation? 1 2 3 4 5 6

8. How easy do you think it would be to replace ……………….…. in the post? 1 2 3 4 5 6

Overall how satisfied are you with ……………….…. 1 2 3 4 5 6

Any other comments?

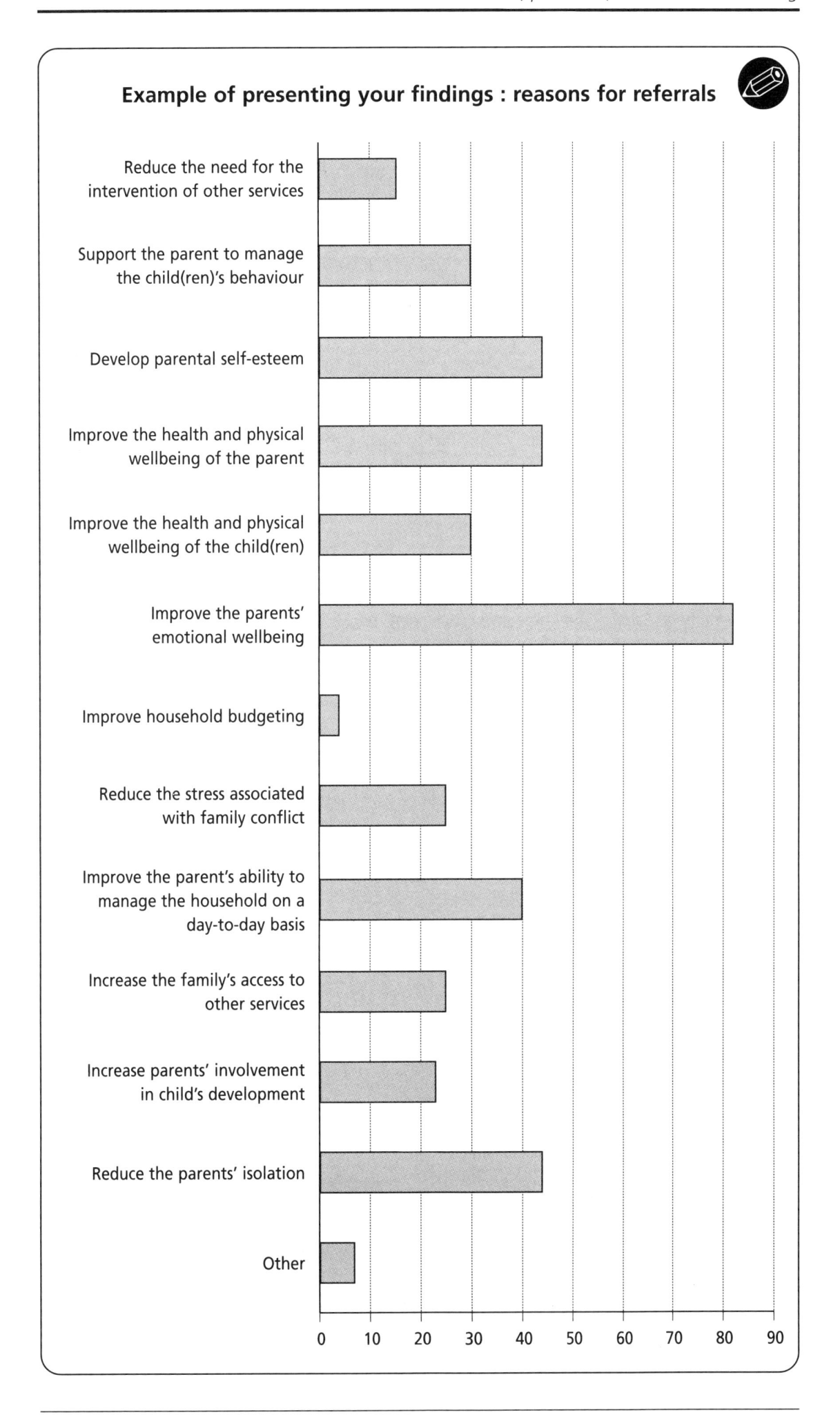

Example of presenting your findings : reasons for referrals

Reason	Value
Reduce the need for the intervention of other services	~15
Support the parent to manage the child(ren)'s behaviour	~30
Develop parental self-esteem	~43
Improve the health and physical wellbeing of the parent	~43
Improve the health and physical wellbeing of the child(ren)	~30
Improve the parents' emotional wellbeing	~82
Improve household budgeting	~3
Reduce the stress associated with family conflict	~25
Improve the parent's ability to manage the household on a day-to-day basis	~40
Increase the family's access to other services	~25
Increase parents' involvement in child's development	~23
Reduce the parents' isolation	~43
Other	~7

Section 11
Conclusion

There are now qualifications available for those working with parents, training packs are being produced, conferences held. What is needed now are standards to be set, monitoring and evaluation to take place and recommended changes made as appropriate in all areas of working with parents and families.

The present government in the UK has shown a keen interest in improving the quality of foster care and in decreasing the waiting times for those wishing to adopt. Children in Need strategies are also being developed. The time is right for change in many areas of child care work but first we must change the mindset of those working in the field to looking at prevention and support as the first option for children and families. There is, as never before, an opportunity for creative thinking and for 'joined up' working amongst different professional groups in order to help children.

However, Mary MacLeod, the Chief Executive of the National Family and Parenting Institute warns that:

We are in danger of becoming a nation of paranoid parents who have forgotten how to trust our judgement. Families are bombarded with conflicting advice about everything from what kids should be eating to how long they should be sleeping. Alongside this, just about everything in modern life is supposed to be bad for our children. Computers, TV, the Internet, how long we spend at work, not working at all, being a lone parent, being divorced. The list is endless and it is easy to forget that most parents know a lot about what is good for their children.

Parents don't raise their children in isolation from the world around them. They need help, support and recognition that what they do as parents is important and valued. They don't need more blame for the difficult times they find themselves in.

The Rt. Hon. David Blunkett, MP, launching the above organisation's Parenting Week in 2001, said that children want parents who show:
- fairness
- care
- respect

It is hoped that this book may help all those working with parents or offering family support to meet the children's criteria and also to help build up the self-esteem and confidence of all parents in their own ability and skills.

Useful names and addresses

Childcare Northern Ireland provides policies, membership, information and training for the voluntary sector in Northern Ireland. It works closely with NCB in the UK.
216 Belmont Road, Belfast, Northern Ireland BT4 2AT, tel: 0289 065 2713, fax: 0289 065 0285.

Children in Scotland is the national agency for voluntary, statutory and professional organisations and individuals working with children and families in Scotland. It exists to identify and promote the interests of children and their families and to ensure that relevant policies, services and provisions are of the best possible quality and able to meet the needs of a diverse society. **Scottish Parenting Forum** is based in their offices, as is **Enquire**, a national special educational needs advice and information service in Scotland. Children in Scotland publish widely on a variety of subjects including childcare, special needs, children's participation, health and work and family life. They also promote research publications as a way to inform practice. They work closely with the NCB in England.
Princes House, 5 Shandwick Place, Edinburgh EH2 4RG, tel: 0131 228 8484, fax: 0131 228 8585, e-mail: info@childreninscotland.org.uk, web: www.childreninscotland.org.uk

Children in Wales is a similar organisation to Children in Scotland. They also work closely with NCB in England.
25 Windsor Place, Cardiff CF1 3BZ, tel: 0292 034 2434, fax: 0292 034 31134.

Home-Start UK is a registered charity. Home-Start schemes attempt to prevent families breaking down, and to enrich the life of all family members. Where problems are deep-rooted, the role of the Home-Start volunteer is complementary to that of the professional worker. The time which volunteers can spend with a family, their informal role, their friendship, spontaneity and common-sense approach can all be focused on the family members rather than on their problems. Through the privilege of getting to know a family really well, Home-Start volunteers can encourage the family's strengths while also developing their own, to the mutual benefit of both, and certainly to the long-term advantage of the children.
2 Salisbury Road, Leicester LE1 7QR, tel: 0116 233 9955, fax: 0116 233 0232 or contact your local Home-Start scheme.

National Children's Bureau (NCB) works to identify and promote the wellbeing and interests of all children and young people across every aspect of their lives. NCB encourages professionals and policy makers to see the needs of the whole child and emphasises the importance of multi-disciplinary, cross-agency partnerships. NCB undertakes high quality research, promotes good practice, and ensures that the views of children and young people are taken into account. Children In Scotland, Children In Wales and Childcare Northern all work closely with NCB.
8 Wakley Street, London ECV 70E, tel: 020 7275 9441.

National Family & Parenting Institute. The NFPI is a national charity set up to enhance the value and quality of family life and to increase investment in it by government, media, industry and public services. The NFPI works together with other organisations involved in family support; they publish and publicise information about relationships, marriage, parenting and the parenting needs of children, carry out research, advise government and influence policy on parenting and the family. Much of the information produced is available on their websites at: http //www.nfpi.org and http://www.e-parents.org.
430 Highgate Studios, 53-79 Highgate Road, London NW5 1TL, tel: 020 7424 3460, fax: 020 7485 3590.

Parenting Education & Support Forum was launched in June 1996. The Forum brings together those concerned with, or working in the field of, preparation, education and support for parents. It promotes and maintains a high profile for parenting education and support, where education means learning in the fullest sense: of growing in knowledge, skills, understanding and personal developments. The Forum presses for effective policies and practice at local and national level, with the aim of serving the best interests of all children and their families. The Forum publishes a bimonthly News Bulletin.
For more information contact: Unit 431 Highgate Studios, 53-79 Highgate Road, London NW5 ITL, tel: 020 7284 8370 Main Office, 020 7284 8389 Information, fax: 020 7485 3587, e-mail: pesf@dial.pipex.com, website: www parenting-forum.org.uk

Parentline Plus provides practical help and information for parenting; confidential, freephone helpline supporting anyone caring for children – parent, stepparent, grandparents, young carers; parenting groups workshops and courses; accessible information on a variety of family issues; interactive website for parents and professionals in addition to training for professionals working with a diversity of families.
520 Highgate Studios, 53-79 Highgate Road, London NW5 1TL, tel: 0207 2845500 (business only), 0207 2845501, e-mail, centraloffice@parentlineplus.org.uk (business only), website: www.parentlineplus.org.uk, National Helpline: 0808 800 2222, Textphone: 0800 783 6783.

The Willows Nursery School (Early Excellence Centre and Beacon School) works with children with special educational needs aged 2 – 5 and their families. They provide education, practical advice and support for parents both in school and during regular home visits. They also run an outreach service for children and families offering early language work and lifelong learning. They aim to empower parents and to increase the parents' confidence in managing their children's needs. The Willows also offers training for anyone working with, or caring for, a child with SEN and produces practical publications to assist colleagues in meeting children's needs (available free except for p&p).
Battenburg Avenue, North End, Portsmouth, Hants PO2 OSN, tel: 023 9266 6918, fax: 023 9265 2247, website: www.willows.org.uk.

Note: any of these organisations may be able to signpost you to other more specific organisations appropriate to your needs.